Private Wheeler

Private Wheeler

The letters of a soldier of the
51st Light Infantry during the
Peninsular War & at Waterloo

To Dad

Wishing you a very
Merry, weird and scary
Christmas —

William Wheeler

and a Happy New Year

All at here

Gary & Kathy
+ +

LEONAUR

Private Wheeler: The letters of a soldier of the
51st Light Infantry during the
Peninsular War & at Waterloo
by William Wheeler

First published under the title
The Letters of Private Wheeler
1808-1828

Leonaur is an imprint
of Oakpast Ltd

ISBN: 978-1-84677-634-2 (hardcover)
ISBN: 978-1-84677-633-5 (softcover)

http://www.leonaur.com

Contents

Preface by the author

As these letters may fall into many hands who will form many different opinions respecting their origin, I have only to say, that on my return home I found the whole of my letters carefully preserved. From these letters, and from hasty notes made at different times, I have endeavoured to give a faithful and impartial record of the services of the regiment during my time, in which I spent so many happy years. The anecdotes are all original, none ever having appeared in print. Such is their simple history.

If it should meet the eye of any veteran who served his country during the eventful period here recorded, I hope it will prove a source of pleasure in recalling to his recollection many glorious achievements time have obliterated from his memory.

Bath,   W. Wheeler
26th February, 1837.

The Letters of Private Wheeler

The first page of Wheeler's first letter does not exist, but it is clear he is already a private soldier in the Surrey Militia.

on the edge of the Rumley (Romney) marsh, which is said to be the cause, I was dismissed from drill at this place, and went to my duty as a soldier; in September we marched to Ramsgate, where we are at present stationed.

Viscount Cranley the Lord Lieutenant and Colonel of the 2nd Surrey is present and commands the Corps. His Lordship is a great favourite amongst us, his character contrasted with Major Hudson's, who is generally in command, is as opposite as light and dark. Lord Cranley is quite an eccentric character, and I think a much better coachman than soldier. He rides a low poney when on parade and his dress being of the fashion some forty years ago, he has a droll appearance. He has acquired the cognomen of 'Punch on a Pig.' This it seems had come to his Lordship's knowledge, for one morning he rode up to Major Hudson and said to him loud enough to be heard, 'Major what do you think the men calls me?'

'I don't know my Lord' was the reply.

'Why it is Punch on a pig.'

The major began to smile but he was soon stopped by Lord Cranley asking the major if he knew what the men called him. The reply was in the negative.

'Well then I will tell you it is B——y Bob.'

I will close this letter by giving you an anecdote of his Lordship, it will at one view shew you the goodness of his heart. The summer before I joined, the regiment with several other Militia Regiments were encamped at Ashford. Lord Cranley was on his journey to the camp to take the command of the whole. A short distance from London he overtook a soldier very lame, His Lordship hailed him and found he was on his journey for Ashford Camp—he soon persuaded the man to mount the dickey and as he drove along the soldier related to the supposed coachman a long story respecting his fears, that he was two days over his time and that his commanding officer was a ———, and that he was sure to be punished when he arrived at the camp.

'That you shall not' said his Lordship I will speak for you.'

The man said his commanding officer was such a proud tyrannizing fellow that by his speaking it would only make matters worse etc. and he would perhaps speak to his master and get him turned out of his place, for the soldier took Lord Cranley for a coachman, and his Lordship took care not to undeceive him. When they arrived at the camp the carriage and four was driven up to the tent of the officer this man so much dreaded, but what must the man's astonishment be when he heard the old coachman say to this officer commanding the troops, 'I have picked up one of your poor fellows on the road completely broken down. If I had not fell in with him, By ——— he would not have been here this week. I request you will not punish him for being over his time.'

The officer so much dreaded stood as humble as a lamb, cap in hand, bowing and scraping. Lord Cranley said to the man 'get down my good fellow, did I not tell you I would speak for you.' What followed is natural to suppose.

No. 2. Riding (Reading) Street Barracks, 13th February 1809

You will see by this letter that we are removed to our old quarters, a short time before we left Ramsgate. Lord Cranley preferred a long string of charges against Major Hudson, who had the choice either to stand a General Court Martial or retire from the service. The major chose the latter.

Thus the regiment is ridded of as great a tyrant as ever disgraced the army. This man delighted in torturing the men, every man in the corps hated him, when once a soldier came under his lash it was no use for any officer to plead for him. If he was young, his reply was: 'It will do him good, make him grow and make him know better for the future.'

On the other hand if he was getting into years, the brute would say. 'Oh! he is old enough to know better.' He delighted in going round the barracks on a Sunday morning to see if he could catch any of the married people roasting their meat. If he saw any meat roasting he would cut it down, and carry away the string and nail in his pocket, observing they should boil their meat, it was more nourishing. Once he paid a visit to the hospital and saw a cat.

'Whose cat is this?' said he.

'It is mine, Sir' said the hospital serjeant's wife, 'We are very much troubled with rats and mice.'

'I don't care a d——' was the reply, 'you know my order, I will neither have dogs, cats, rats, or mice here.'

Beside the name of B——y Bob he had acquired the cognomen of 'Wheel 'em again,' from the habit of calling to the serjeant major, 'Do they grumble?'

The answer would be 'Yes, sir'—

'Then wheel 'em again.' He also has got the name of the 'Lion and the Bear'; the following lines are part of a song some one of the men composed on him and a young sub—a great favourite of the majors.

'The lion one day to the jackal did say,
The colonel from the regiment is gone;
I'll drill them I swear,
With the voice of a bear.'
Secure arms with your bayonets fixed on.

His departure was quite a jubilee to the regiment. Captain (later Lieutenant-Colonel Richard) Frederick is appointed major in his place.

To fill up the remainder of this letter I must trouble you with another anecdote of Lord Cranley. A muster of the troops in the district took place, a grand field day and sham fight was the consequence. Lord Cranley had the command of a brigade. After some manoeuvring, which his Lordship as well understood as the nag that carried him, the line halted and a general discharge of musketry took place. Lord Cranley was delighted. He rode up and down the line, calling to the men to load and fire as quick as possible. At length the fire slackened. He enquired the reason the men did not fire brisker.

When he was informed the ammunition was nearly expended. 'Well' said he, 'let the men stand at ease.'

The troops had now began to advance but Lord Cranley's brigade remained stationary. The staff was despatched to order Lord Cranley to push forward his brigade. It was all to no purpose. His Lordship was inflexible. 'We want powder' was his reply, 'what use is going into battle without powder etc.'

At length the general came galloping calling on His Lordship to move on. He might have saved himself the trouble. It was vain to try to persuade Lord Cranley that he should move on. 'I want more powder.'

'You have spoiled the line and in the event of a real fight you would endanger the safety of the whole army. Let me entreat your Lordship to move on.'

'D—— it, man, what is the use. I want powder.'

At length Lord Cranley told the general to appoint someone else to command the brigade, observing: 'D—— it, General, I don't see the use of going into battle without powder.'

He then called for his carriage, mounted the dickey, saying if the general would learn him to be a soldier he would learn the general to be a coachman.

The day we marched into Canterbury His Lordship drove into the city with his carriage completely crammed with the soldiers wives, whom he had picked up on the road.

No. 3. Maidstone, 12th April 1809.

I have at length escaped from the Militia without being flayed alive. I have taken the first opportunity and volunteered together with 127 of my comrades into the 51st Light Infantry Regiment. I had made up my mind to volunteer but into what regiment I cared not a straw, so I determined to go with the greatest number. The latter end of March the order came. On the 1st April I gave in my name for the 51st. The 2nd and 3rd was occupied by the Doctor's inspection and the general's approval, and on the 4th I was attested for seven years.

The regiment is laying somewhere in Devonshire. I have not seen a single man belonging to the corps, except Lieutenant (Edward) Frederick, brother to the major of the Surrey Militia. Upwards of ninety men volunteered to the 95th Rifle Regiment. I was near going to this regiment myself for it was always a fancy corps of mine, and another cause was that Lieutenant Foster a good officer beloved by every man in the corps I had left, volunteered into the 95th. But I had made up my mind to go with the strongest party.

Maidstone is full of volunteers, belonging to every regiment in the service. It will not be long before we shall leave this scene of drunkenness and riot, and the sooner the better. When I join the regiment I shall write again. I shall then have more time and shall have collected something that will enable me to spin out a long letter.

No. 4. Kingsbridge Barracks. 18th May, 1809.

Two days after I had written my last letter we marched for Kingsbridge Barracks. Devonshire, and joined the regiment. We could not have had a more pleasant march. The weather was fine and not being encumbered with baggage, and not under any restraint, we performed our days march at what time we pleased. In marching through Surrey we lost nearly all the party, some mornings only two or three would muster to march with the officer, who had command of us. But by the time we got to Salisbury the whole of the party had again collected and we found we had increased in numbers, having picked up several smart young fellows on the road.

We had one incident of rather a ludicrous nature happened on the road; before I say anything of the 51st Regiment. I will relate it to you. It was as follows—Corporal Shortland, one of our voluntiers, had began at Maidstone to shew symptoms of madness. We all thought that he was acting the old soldier, whether it is the case or no, it would be improper for me to judge. The morning we marched out of Salisbury, poor Shortland presented one of the curiousest characters I ever saw. As we were assembling in the morning he made his appearance dressed in the following droll manner; his head was ornamented with an old bee hive and the other part of his dress consisted of an old blue petticoat, tied round his neck, the bottom scarcely reached so low as a Highlander's Kilt, his legs and feet were bare, in his right hand he carried a shepherd's crook.

Thus dressed and equipped he was hailed with three cheers, and off we marched with Shortland in our front, but it was soon found that not being accustomed to march without shoes, he would not be able to proceed far, so it happened that a luckless donkey was feeding by the side of the road. Of course he was pressed into the service and poor Corporal Shortland was mounted on him; in this manner he performed the day's march. The poor fellow is now in hospital.

I must now say something of the corps I have joined. We are about eight hundred strong, about one hundred and fifty of this number are old soldiers, the remainder being volunteers from the Stafford, South Gloucester, 1st and 2nd Surrey together with some half dozen Irish Militias. The facings of the regiment are green, but all the volunteers at present wears the facings of the different regiments they have left. It will be impossible for me to say anything of the regiment, that is if it be good or bad, but I rejoice to say I have escaped from the one I left with a whole skin. If the old soldier's reports of the treatment and discipline of the 51st be correct, I shall have no cause to repent.

From the little I have seen I am inclined to believe I shall find this to be a good corps. The regiment was employed on General Moore's expedition in which they in common with the army suffered much indeed, if half be true what I have heard from the old hands. I am at a loss to account that so many has returned. The regiment is commanded by Lieutenant Colonel Mainwaring, a very humane man. He is no advocate for the cat o'nine tails. I have more than once heard it remarked that if he could not stand fire better than witness flogging he would be the worst soldier in the army.

No. 5. Berryhead Barracks. 20th June, 1809.

What a funny droll set of beings the old soldiers of the regiment are. They are continually relating such marvellous tales of murders, rapes, and robberies that would frighten Old Devil Dunk himself if he could hear them. I listen to their tales, with some degree of interest often doubting the truth of the fatigues etc. they seem to delight to relate.

Colonel Mainwaring is one of the most eccentric characters I ever met with. I make no doubt but I shall be able to amuse you with many anecdotes about him, in some future letters. I will relate one to you as I heard it myself, it happened in the summer of 1807. The regiment at the time was stationed at Chichester Barracks, several boys from the Duke of York's school, with others born in the regiment were put on pay. Near the barracks was an orchard well stocked with cherries. Several of the boys got into the orchard, but the vigilant eye of the owner soon discovered the marauders, but before he could even identify one, the whole bolted over the opposite hedge. The farmer came to the colonel to lodge his complaint. All the boys were assembled but the farmer could not tell one from the other, they being all about the same height and dressed alike.

'I see, was not this the case," said Colonel Mainwaring 'When you looked over the hedge, they young rogues popped over the other opposite.'

'Just so, Sir' was the reply.

'I thought as much. They have learnt something from the

crows that robs you of your corn. Like them they had thrown out their sentries, so they out generaled you, but I am too old a soldier to be done by such a set of young spalpeens. If I cannot find out the thieves I will soon see who has eaten the fruit. I will make the whole of the rascals disgorge the contents of their stomach at our feet.' Then turning round, he shouts for the serjeant of the hospital to bring fourteen emetics immediately.

The boys turned pale. One called out 'I ate some, sir, but I was not there. I was in the barrack room. Bob —— gave me a handful.'

Bob —— endeavoured to excuse himself by saying he did not get up into the tree, he only held his cap while Bill —— threw them down. In short everyone had his excuse. The colonel separated the innocent from the guilty, and the old man was struck dumb with astonishment at the superior sagacity of the colonel.

This morning we had a field day. It was performed so much to the satisfaction of Colonel Mainwaring that it put him into one of his best of good humours, so he imparted a secret to us, which he said would 'make our hearts leap with joy. He had written to the Duke of York to inform him we were all tired of eating the bread of idleness, and was longing to go out on service. He had received an answer saying that our request should be attended to, and that we were to hold ourselves in readiness for a general inspection preparatory to our embarkation.

He was full of chat and amused us by relating many curious anecdotes of himself and of others. He added how happy we should feel when we saw another wreath of laurel added to our colours, and that to, by our own exertions. He finished by telling us how proud he felt to have the command of such a fine body of men. 'Here' he exclaimed, 'is John Bull from England; Swaney from Scotland, and Paddy from my own country. By J——s, we will not only beat the French but we will eat them afterwards.'

I have said the colonel is adverse to flogging, yet he has been under the necessity of whipping one man since I joined. This fellow had deserted when the regiment was under order for Corunna. He was sentenced five hundred lashes he only received seventy-five he was then taken down, our ranks opened, and the poltroon, as the colonel justly called him, was ordered to march between the ranks. At the same time Colonel Mainwaring kept shouting 'soldiers spit on the cowardly poltroon, you should all p—— over him if it were not too indecent.'

No. 6. Berryhead Barracks. 30th June 1809.

The inspection is over it took place the 23rd inst. and we are under orders for service. The vessels intended to convey us to Spithead are expected every moment. It is the general custom of most regiments to shut up the gates, and confine the men to barracks when under orders for Foreign service. Not so with us. Colonel Mainwaring does not approve of this plan. When he received the order the gates were thrown wide open that the good soldier might make merry and enjoy himself, at the same time adding that if there should be any poltroons in disguise amongst us they might be off. It was only the good soldiers he wished to take with him. We were going to reap laurels, therefore he should not hinder the good soldier from enjoying himself for the sake of keeping a few good for nothing fellows. If any such had crept unto the corps, they would only cover the regiment with disgrace. The confidence reposed in us was not in one single instance abused, not one man having deserted. I have been detained two hours since I began this letter, about the baggage, and now I am about to recommence two vessels are coming round the point, the wind favourable and all in high glee. I must close this by promising to write you all particulars in my next.

No. 7. Spithead. H.M. Ship l'Impetueux. 15th July, 1809.

We embarked on board several cutters and sailed in a few hours after my last. I am now about to fulfil my promise, my will is good but I fear my ability is insufficient to keep pace with my pen. However I will be as communicative as possible and give a faithful detail of passing events, I must crave your indulgence if

I prove tedious, my only wish is to amuse.

It being the first time I was ever on salt water nothing could be more pleasant; our little cutter skimmed over the waves like a seagull. I had not the least symptom of sea sickness; never did I pass so agreeable a morning. I was on deck at daybreak. We were running close under the land; it was quite a fairy scene. The only thing that disturbed my mind was that I had entered the army. I would have given the world to have been a sailor. We continued sailing without altering rope or sheet, until we run alongside the *Pompey* (74). We went on board this vessel but was soon shifted to the *l'Impetueux* (80). (H.M.S. *Impeteuse*)

The whole regiment was put on board, she had her lower deck guns taken out and the larboard side of the lower deck was all the room allotted to us, the remainder was occupied by the ships company. Your having been to Spithead relieves me from the task of attempting to describe this place. I remember what you often told me in the garden, that the masts of the ships appeared as thick as the kidney bean sticks, from that time my curiosity increased to see this grand sight, you will therefore excuse me if I say that being in the midst of such a novelty, instead of attending to my own comfort in seeing where my berth was below, I remained on deck, feasting my eyes on the wonders that surround me until *taptoo*, it is true I had been below and put up my appointments. I knew that the company I belonged to was stationed forward close to the manger.

When the gun fired all the soldiers were ordered down except the watch. I descended by the main hatchway, all was darkness, and the deck completely covered with the troops. The first step I took off the slips was on someone's leg, the second on an Irishman's face, who swore by —— that some 'tundering tief' had murdered him, I made another stride and found there was nothing but living bodies to walk on, I was soon arrested in my course for someone seized hold of my leg and down I threw myself across half a dozen of my comrades, a battle royal instantly commenced in the dark.

I remembered the old adage, 'The biggest coward has the

best luck, in those kind of broils.' I lay still, so by the time the battle was over I had contrived to get the length and breadth of my person on the deck where I lay 'til morning.

But the best is to come. The decks had been newly caulked, the heat of so many bodies had drawn the pitch and tar, so that we were stuck fast in the morning. It was the most ludicrous sight imaginable, some were fast by the head, others had got an arm secured, those who had laid on their backs were completely fast, some who were wrapped in their blankets came of best, but their blankets were completely spoiled. It was a fine treat for the blue jackets to see all the lobsters stuck fast to the decks. Better arrangements have since been made and we are now comparatively comfortable.

I have found a townsman on board, young Alexander. I eat and drink with him so that I am much better off than many of my comrades. I said I wished I had entered into the navy but I am now satisfied with the choice I have made. What a difference is there in the treatment of the men on board this ship compared to our regiment, if the discipline on board the *l'Impetueux* is a correct index of the other ships of the navy. I will always stop my ears when 'Britons never shall be slaves' is sung.

The first lieutenant who goes by the name of 'Ugly Betty' is a tall thin meagre ugly looking fellow, and what is worse than all his mind is as evil as his person is disagreeable. The captain comes on board every Wednesday to punish, and Ugly Betty never fails to have a long list to present to him. The captain is no niggard at serving out the rope yarn, Ugly Betty's word is always taken, very few ever escapes, until their backs are lacerated in such a manner that causes many a hardy tar to faint at the sight. This is done without asking any questions as to the truth or falsehood of the charge, or with the mock shew of a trial. When a poor fellow is tied up he is ignorant how many lashes he is to receive, the boatswains mates keep tearing the flesh until the captain order the man to be taken down. The boatswain if not a twin brother of Ugly Betty, seems to be possessed with the same evil genius. Nothing can be done by this worthy disciple of the

Devil Credulous, without the ropes end, and plenty of curses, —— .

Spithead is all bustle, crammed with vessels, from the huge three decker to the smallest craft, thousands of lighters and boats are on the move continually. A certain number of seamen from the different line of battle ships are to serve on shore with us, they will be employed in dragging guns, ammunition stores etc. These men are to be equipped with a cutlass and pistols, a broad canvass belt to fasten to the gun. Alexander will be employed on this service. This will prove a treat to the seamen, some of whom has not been on shore many years.

No. 8. H.M. Ship l'Impetueux. Downs. 28th July, 1809.

You will perceive by this we have left Spithead and have arrived at the Downs, where the whole expedition is assembled. Colonel Mainwaring joined us a few days after I wrote you last. He was no sooner on board then he ordered us all to parade to see how we all were, he expressed great pleasure on finding us all in good health. He said the 'Old Poltroon' was come at last, he was not going to stay behind to disgrace himself. This must have been a thunder-stroke to the men whom the cap fitted.

To make you acquainted with this odd expression I must tell you that at the time we embarked at Torbay, Colonel Mainwaring came round the different vessels we were on board, to see how we were situated, this done he got into his boat and pushed off for the shore wishing us a pleasant passage to Spithead. Some of our men who had been sacrificing to the shrine of Bacchus, called after the colonel. 'There goes the old poltroon, we will go on service ourselves, we will leave him at home to disgrace him.' This was going too far with a joke, but Colonel Mainwaring knew it was what he had often repeated himself, he therefore took no further notice of it. The fact was Colonel Mainwaring was going to Portsmouth by land with his lady and intended to join us at Spithead. Some of the sailors observed that it would be a serious joke for any of them to practice with their captain, it would cost them buckets of blood.

Now I am writing the colonel has just passed by and he has had a row with one of the men. I do not know what the offence was, but Colonel Mainwaring patted the epaulette on his shoulder, saying 'If it was not for this.'

Then clenching his fist and putting it up to the man's nose, said 'I would let you know that Colonel Mainwaring has got an iron fist.'

The Earl of Chatham commands the expedition and is on board the *Admiral*. Everybody is ready, the wind blowing up the channel, the Blue Peter flying and the fleet unmooring, we shall soon be off. Our destination is still a secret.

No. 9. Camp near West Zuburg.
5th August 1809.

On the 30th *ultimo* we dropped anchor off the Island of Walcherien after a pleasant passage of nine hours. Our berth was next to the *Eagle,* 74, at the turn of the tide, we got foul of each other, our stern was aground; in order to remedy the evil the guns on the quarter deck were run forward to lighten her stern. Ugly Betty had stationed himself on the poop awning with the speaking trumpet, swearing and growling like ——. The repeated strokes we every moment received from the *Eagle* shook us violently, one of these strokes sent Ugly Betty's head foremost on the quarter deck and broke both his legs. The news flew like wild fire, and with it universal joy at his fate. I should not have thought it worthwhile to have said anything of the matter, but a few hours before, Ugly Betty kicked some of our men who were in his way and called them 'a —— set of lobster-backed ——,' adding 'some of us would be in hell before tomorrow this time.'

The next morning we were all ready for landing, but as our regiment was to disembark with the 2nd Division I had a good opportunity of observing the preparations of the 1st Division, and the manner they effected their landing. The gunboats had taken up their position along the shore, the flats full of soldiers and towed by the ship's boats, formed in rear of the gunboats. On a signal the flats advanced. All now was solemn silence, saving the gunboats, who were thundering showers of iron on the enemy. Their well directed fire soon drove them to shelter, behind the sandbank.

The flats had now gained the gunboats, shot through the intervals and gained the shallow water, when the troops leaped out and waded ashore, drove the enemy from behind the hills where they had taken shelter from the destructive fire of the gunboats. Some batteries and forts were soon taken, the enemy fled and we lost sight of the contending parties. After this we soon landed and on the beach our brigade was formed. It consisted of the 14th, 51st and 82nd Regiments commanded by Major General Houston. We then moved on some distance and encamped for the night.

The next morning, 1st of August, a remarkable day, it being the fiftieth anniversary of the Battle of Minden. Colonel Mainwaring could not let this opportunity slip without addressing us. I wish I could give you his speech, that is impossible. He told us that all the pleasure and happiness he had ever felt fell short of the pleasure he now felt at being at the head of that corps, who on that day fifty years had by their native valour repulsed and defeated the whole body of the enemy's cavalry before Minden. He shewed us the word Minden on our colours, and reminded us it was inscribed on our breast plates. He said it was probable we should fall in with the enemy that day, and if we did not give them a good drubbing, how could we ever return home to our fathers, mothers etc.

Our country expected much from us, the regiment in its infant state had performed prodigies of valour on that day, and now that we had grown grey (some of us) in the service, would it not be expected we should eclipse them in glory etc. etc. etc. In the course of his address he recurred to his old favourite maxim of firing low, you will then hit them in the legs and there will be three gone, for two will pick him up and run away with him, we shall soon thin them this way, then we can dispose of the remainder at our ease.

Soon after this harangue we advanced on Middleburg, a neat clean little city, the capital of the Island. The gates were soon opened to us and we remained some time halted in the street. At length we marched out on the great road to Flushing.

Colonel Mainwaring with one of our comps. and the Light Company of the 82nd Regiment formed the advance guard. The 82nd was in front this day, we had taken the front the day before.

Before the rear of our brigade had cleared the city, we received a volley of musketry on our pivot flank (we were marching in column of subdivisions right in front). The word was now given 'Wheel into line,' 'Prime and Load.' Before we had time to load, another volley was fired. The contents of this as of the first passed over our heads. We could see from whence the fire came but could not see the enemy. To advance upon them was impossible, there being several deep ditches between us. We then broke into open column of subdivisions and continued our route in double quick time.

We soon came to a wind mill, here the road turned suddenly to the left, we now saw it was crowded with the enemy in full retreat for Flushing, we followed hard in pursuit about two miles without meeting with anything to retard our progress, when we were suddenly stopped, and the fire from the enemy increased; it was now evident that some impediment was in the way. We could not form into any other order, neither could we render much assistance to the advance as there were deep ditches full of water, each side the road. A few of us did manage to get across into the field on our left, but was soon obliged to return for we met other ditches, wider and deeper, than those beside the road. The enemy at this place had thrown up a breast work and had dug a trench.

After passing this place we jogged on at a smart pace until we came to the village of West (actually East) Zuberg. The enemy had now formed, Colonel Mainwaring with the advance guard charged, drove them through the village, and took two 9 pounders. We followed them as far as the Swan Inn, here we were obliged to halt, or we should have been exposed to the guns of the garrison; Piquets was now thrown out, and the brigade fell back near to West Zuberg and encamped. I believe the distance from Middleburg to Flushing is about four miles.

No. 10. Camp West Zuburg. 12th August, 1809.

I wanted to say more in my last, want of room obliged me to cut short the latter part of my letter. I told you that Colonel Mainwaring charged at West Zuburg and took two guns, it was well he did, for it appeared to be the intention of the enemy to keep possession, at least for the evening, of the village, for here their whole force was formed. At the entrance of the village they had planted two 9 pounders, equal to our 12 pounders, these were loaded with grape, in a few seconds more their contents would have been discharged on us, but such was the impetuosity of the charge they were driven from their ground leaving the guns behind loaded, we punished the enemy severely from this place to the Swan Inn, distance about a quarter of a mile, the road was strewed with their killed and wounded and a great many prisoners were made, from the buttons on the prisoners clothes, it appeared they belonged to the 1st and 2nd Battalions Irish Legion and the 1st Colonial Battalion.

As soon as our camp was formed I was sent on fatigue party to West Zuburg. I had not in the hurry of the fight noticed many of the killed and wounded, but now I had time, I could not without pity and some degree of horror look at the desolating scene around me. The inhabitants had fled, taking some trifling movable things with them, the remainder is either carried off or destroyed by the enemy, the dead and dying laying about covered with blood, sweat, and dust looks frightful, the wounded some in their last agony begging for water, others writhing under pain, calling on someone to shoot them. But amidst all this pain and misery, it is delightful to see the very same soldiers, who an hour before were dealing destruction about them, tendering all the assistance in their power to a fallen enemy. What a boast to belong to such a country.

I shall relate one anecdote to you that will be illustrative of the temper and good feeling the British soldier manifests towards an enemy in distress. We found a poor Frenchman badly wounded, his leg appeared to be fractured in two places, he was laying as he dropped, which caused much pain, we removed him to a house, put him on some straw, the poor fellow fainted.

'D——— it,' said Perkins 'is there no gin amongst us, the poor fellow will die.'

Finagan who was supporting his head called out 'B———d and U———ds here take this shilling one of ye and see if you can get some gin.'

The poor fellow revived and expressed his gratitude in a language none of us understood. My attention was now arrested by a voice in broken English, I turned round, and saw a gentleman, an inhabitant of the place, he was standing with his hands clasped together ejaculating in English 'Merciful Heaven, what do I see, these men who a short time since fought on this spot with the fury of lions, has cast aside their ferocity and assumed the character of the lamb, they make no distinction, their enemy is treated with the same tenderness and compassion as their own comrades, come with me, I will fill all your bottles'. We got our wooden canteens full of gin, then after securing the commissariat stores returned to camp. This place we have made as comfortable as possible by erecting huts.

The enemy is completely shut up in Flushing, and we are going on with the necessary work for the destruction of the town. There is not an idle hand to be found, some are building batteries, digging trenches, filling sand bags, making large wicker baskets, carpenters making platforms, sailors bringing up guns, mortars, howitzers, ammunition, shot, shell etc. All this work is going on under the beautiful music of all the guns and mortars the garrison can bring to bear on any of our works. Our duty has chiefly been on picquets, and covering parties to check the enemy should they sally out to destroy our works.

I have seen Alexander, he was well and in good spirits, highly pleased with the treat of being on shore. Two nights ago we were visited by a dreadful thunder storm, such were the torrents of rain we were washed out of our camp, the barns and out houses of two farms near gave us shelter for the night. This has slightly hindered our work, but the progress made under so many difficulties is astonishing, everything is nearly complete, and begins to assume a very formidable appearance. I am just come off duty from the advance works, we were covering a battery that will be complete tomorrow, there will be twenty 32 pounders mounted in this battery.

No. 11. East Zuburg. 17th August, 1809.

Flushing surrendered yesterday, you will learn but little from me. You must gather the particulars from the papers. I must confine myself to what passed under my own eye, that cannot be much. 'Corporal Trim' justly observed to 'My Uncle Toby that a soldiers observation cannot extend far beyond the muzzle of his firelock'—but I hope the little I shall communicate for your information will prove interesting.

On the 13th inst. I was on picquet at the Swan Inn, in the afternoon a Congreve rocket was fired from a battery we were covering, it dropped short, this drew a heavy fire on us, without doing mischief. This appeared as much as to say, we are ready, and the enemy's fire, plainly said so are we. The work of destruction soon began after this and both sides seemed determined. At dusk we were relieved off picquet and marched to camp, where I slept as comfortable as if I had been at home in my bed in the corner.

The firing was very brisk the whole of the night. In the morning, agreeable to practice, we marched to our alarm post. The roaring of the guns was somewhat slackened, and the town was on fire in several places. A great confusion of voices could be heard from the town, this no doubt was occasioned by the people endeavouring to extinguish the fires.

One of our men who was from the land of Saints, was to use our colonel's expression 'The D—l of a boy for a drop of the crature.' Doherty, for that is his name, had found some gin, and had made too free with it. The colonel soon noticed what was the matter, and said 'How now, Doherty, what is the matter you are not well.'

'Not at all your honour, Doherty was never better in his life. I have only just been taking a wee drop to the health of my comrades, who are battering down the cursed town about the ears of the blackguards in it, and if that is not the truth of the story then bad luck to me if I do not give your honour leave to tell me of it as long as I live.'

'But Doherty that wee drop was a large one I am afraid, besides you should have watered it.'

'Water it, did your honour say, why it is yourself you know that would never again own Doherty for a countryman, if he had been guilty of sich a thing.'

'Well if you would not water it yourself, I must.'

'Serjeant major get me a rope, and you sir strip.' The rope was tied by the centre round Doherty's waist, one end thrown across a ditch, and some men sent across to take hold of it. In Doherty jumped like a Newfoundland dog, and the men each side by pulling him backward and forward, gave him such a complete sousing as ever mortal had before.

He was then ordered out, when he exclaimed 'Och by J——— and it's your honour that knows how to do everything, may your honour never die. But the D——— burn Doherty if he ever wishes to trouble your honour to mix any more grog for him.' We were all laughing pretty heartily before, but this finisher set us all into a roar in which the colonel and poor Doherty joined. At the bottom of the ditch was a great depth of black mud; this being well stirred up, he appeared as black as His Satanic Majesty.

The bombardment continued all day, and increased at night. This night I was on picquet, it was beautiful and fine, one half of Flushing was in flames, the fleet and the whole of the batteries were at it pel mell. At midnight, when on sentry, I often counted fifteen shells and twelve rockets at one time hovering over and descending in to the devoted town. The roaring of guns and mortars, the hissing of rockets, shot and shells, the chiming of the church bells, the French sentries calling at intervals 'Alls well,' the noise of the people trying to extinguish the fires, but above all, the heart rending cries of the poor women and children, beggars description.

The enemy sustained our fire with great fortitude until the morning of the 15th inst. when they surrendered. The gates and principal places were taken possession of by our troops this day and the enemy marched out with the honours of war, that is with fixed bayonets, colours flying, drums and music, and several field pieces loaded. They laid down their arms outside the garrison and were marched to the waterside to be shipped for England. I did not see this grand sight, being on the Provost Guard at East Zuburg. The men who had been up to the gates gives a frightful account of the destruction of the town.

No. 12. Anne Transport. Before Antwerp. 26th August, 1809.

You see we have not been idle. As soon as we had reduced Flushing and the Island of Walcherine was our own, all the disposable part of the army embarked, and proceeded up the Scheldt to Antwerp. We are at present anchored before the city. The whole of the French fleet are strongly moored in the harbour, where they are as snug as their hearts can well desire, protected by formidable batteries and two large chains drawn across the mouth of the harbour, to make themselves doubly secure.

The city is protected on the land side by an immense army, and troops are daily arriving to reinforce those already in camp. It is evident we are a day behind. Some heavy cannonading takes place every time the tide serves, between our light vessels, and gunboats, and their batteries outside the entrance of the harbour. This does not appear to be of any service and must be attended with loss of life and an useless expenditure of ammunition. We should have run up here first, reduced Antwerp and then we might have taken Flushing.

We are getting tired of being stowed up in the transports, and many of our men has been attacked with a severe ague, which seems to threaten the whole army, it being on the increase. It is reported that the object that brought us here cannot be attained, and it is the general opinion if we should land that we should be very glad to get on board again, So if there is no more work cut out for us, we shall soon, as the Irishman says, be after returning home again.

I cannot refrain from relating to you an anecdote so strikingly illustrative of the British Tar's character, although it cannot be done without telling a dirty story, as it was from a dirty trick the anecdote had its origin. Some of the dirty rascals on board the French fleet has been amusing themselves by ——— on the Union Jack, on board one of their ships in the mouth of the harbour.

In sight of the whole of our fleet, they have placed the British Jack under their bows for the ship's company to evacuate on. I could not help laughing at one of our honest Jacks, who feeling a personal insult at such an unwarrantable dirty trick, could not help exclaiming 'D———n their s——n cowardly eyes and limbs, if it was not for the cursed chain across the harbour, we would soon make the frog eating sons of B———s lick the filth off with their tongues.'

'But the batteries, Jack, how could you pass them?'

'D———n the batteries, we would soon blow them to hell, it is the chain that keeps us out, we have volunteered to try our hands at breaking it but the lubbers won't listen to us.'

No. 13. Horsham Barracks. 20th September, 1809.

Here I am returned safe and sound after encountering the dangers and fatigues of the late campaign. I hasten to relieve your anxieties, you will therefore excuse a short letter, we arrived here yesterday, our second division marched in today.

We have left many sick at Portsmouth, and many fresh cases of ague are occurring daily. As soon as we are settled I shall write again.

No. 14. Horsham Barracks. 15th October, 1809.

My last letter on board the *Anne* transport informed you it was rumoured that we should soon return. Nothing worthy of notice transpired, until we left our anchorage and sailed for England, this was on the 9th. September; we reached the Downs in twenty four hours, our adjutant died on the passage. What his abilities might have been in the Household troops it is hard to say; he had been one of these lucky mortals whom dame fortune had selected from the ranks; with us he was a sort of harmless creature. Colonel Mainwaring was both colonel and adjutant. Had he some colonels to deal with, no doubt he would have appeared in a different character, which I am led to think would not have been the best.

The 12th we disembarked at Portsmouth and marched for Horsham. The regiment is in a very sickly state, the hospital is full, and two barrack rooms each holding sixty men is occupied with convalescents; a great many has died and numbers who have recovered will never be fit for service again. I am the only man in the company to which I belong that has escaped the ague. Poor Corporal Shortland, who I mentioned in a former idler had shewed symptoms of madness, when on our march to join the regiment from Maidstone, has hanged himself. He was found one morning suspended by his stockings to the accoutrement rack, in the setting room. Although his toes touched the ground he was quite dead.

No. 15. Two Brothers transport, Off Walcherine. 8th November, 1809.

On the 17th *Ultimo* we received orders to prepare a detachment of every man fit for duty to hold ourselves in readiness to march to Portsmouth. All we could muster was about 300. These were formed into six divisions, and under the command of Major Dunkin we marched to and embarked at Spithead, sailed for this place, dropped anchor between the Islands of Walcherine and South Beveland. Since we left these islands our people have evacuated South Beveland and the enemy has taken possession of it, the troops are so sickly in Walcherine. It is intended to destroy the works and dock yards together with every place belonging to the French Government, then leave the place; we are to remain on board to act as circumstance shall require; the enemy is throwing up works on the Island they occupy, and it is said they are meditating an attack on Walcherine. The river is full of our gunboats, which are constantly annoying them, and they in return keep up a constant fire on our boats, so nothing is heard all day and night long but the clang of war, and seemingly without effecting any purpose whatever. Our situation here is not very pleasant, the weather is cold and we have not much room to exercise ourselves on deck; one comfort attending us is gin, and tobacco is cheap, so we can enjoy ourselves over a pipe and glass; the cause Of our remaining on board is for the preservation of our health.

No. 16. Horsham Barracks. 17th February. 1810.

We remained in our uncomfortable station on board the *Two Brothers,* until the beginning of January instant and then sailed once more for old England.

Some time before our departure the enemy were making active preparations for a descent on Walcherine, everything worth moving having been removed on board the fleet. The works at Flushing, Dock-Yard etc. being destroyed, the army of occupation embarked, we bid *adieu* to this land of sickness and death.

The headquarters of the regiment being still at Horsham we received orders on our landing at Portsmouth to proceed to this place; about a mile from the barracks we were met by Colonel Mainwaring. This was another of the colonel's proud days, he had brought the colours and band with him, as he said to do us honour. He welcomed us a hundred times, saying give each man a sprig of laurel, he delighted to honour such men. The day was to be devoted to feasting and mirth; he had ordered the 'fatted calf' to be killed and it was now smoking hot on the tables in the barracks, so we jogged on to the tune of 'See the conquering hero comes' to eat the 'fatted calf.'

We found our dinners ready and sat down to it with a good appetite, cans of beer were going round merrily, and we were asking and answering questions, when who should pop in but Colonel Mainwaring, shouting 'It's just as I thought serjeant, why are not these poltroons cleaning my good soldiers appointments instead of robbing them. The service detachment wants an hour's rest after dinner over the can and pipe. We who have been staying at home eating the bread of idleness should think it on honour to wait on such men. If you do not make them all as clean as new pins, your port liberty shall be stopped, not one of you shall have the honour of spending the afternoon with them.' The remainder of the day as a matter of course, was devoted to the jolly God; the ague is still making great havoc in our ranks, I have escaped as yet.

No. 17. Horsham Barracks. 17th June 1810,

For the want of something better I shall fill up the remainder of this letter with an anecdote or two of Colonel Mainwaring. The 4th of June being the grand jubilee or King's birthday June 1810 we marched through Horsham to a gentleman's park, had a field day to amuse several ladies and gentlemen, then fired a *feu-de-joi*, and marched home. We formed square in the barrack yard, when the colonel began a lecture that lasted some time, he was in one of his best of good humours—an act of grace was to be performed, the prison doors were to be opened and the prisoners set free, but there was one unfortunate man whose crime was so great, that it required something extraordinary to be done before he could be purged from his guilt. It was Serjeant Harrison, he had been on command and had lost or spent the public money intrusted to him, about £2—and deserted. He had been brought back on the 2nd inst. The colonel lectured poor Harrison a long time, was afraid if he released him without thoroughly wiping away all his guilt, it would be of little or no benefit to him or to the service. After a little consideration, he shouted out, 'is there none can advise me in this important affair?'

All was silent, no one tendered their advice. 'What' he cried 'will no one put their shoulders to the wheel? Then I must lift the wagon myself, spread the colours.'

The colours were brought to the middle of the square, the tops put together, thus forming a kind of arch.

'Now Harrison' said the colonel 'pass uncovered under those honourable colours.'

This done, he shouts out, 'He's half clean, he must pass under them again, let the colours touch him this time, now his crime he's blotted out forever he is regenerated, the new born babe is not more innocent, and, woe to the first man who ever mentions the affair to him.' No one had been appointed in his place, he was therefore ordered to join his company and retain his rank. He was not disliked, so everyone was pleased to see him restored in his former situation again.

The following is of a different complexion. The colonel was in one of his worst of bad humours, it happened, after a field day when everything went wrong, as we were returning home and was just entering the town. As is usual, the music struck up a quick march. The colonel spurred his horse and dashed into the centre of the band, nearly upset the big drummer, whirled his horse about, drove the musicians in all directions, shouting 'They shall have no music, the poltroons, let them sneak through the town like a set of thieves. I would not give a bunch of dogs' meat for the whole corps. I will not disgrace myself with remaining with such a set of scoundrels, I will exchange or resign etc.'

We marched into the barracks as quiet as if we were going to surprise the enemy, there we got it 'hip and thigh' until the colonel was quite exhausted. He then dismissed us saying 'a bird that can sing and won't, must be made sing.' An order appeared directly after that convinced us he was not joking. It was for four hours extra drill per day, for a month.

No. 18. Stenning (Steyning) Barracks. 30th August, 1810.

The 10th. inst. the regiment marched to Brighton to be present at the celebration of the Prince of Wales' birthday. We were quartered in the town, the other troops about 16,000 were encamped in the neighbourhood. On the 12th the army assembled on the hills near Brighton, fired a *feu de joi*, and marched past the prince in review order, then returned home to the different encampments and quarters. The next day the troops marched to their respective stations in the district, except our corps. We remained in Brighton two days, to perform some evolutions before the prince, who was pleased to signify his approbation of the manner we had performed every movement. This piece of intelligence was imparted to us by Colonel Mainwaring who swaggered in front of the corps like a bashaw with three tails. We then returned to Stenning.

Perhaps I have too often troubled you with anecdotes of Colonel Mainwaring, you must excuse me if I trouble you again. This I trust you will do when I inform you, if I am not the principal performer, I am at least the second in the farce. We had not been long at Stenning Barracks. before the ophthalmia made its appearance in the corps. It began to spread rapidly and many men were sent to Bognor, where an ophthalmia hospital is established, every precaution that wisdom and experience could devise was taken, but for all the dire disorder increased. Colonel Mainwaring was going mad. He said the men were making their eyes bad, to prevent the regiment going on service. One morning he said the next case should come under his own hand, the next man whose eyes should become bad should be locked up in the dead house for twenty four hours, his hand tied behind him and kept on bread and water, then if his eyes got better he would flog him, for it would then be evident that the men were making their eyes bad by applying something to them.

At this time my eyes were weak, but no sign of inflammation in them, so they had escaped the colonel's notice, but I was in continual fear least he would select me to try his new experiment on. It happened one night I was on guard, there came on a heavy storm of thunder and lightening. It instantly struck my mind that by going to the doctor and complain that the lightening had hurt my eyes, I should be a day's march in front of the colonel. Accordingly the next morning I saw Dr. Johnstone and told him my tale. He said my eyes were only weak, that a dose of salts would set them to rights. Thus far I had succeeded.

The next morning, however, 'Old Spunk' (for that is one of the names he goes by) came down the ranks, made a dead halt in front of me (at this time my eyes were running with water, owing to the excessive heat of the sun, and its reflection from the shingles with which the barrack yard is covered). The old boy seized hold of my shoulder strap and began lugging me out of the ranks, shouting 'I've got him, set a rogue to catch a rogue he's sure to find him, I saw this fellow winking and blinking when I was in front of the battalion, away with him to the dead house etc.'

As he was leading me along, I mentioned Dr. Johnstone's name and that I had reported my eyes to him etc. He then called Dr. Reid, who was on parade. Dr. Reid said Johnstone had been speaking to him about me and confirmed what I had told the colonel; he also said it was only weakness, increased from the reflection of the sun and said I had better be kept away from the hospital etc. This so pleased the colonel that he turned round and shouted 'I was mistaken in this lad, he is the best soldier in the corps, he has been to the doctor, he has done as you all should do, he has put his shoulder to the wheel, etc., I will be kind to him, no more parades or drills till his eyes are well, he shall take his walks in the cooling shade'. This and much more blarney took up his time a few minutes.

When I was ordered to fall in, I took up my place, and the colonel went in search of another victim for the dead house. He shortly returned to me saying I must drink 'Three ounces and a half of the bitter gall Epsom salts, and two hours knapsack drill in double quick time would open my back door, and when the back door was opened we could not err'—then calling the serjeant of the hospital, whom he ordered to mix up the dose. Some salts were brought to me in the ranks in a tin quart pot.

As I was about to drink it he said 'stop, come out six paces in the front to set an example.' I was walking out carelessly, when I was ordered back again, to take six paces in ordinary time for he observed when we were under arms everything must be done with double celerity. Out I marched with quart pot in one hand and firelock shouldered. When I had halted, I had to wait for the word to drink, for Colonel Mainwaring never does anything by halves. He stood in front of me, putting his hand on his sword, shouted out 'drink it up'—'drink it up'—as often as he saw me swallow, the words 'drink it up' was repeated and the sword drawn an inch or two.

When I had taken the cup from my mouth, the sword was plunged back into the scabbard, with this exclamation 'You're a lucky fellow, if you had not finished it before I had drawn my sabre, I would have cut you down.' I gave the cup to the man who brought it from the hospital, he was swaggering away when some lumps at the bottom of the cup made a rattle. (The salts in use in military hospitals at that time was very course, and a brownish colour.)

The colonel ran after him, kicked his seat of honour, seized the cup, shouting—'set a rogue etc.' He then rammed his hand into the cup, and took out what had not dissolved, brought it to me and made me eat it, repeating 'about opening the back door etc.' I did not have the two hours' drill, my eyes got better and Colonel Mainwaring does not forget to take the whole credit to himself.

No. 19. His Majesty's Ship Revenge, Spithead. 9th February, 1811.

On the 22nd January we embarked on board the *Revenge* (74). Headquarters and five companies. The *Denmark* (74), three companies, and the *Vengure* (74), two companies. The first thing that caught my eye on board, was the signal made by the immortal Nelson, when going into action at Trafalgar: 'England expects every man to do his duty.' This Motto appears across the after-part of the quarter deck in large bold characters of gold. I am told that every ship that was with Nelson that day bears this distinguished honour as a memento of the glorious action. We are much more comfortable on board this ship then we were on board the *l'Impetueux*. Our lower deck guns are cleared out and we have only half the number of men on board. A large armament is assembled and our destination is Portugal to reinforce Lord Wellington's army.

When on board the *l'Impetueux* I had formed a very unfavourable opinion of the navy. A short time on board this ship has in a great measure corrected that opinion. The captain goes by the name of 'Father.' Cursing and swearing is not allowed. The good feeling existing between the captain and sailors was fully displayed last Sunday morning, when the ship's company assembled for the captain's inspection. It was truly pleasing to see the good old man, their 'Father' as the men have justly named him, walking through the ranks of sailors, who all appeared as clean as possible, with health and contentment glowing on their faces. As he past the men he seemed to impart to each a portion of his own good nature.

After the sailors, our inspection came on. The good old man accompanied the colonel through our ranks, his affectionate looks and smiles gained all our hearts. After inspection all hands were piped to church. The place set apart for divine service is the quarter deck, which is sheltered from the wind or sun by hanging out different colours. This day the spirit of the fourth commandment was put into force far beyond anything I could have expected, nothing was done but what was absolutely necessary, the sailors neat and clean employing themselves agreeable to the bent of their own inclinations. In one place might be seen a sailor sitting on a gun reading to his shipmates, others reading to themselves, in another place a party could be listening to the hair breadths escapes and wondrous deeds of some well fought battle, while others less careless would assemble in some sequestered spot, offering up prayers and singing hymns of praise to their creator and redeemer. Amongst each party of sailors might be seen a good sprinkling of red jackets, this gave life to the scene. I viewed it with delight, and I might truly say I never passed a day in my life so completely happy.

Through the week all is bustle, every hand is employed, the same cheerfulness prevailed, no cursing or swearing or ropes ends is brought into practice. The word of command or boatswain's pipes is sufficient to set this mighty living machine in motion. Two evenings each week is devoted to amusement, then the boatswain's mates, with their pipes summons 'All hands to play.' In a moment the scene is truly animating. The crew instantly distribute themselves, some dancing to a fiddle, others to a fife.

Those who are fond of the marvellous, group together between two guns and listen to some frightful tale of ghost and goblin, another party listens to some weather beaten tar who 'spins a yarn' of past events, until his hearers sides are almost cracked with laughter. Again is to be found a select party immortalizing the heroes of gone by days by singing songs to the memory of Duncan, Howe, Vincent, and the immortal Nelson, while others whose souls are more refined are singing praises to the God of Battles. Thus my time is passed in the midst of health, pleasure and contentment.

No. 20. Lisbon. 10th March, 1811.

We remained at Spithead until the latter end of February, then weighed anchors and stood down Channel, wind favourable, cleared the land's end, and was scudding away, when the wind chopped round, we tried two days beating against it but was obliged to re-enter the Channel and the whole fleet anchored in Torbay. Here we had to wait for a better wind. At length we sailed again but before we could make Cape Finester the wind became foul again. After many vain attempts to weather the Cape we had to return again to Torbay; we now found the *Denmark* was missing, no fears were entertained for her safety, she was a good sailing vessel, and everyone was of opinion she had weathered the cape, and had proceeded to Lisbon. Let it suffice for me to say we were obliged to put back into Torbay six different times before we could weather Cape Finester, this difficulty being surmounted we soon made the Tagus.

I am now half a sailor, having stood all the bad weather without seasickness, indeed I never enjoyed better health and spirits in my life. I should much wish to describe to you the awful grandeur of being on board a line of battle ship in a heavy gale of wind. If you will make allowances I will attempt it. This mighty Leviathan was tossed up and down and rode on the waves like a cork, one moment we were on the top of a mountainous wave, then the eye would catch others of the fleet, some rising as it were from the bottom of the deep, while others who had gained the summits of the waves was again driven down by irresistible force to the abyss below. Then when below, hemmed in by mountains of water, or casting your eyes upward there would be seen perhaps a three decker that seemed to be suspended in the air, and threatening you with instant destruction, but before the thought had well taken possession of your mind a change had taken place in the fairy scene, the three decker is below, and you had Majestically risen to the top, and in your turn seem to threaten her.

When we were at sea, when the weather permitted the amusements went on the same as at anchor. Once a week a play would be performed by some of the officers and men. On those occasions a Theatre would be erected as it were by magic. The scenery displayed the skill of the artist and the manner some of the characters were sustained would have drawn bursts of applause from a London audience.

On entering the Tagus the wind blew right in our teeth, this gave us much trouble to get up to Lisbon, every minute it was about ship. In making one of these tacks I had a very narrow escape with my life. I had incautiously gone too near the larboard main tack, the ship was going about, the seamen shouted to me. I knew there was danger, but from whence it proceeded or which way to escape I was equally at a loss to know. The tack passed so near my head that one of the sailors said his sight was taken from him with terror. If the rope had struck me instant death would have been the consequence. I remarked to one of the sailors that if it had struck me it would have given me the head ache.

'It would not' said he 'for that same tack would kill an elephant, as easy as it would a cat.'

As soon as we made our anchorage, several of our men came along side, they had been in Lisbon above a fortnight. The *Denmark* had weathered the cape, the haze had prevented her seeing the remainder of the fleet, so she prosecuted her voyage. We came to anchor near to Fort Julian and the next morning the 9th. March landed at Black Horse Square.

Before we left the ship the captain gave us all an allowance of rum. If we were pleased to get on land again, we could not part with the crew without feelings of sorrow at the thought of parting with men who had deprived themselves of many comforts to add to ours; there was one pleasing prospect, we were leaving them under the fostering care of their good old 'Father,' not a man had been flogged during the time we were on board.

The first thing that attracted my attention on landing was the great number of friars and monks, the place swarmed with them. What a pity they are not otherwise employed when their country demands the service of all her sons. How many fine regiments could be formed by these men. We are now quartered in a convent, the monks outnumbers us three to one. It will be some time before we shall march for the army, we have to be provided with many things before we take the field. Horses, mules and donkeys are to be purchased. Blankets, camp-kettles and many other things are to be served to us, but there will be no unnecessary delay in providing those things and as soon as we are complete we shall march.

No. 21. Lisbon. 13th March, 1811.

What an ignorant superstitious, priest-ridden, dirty, lousy set of poor devils are the Portuguese. Without seeing them it is impossible to conceive there exists a people in Europe so debased. The filthiest pigs sty is a palace to the filthy houses in this dirty stinking city, all the dirt made in the houses is thrown into the streets, where it remains baking for months until a storm of rain washes it away. The streets are crowded with half starved dogs, fat priests and lousy people. The dogs should all be destroyed, the able-bodied priests draughted into the army, half the remainder should be made to keep the city clean, and the remainder if they did not inculcate the necessity of personal cleanliness should be hanged. Then would the people be relieved from a heavy tax, the army so reinforced that in one campaign we should, to use one of Colonel Mainwaring's old sayings, 'not only be able to beat the enemy but eat them afterwards.'

In the middle of the day the sunny sides of the streets swarms with men and women picking the vermin from their bodies, and it is no uncommon sight to see two respectable dressed persons meet and do a friendly office for each other by picking a few crawlers from each other's persons. How is a stranger surprised to go into one of their places of worship, his eyes dazzles with the costly ornaments, and the great number of lighted lamps and candles (this is what I call a burning shame), better the money was laid out for the poor then in such gewgaws. This time of the year is the priest's harvest, numbers of processions are daily parading the streets.

There is nothing so degrading to human nature as the conduct of the people on those occasions. As the processions pass, the people fall on their knees, smite their breast, 'knock head' as the Chinese do to Jos. Remain in this humiliating posture until the host has passed one. Half of their religion consists in ringing of bells. Such a confounded clatter is kept up all day and half the night, that it is enough to drive one mad. Woe to any poor soul that has got an headache.

A few days ago I was struck with a pleasing sight, it was one of the holy thieves clothed in nothing but a pair of inexpressibles. In every other respect he was quite naked, crawling on his hands and knees, and a great ill-looking fellow with a cat o'nine tails whisking the flies off his back. In front a priest carried a crucifix while some others followed in the procession. What he had been guilty of I was not able to learn no farther than he had given offence to some of Holy Brotherhood.

41

We are now quite prepared to take the field. We expect to receive the order to march every hour, the weather is beautifully fine, like the latter end of May in England.

No. 22. Villa Mayor. 20th April 1811.

On the 14th March we proceeded up the Tagus on boats to Villa Franca above Lisbon. We passed the *l'Impetueux;* the men had mounted the rigging and yards to see us pass. When we came abreast of her, the crew gave us three hearty cheers, the complement was returned by us, and some of our men did not forget to enquire after Ugly Betty.

Before we left Lisbon we had served to us, seven day biscuit, five day meat, and two days wine. Each man's kit consisted of one blanket, one watch–coat, two shirts, two pair stockings and two pair boots, one pair of soles and heels, besides all the other little etceteras, necessary to make up the soldiers kit. Sixty rounds of ball cartridge in the pouch; all this was load enough for a donkey. We arrived at Villa Franca in the afternoon, received two more rations of bread, meat and wine, and the next morning began our march towards the famous lines at Torres Vedras. These we passed the next day, all around us now was one vast scene of desolation.

On the 16th arrived at the City of Leyria. The enemy had commenced the destruction of this place, but being pushed so close by the advance they were obliged to leave the work of destruction half completed. The town had been on fire in several places, the houses were completely glutted, doors, windows, shutters, and in many places the floors were ripped to pieces for fuel, furniture broken to pieces and thrown into the streets, the churches did not escape, the graves were opened, and the dead dragged out. This was horrible. The dead lay scattered about, some had been buried many years, others only a few weeks. In one of the churches laid an inhabitant and a priest, both stabbed in the side with a bayonet. They were both on the steps leading to were the grand altar once stood. They had no doubt retired here thinking the sanctity of the place would protect them, but no place would shelter the innocent and defenceless from such hell-hounds. There was not a living soul in the place but one solitary female. She was laying on a bed covered with blood, having received from the hands of the French soldiers eleven bayonet wounds.

We left this place next morning, the ruins still smoking. This day we saw several women and children coming from their hiding places. There appearance was frightful, scarcely able to crawl for the want of food, their deathlike countenances and their hollow sepulchral voices would excite pity from savages. They would fall on their knees and beg a morsel of bread for Jesus, Mary and Joseph's sake. Thousands must have died of starvation and thousands more must perish, for there is no help at hand, rich and poor are all reduced to the same state. Towns and villages destroyed, the vineyards, everything the enemy could lay their hands on has shared in the common destruction. This is not confined to their line of march only; parties has been sent out to their right and left for plunder and to destroy, every days advance presents the same sad spectacle, to our view. The demand on our haversacks increased every day until we had completely emptied them; Not a biscuit was now to be found in the regiment.

We were in the midst of a desert a long march in front and no hope of getting more bread until we could gain some place where some commissariat was stationed; thus circumstanced it required all the art of Colonel Mainwaring to keep up our drooping spirits. One day he halted us, called the quarter master, took out a letter and said he had received the welcome news, bread was at hand. The quarter master was to ride forward and purchase enough to last the regiment a week. We then continued our march 'til night, stretching our necks and making the best use of our eyes at every turn of the road to see if we could catch a glimpse of the quarter master. It was all a delusion. At length we turned off the road and encamped for the night; in the morning the colonel wondered where the quarter master could be. He was confident that bread was at no great distance, for he could smell it, it could not be far off. At this moment the quarter master appeared with a loaf. The colonel held it up, saying: 'I knew I was right, my nose never deceived me, there is plenty of this only two leagues distant, come let us away to the feast.'

Two leagues brought us to Carapina Camp. Here a great part of the army was halted, waiting for provisions. We received half an allowance of biscuit and rum with a full ration of meat. This was all we were to expect until the commissariat mules should arrive from Lisbon except meat. Bullocks always travel with us. Three days later we were agreeably surprised to hear our bugle sound to go for bread, meat and rum. This put new life into us.

Two days before we arrived here, we came to the remains of a bridge. This the enemy had blown up before their rear guard and baggage had crossed. The river was full of dead bodies quite naked, they had been stripped by the peasantry and thrown in. The bank of the river was crowded with dead horses, mules and donkeys for half a league.

In this camp the 7th Division was formed. The 1st Brigade consisted of the 51st, 85th and the Duke of Brunswick Light Infantry Regiment and Chasseurs Brittanique Regiment, commanded by Colonel Cayler 85th Regiment. The 2nd Brigade consisted of the 2nd Cussadores, 7th and 18th Portuguese Regiments. The division is commanded by Major General Houston.

The arrival of provisions was a signal to be off, so we marched to Villa Mayor, where we are now stationed. It is the head quarters of the division; this part of the country is not quite so bad as that we had passed, most of the houses have got their roofs on, no thanks to the enemy—they had no time for mischief.

They had orders to quit and they knew if they lingered it would not be John Doe or Richard Roe they would have to deal with; our provisions has run out again but the inhabitants are beginning to assemble and bring in some eatables to the market. The enemy are not far off, they are hanging about Ciudad Rodrigo and Almaida, which places they have very strongly garrisoned.

No. 23. Portalégro, 21st May 1811.

We remained at Villa Mayor until the 2nd inst then marched on Fuentes d'Onor. The enemy had assembled all his force, intending to relieve the garrison of Almaida. On the 3rd about midday we went into position on a height in front of the village of Fuentes. The 71st Light Infantry Regiment with other troops was warmly engaged at the village until night, various was the success of each party, the place was many times lost and won, at last the British succeeded in possessing the place and held it until the 5th when the battle was fought.

On the 4th both armies were occupied in manoeuvring. The morning of the 5th shewed us the enemy in columns waiting for the word to attack us, as they did not seem in much hurry we began boiling some rice for breakfast, but they soon spoiled our cooking by sending some round shot amongst us. We soon took up our position—it was on the right of the line and at some distance from the main body. The enemy came down on our right in an immense body of cavalry, we had to throw back our right wing to oppose them. We had only two Portuguese guns, one of these the enemy dismounted the first round they gave us, and the Portuguese very prudently scampered off with the other for fear it would share the same fate.

Our position after throwing back our right wing was about twenty paces under the brow of a gentle descent, beyond which was a large plain covered with the enemy. A little distance in our rear the ground began to rise rather abruptly, it was covered with cork trees, rocks and straggling bushes, there was also a long wall behind us. On the high ground this was occupied by the Chasseurs Brittanique Regiment and the Portuguese Brigade. We had some men in our front skirmishing, but they were soon driven in and formed with us, thus situated we anxiously waited the attack.

An officer of hussars soon shewed himself on the brow, he viewed us with much attention then coolly turned round in his saddle and waved his sword. In an instant the brow was covered with cavalry. This was a critical moment, the least unsteadiness would have caused confusion. This would have been followed with defeat and disgrace. The enemy had walked to the brow, and their trumpeter was sounding the charge, when Colonel Mainwaring gave the words 'Ready, Present, Fire.' For a moment the smoke hindered us from seeing the effect of our fire, but we soon saw plenty of horses and men stretched not many yards from us.

The Chasseurs Brittanique Regiment now opened a fire, as did the Portuguese over our heads. It was a dangerous but necessary expedient, for our fire was not sufficient to stop the cavalry, so we were obliged to lay down and load. The confusion amongst the enemy was great, and as soon as the fire could be stopped a squadron of the 1st Royal and of the 14th Light Dragoons gallantly dashed in amongst the enemy and performed wonders, but they were soon obliged to fall back—for the enemy outnumbered them twenty to one or more; we now sorely felt the want of artillery and cavalry.

The enemy had formed again and was ready for another attack, our force was not sufficient to repel such a mass, so the order was given to retire independently by regiments. We retired through the broken ground in our rear, crossed the wall, and was pretty safe from their cavalry, but they had brought up their guns to the brow and was serving out the shot with a liberal hand. We continued retiring and soon came to a narrow rapid stream, this we waded up to our armpits and from the steepness of the opposite bank we found much difficulty in getting out. This caused some delay so the regiment waited until all had crossed, then formed line and continued our retreat in quick time; it was now the division was suffering much from the enemy's fire, the Portuguese in particular, the Chasseurs Brittanique Regiment came in for their share.

Thanks to Colonel Mainwaring we came off safe, although the shot was flying pretty thick, yet his superior skill baffled all the efforts of the enemy, he took advantage of the ground and led us out of a scrape without loss. I shall never forget him, he dismounted off his horse, faced us and frequently called the time 'right, left' as he was accustomed to when drilling the regiment.

His eccentricity did not leave him, he would now and then call out 'That fellow is out of step, keep step and they cannot hurt us.'

Another time he would observe such a one, calling him by name, 'cannot march, mark him for drill, serjeant major.'

'I tell you again they cannot hurt us if you are steady, if you get out of time, you will be knocked down.'

He was leading his horse and a shot passed under the horses belly which made him rear up. 'You are a coward' he said 'I will stop your corn three days.'

At length we came to Alamadela. Here the division went into a strong position behind the village, our regiment was posted in the vineyards in front of the village, this put a stop to the further progress of the enemy. The 85th joined us here, they had been employed on out duty, unfortunately the cavalry came upon them when they were extended. They had lost upwards of three parts of the regiment, I believe mostly prisoners. The battle lasted until night but the enemy could make nothing of us, indeed with some skirmishing against a few parties they sent to reconnoitre is all we had to do after.

On the 7th at night the garrison of Almaida blew up some works and managed to get away, the reports in circulation do not reflect much credit on the troops employed before the town. The object of the enemy being to relieve the garrison, and as the works was now in our possession, they retired across the Agueda.

The 3rd and 7th Divisions marched to Villa Velha, here we crossed the Tagus and proceeded to Portalegra where we have halted for a few days, having received the intelligence of the defeat of Soult at Albuera. Soult was aware of our approach, he therefore tried his luck before we could arrive. It was well for him he did, if we had joined the army we should have overwhelmed him. My letter is almost full, I have many anecdotes to you that came under my notice.

One of our men shot a horse, the dragoon made an attack on

him with his sword but Maxwell, for that is his name, ran him through his body with such force that he could not extricate his bayonet without placing his foot to the fellow's ribs. General Houston was separated from us by the enemy; when our cavalry charged, his orderly Dragoon (1st Royal) cut a lane through the enemy and they both escaped. One of the 14th Light Dragoons behaved gallantly, he was attacked by five at once, he managed to kill and wound the whole and rejoined his comrades in handsome stile.

Our loss is trifling only having the bugler and fifteen rank and file killed and wounded.

No. 24. Camp before Badajoz. 6th June. 1811.

We halted but two days at Portalegra then marched and laid siege to Badajoz. The 3rd Division is encamped on our left across the river, the 7th Division in front of Fort San Cristoval and the 4th Division, on the Spanish side of the town. This place is very strong and the general commandant is said to be the best engineer in the French service. The work of digging trenches and building batteries soon commenced. After our arrival it is a saying the more danger the more honour, if so this must be the most honourable job we could have been set about.

Fort San Cristoval is an out work of great strength, close to the garrison, but is separated from it by the river, its communication is by a bridge. It is against this fort we are throwing up our works. Under the cover of night we commence throwing up any new work, as soon as the enemy hear the pickaxe they give us a light by throwing out a quantity of fire balls. This would be very accommodating on their part if they did not open as many guns as they can bring to bear on the place. These balls give a great light around the place where they fall and enables them to point their guns with greater precision.

The other night we began to brake ground in a fresh place, they very politely gave us a light by sending out six beautiful fire balls, the word 'down' was given, but before we had time to stretch ourselves on mother earth they discharged a volley of round and grape shot. One of the round shot must have passed pretty near my cranium, I thought I was wounded, my head ached violently. I felt the pain a long time and it was with difficulty I could perform my duty. Had I been working in a place where there was no danger I certainly should have given up, but here I was ashamed to complain, lest any of my comrades should laugh at me.

It is astonishing with what rapidity our works advances, in a short time we had four batteries ready. When off duty, in our camp we are exposed to the scorching heat of the sun, we have no tents, not a tree or bush to shelter us, we have to fetch every drop of water we use at the distance of three miles, we must be ready at a moment's notice should the enemy sally. The other day an accident of an alarming nature occurred, a fire broke out in our camp, the ground being covered with a sort of thistle that was completely dried by the sun, and caused the fire to spread alarmingly. It was making rapid progress to the spot where the whole of the ammunition was deposited. Fortunately we subdued the fire before it caused any mischief.

The day our batteries opened on Fort San Cristoval I was on covering party and stationed in the trench in front of No 4 Battery. The first hour the shock of the guns would almost lift us off the ground, but we soon became so used to it that we could sleep as comfortable as if we had been in a feather bed. The duty in the trenches by day is very fatiguing, almost suffocated for the want of air and nearly baked by the sun, parching with thirst, with a beautiful river close to us but might as well be an hundred miles off—for if anyone only indulged the eye with a peep, bang goes half a dozen muskets at his head. Then we are kept in constant motion by swarms of flies, to say nothing of the vermin that has stationed themselves inside our clothes, who are as busy as possible laying siege to our bodies, while we cannot bring a finger to bare on them.

Yesterday about midday I was in the trench in front of No 2 Battery. An old Portuguese had just arrived with a car loaded with ammunition drawn by two oxen, he had just got his load deposited in the magazine when the enemy favoured us with a shell from the 'big Tom of Lincoln' (the name we have given to one of their tremendous mortars – after the 5 tons 8 cwt bell at Lincoln Cathedral). I watched its progress and saw it burst a few feet over the oxen, they were cut to pieces with the car. When the cloud of dust and smoke had cleared away we observed the old fellow running like a deer, he had miraculously escaped unhurt. Besides killing the oxen, one of our guns in the battery was dismounted. Another was soon mounted, but it caused some trouble as they dapped another shell into the battery and wounded several men.

This afternoon the fort begins to present a wide breach. The firing is going on with great spirits on both sides, we have heard that Soult is collecting all the force he can get together to come to the relief of the garrison.

I shall close with relating an anecdote of one of the artillery. This man had been severely wounded in one of the batteries by a shell. It was necessary to amputate an arm and both legs. Doctor Webster commenced the operation with a leg, this done the arm followed. It was thought proper that the man should rest awhile before the other limb should be cut off, but the man insisted that the doctor should proceed, observing 'it's no use to make two bites of a cherry, what use is it in making so much fuss about a leg that will be of no service to me or anyone else again.' It was soon off and he dropped into a deep sleep.

Early the next morning the doctor visited him, he found him leaning on the only elbow he had left smoking a short black pipe, and was apparently as comfortable as if the amputations had taken place a month.

No. 25. Campa Mayor. 20th June 1811.

My last informed you that the breach in Fort San Cristoval was near complete. The incessant fire from our works soon rendered it fit for storming. In the afternoon of the 7th inst. (actual on evening of 6th) three divisions of our corps each containing twenty-five men and one division of the 85th containing twenty-five men, were paraded in the camp—this made the party hundred rank and file having a due proportion of officers with it. Ensign Dyas, 51st Regiment, a young officer of great promise, of a most excellent disposition, and beloved by every man in the corps—an Irishman by birth and whose only fortune was his sword—volunteered to lead the forlorn hope.

We were commanded by Major Macintosh, 85th Regiment, and supported by the remainder of the division. In the evening we advanced towards the fort, but lay hid until the shades of night had cast her mantle over us, then moved on towards the breach observing the strictest silence. To divert the attention of the enemy all our guns were opened on the fort, but the French commandant was not to be duped, the sly old fox had anticipated our visit and had prepared everything to give us a warm reception. Each man in the fort was provided with six loaded firelocks. Live shells were placed so as to be rolled into the trench. In short, nothing that would annoy us was forgotten.

We advanced up the glacis close to the walls. Not a head was to be seen above the walls, and we began to think the enemy had retired into the town. We entered the trench and fixed our ladders, when sudden as a flash of lightening the whole place was in a blaze. It will be impossible for me to describe to you what followed. You can better conceive it by figuring to your mind's eye a deep trench or ditch filled with men who are endeavouring to mount the wall by means of ladders.

The top of this wall crowded with men hurling down shells and hand grenades on the heads of them below, and when all these are expended they have each six or seven loaded firelocks which they discharge into the trench as quick as possible. Add to this some half dozen cannon scouring the trench with grape. This will immediately present to your imagination the following frightful picture. Heaps of brave fellows killed and wounded, ladders shot to pieces, and falling together with the men down upon the living and the dead. Then ever and anon would fall upon us the body of some brave Frenchman whose zeal had led him to the edge of the wall in its defence, and had been killed by

51

their own missiles or by the fire of our covering party.

But in the midst of all these difficulties, great as they were, we should have taken the fort but for an unforeseen accident that could not be remedied—it was the ladders were too short. Several men who had gained the top of the ladders could not reach the top of the wall with their firelocks. As soon as this was discovered all hopes of gaining possession was abandoned, and the order was given to retire.

The next morning our little party of hundred were reduced to between twenty and thirty, a cessation of arms for two hours took place to remove our killed and wounded. All the day of the 9th our guns were battering away at the fort, more ladders were prepared and another party consisting of double the numbers from the same corps were formed. Ensign Dyas again volunteered to lead the 'forlorn hope.' This party was commanded by Major McGeechy, 18th Portuguese Regiment. (Wellington's Despatches say 17th.)

This second attempt was attended with the same ill success as the first. It is true we had profited by the discovery of the ladder being too short, but the old fox inside was too deep for us. He had caused all the rubbish to be cleared out of the trench. This again placed us just in the same predicament, our ladders were again too short and if possible we received a warmer reception then before.

The ladder I was on was broken and down we all came together, men, firelocks, bayonets, in one confused mass, and with us a portion of the wall. After some time the fire slackened, as if the enemy were tired of slaughter, when an officer Lieutenant Westropp came running from the western angle of the fort calling out to retire— the enemy were entering the trench by the sally port. We then began to leave the trench. Poor Mr. Westropp was assisting a wounded man in getting out, when he was shot dead just as he had effected his purpose.

I now saw Ensign Dyas calling to the men to leave the trench and retire to our rallying post. As we were retreating down the glacis, a misfortune befell me and I had a very narrow escape of being made prisoner, being cut off from my comrades by the party who sallied. There were eight or nine in the same mess. These the enemy obliged to go into the fort. However, I hit upon an expedient that answered well. I threw myself down by a man who was shot through the head and daubed my white haversack with his blood. I shewed this to the enemy when they ordered me to get up and go into the fort. From the appearance of the blood they must have thought I had a very bad wound in the hip, so they all left me—except one who searched my pockets, took off my shirt, boots and stockings. But more of this in my next, let it suffice that I am safe and was never in better health and spirits.

No. 26. Campa Mayor. 16th July, 1811.

Want of room in my last obliged me to break off short in the midst of my account of the storm. I shall now take up the subject where I was left barefooted and without a shirt on the glacis. The enemy having retired within the fort, the moon rose, which cast a gloomy light round the place. Situated as I was this added fresh horrors to my view, the place was covered with dead and dying, the old black walls and breach looked terrible and seemed like an evil spirit frowning on the unfortunate victims that lay prostrate at its feet.

As the moon ascended it grew much lighter and I began to fear I should not be able to effect my escape, for the enemy kept a sharp look out and if anyone endeavoured to escape they were sure to discharge a few muskets at him. I soon perceived that as often as our batteries fired they would hide behind the walls. I made the most of this by sliding down as often as I observed a flash from our works. By daybreak I had got to the plain below the fort. I had nothing to do but to have a run for it across the No. 1 Battery. This plain, like our camp, was covered with small dry thistles. The enemy discharged two guns loaded with round shot, and several muskets at me. My comrades cheered me and I bounded across like a deer, the devil take the thistles. I felt none of them until I was safe behind the battery.

Captain Douglas gave me a drop out of his bottle, and I made for camp where I arrived just in time to have my name struck out of the killed and wounded list, '*sans*' shirt, '*sans*' boots and '*sans*' stockings. Lieutenant Dyas [1] was in camp. How he had escaped unhurt is a mystery. He was without cap, his sword was shot off close to the handle, the sword scabbard was gone, and the laps of his frock coat were perforated with balls. Indeed everyone who returned bore evident marks where they had been. Their caps, belts, firelocks etc. were more or less damaged. I had three shots pass through my cap, one of which carried away the rosehead and tuft, my firelock was damaged near the lock, and a ball had passed through the but.

This morning, as before, was devoted in collecting the wounded and burying the dead. Major McGeechy was killed, the few that remained of his party carried and followed him to the grave. The loss of the regiment was—killed: Lieutenant Westropp, two serjeants and 130 rank and file; wounded: Captain Smillie, Lieutenant Beardsley and Hicks, seventeen serjeants and 154 rank and file. Besides this we had killed and wounded at work and in the trenches about thirty-four men.

It is truly astonishing with what indifference to personal safety the duties of so dangerous a service is carried on. We soon became familiar to the hissing of shot and the bursting of shell. To pass a dreary hour in the trench we found amusement in putting our caps on the muzzle of our firelocks and just shew them over the breastwork. This would always draw a fire on the cap. We soon turned this sport to advantage—this was stationing some good shots under cover, then shew a few caps for a decoy, some of the enemy eager to make us pay for peeping would expose themselves, thus many brave Frenchmen fell behind their walls to rise no more.

---

1. Mr. Dyas obtained his Lieutenancy vacant by the death of Mr. Westropp, he being the senior ensign. Promotion for leading forlorn hope see 89th Letter dated Portsmouth, 5th May, 1821. I have not returned Ensign Dyas as wounded. I never heard he was until I saw it in the *Adventures of the 88th*. It is very probable he was, slightly. I have described the state the few who returned were in. It is true all were covered with blood. W. W.

As we became more fire proof, the river near us became too great a temptation to be resisted. To the left of No. 1 Battery there was a curve in the river, on the bank stood a small chapel, thirst tempted some of our men to go for water.

They returned safe, but not like the Jews of old, for their report was favourable. They said the chapel and the bank was an excellent cover from the fort, they had bathed and was returned like 'giants refreshed.' What a luxury, several of us made up our minds to taste of its sweets, even should old Beelzebub and all his legions stand in the way.

In half an hour seventeen of us was in the river sporting and knocking the water about like ducks, as thoughtless as if old Fort San Cristoval had changed masters. But this was not to be tolerated—in the middle of our sport we were informed, by a shot that struck against the corner of the little chapel, that we were trespassing, and lest we should not understand its meaning, the enemy dapped a ponderous shell into the river. This rose such a vortex of water that we were whirled about as if some water God had surprised and was about to punish us for our intrusion. Of course we scrambled out and gathered up our clothes, and scampered away to our post, naked—to the no small diversion both of our own comrades as well as the enemy.

Soult, having reinforced his army, advanced to the relief of the garrison. This caused us to raise the siege. After destroying our works and removing the guns, we retired into Campa Mayor. This place is four and a half leagues from Elvas and the same distance from Badajoz. It has been a place of some strength but at present there are no guns mounted, the town is large enough to provide quarters for the 3rd and 7th Divisions.

The enemy has shewn themselves three times in our neighbourhood. Each time we marched out and took up position on the road to Elvas, on high ground. On each occasion we were spectators of some sharp skirmishing with the enemy's advance and our light Cavalry. In these affairs the 11th Light Dragoons has suffered much. The 1st and 2nd German Light Infantry has joined us—these with the Duke of Brunswick's Light Infantry forms our third Brigade, so that our Division is now complete. Colonel Mainwaring is gone to England, it is said for the benefit of his health. Major Rice commands the regiment.

No. 27. Villa Mayor. 5th Sept. 1811.

We marched from Campa Mayor the latter end of July, the enemy having entered Portugal by Ciudad Rodrigo, with a strong force, and advanced to Villa Velha—repeating their old tricks of plundering and destroying everything they could find. At the Tagus they found the bridge removed, and as our advance was not far from them they retired back to the neighbourhood from whence they came.

Our army now went into cantonments on the frontier, we at Villa Mayor. Our men soon began to be very sickly. So great is the number of casualties this moment that we cannot muster 200 men fit for duty. It is now getting late in the season and it is a chance if the army should take the field again. Want of room in my last prevented me informing you that nine men of the Chasseurs Brittanique Regiment were shot for desertion. This corps was originally formed of French Loyalists, but the old hands are continually dropping off and they are replaced by volunteers from the French prisons.

A great number of these men enter our service for no other purpose then to go over to their army as soon as an opportunity offers (and who can blame them). The consequence is the major part of the corps cannot be trusted. I wish they were at the devil or anywhere else, so that we were not plagued with them, for we are obliged to perform all the most dangerous and fatiguing duty of the campaign—for if these men were intrusted on the out posts, more would desert than they do at present. Colonel Custis and Captain Napier are the only British in the regiment.

The Duke of Brunswick's Oels are almost as bad, they too get many from the prisons, this corps had two men desert from Campa Mayor and three shot for desertion. The method of carrying the sentence into execution is as follows. The division is formed into a square having three faces, the prisoners are formed into line, in the square with their backs to the opening, the firing party composed of men from the regiment are drawn up in front of the men only a few paces from them. After the court martial is read, and the men have received spiritual assistance from the chaplain, or if he be a Roman Catholic from a priest, their eyes are bound and they kneel down. When they have made a signal, the firing party—who are ready loaded and firelocks cocked—watch the provost martial who stands with a handkerchief.

At the first signal the firing party presents, and at the next they fire. The muzzles of the pieces are so close to the unfortunate culprits that it is impossible any one can miss the mark, but to make doubly sure the muzzle of a firelock afterwards is put close to the head of each as they lie on the ground and discharged. The division then march past the dead bodies in sections of threes, as the men pass the dead bodies the word of command is given 'Eyes left.' I shall not attempt to describe to you the frightful appearance of the mangled bodies. You can easily imagine that when you are informed that a party for one man contains ten and for every additional culprit four or six are added.

What an unfortunate country this is, most of the towns are in ruins and but few inhabitants are to be met with. There has been, and is, abundance of grapes. The vineyards are loaded, but where are the labourers for the harvest?

This part abounds with lizards of various sorts, some are very beautiful. Amongst these beautiful creatures there is a very large sort—our men who were in India calls them 'Goannas.' It is curious if a man lies down several of them will come round him, always keeping at a humble distance; they will raise themselves on their fore-feet and stretch up their necks and watch him; if he moves they will scamper away in all directions. It is said they are harmless.

No. 28. Penamacor. 10th November, 1811.

We remained at Villa Mayor until the middle of October, then moved a few leagues in advance, where we remained until the 24th. The enemy had collected a great force, and was moving on Ciudad Rodrigo, to throw in supplies. This caused some sharp fighting. On the 25th, 26th and 28th, our division being in reserve, we did not take an active part in any of the skirmishes.

The enemy succeeded in their object, and retired into Spain, and we into Portugal for winter's quarters. On our march I was struck with astonishment at the enormous size of a great number of olive trees, whose bodies appeared like the ruins of some ancient buildings. Every tree represented a spacious arch, some complete, others in a very ruinous state. Our officers rode through them, and several were large enough to allow two to ride through abreast.

One tree in particular took everyone's attention—the arch was full twenty feet in height and so wide that two of our men having hold of hands could not reach its sides with their arms extended, the grandeur of its foliage ran up to an amazing height and spread to an incredible distance in all its beauty, this was a pleasing contrast. While the body seemed dead with age, the young branches shot out above as beautiful as ever I saw any from a young tree. Various were the conjectures respecting the age of these trees, some of our officers were of opinion that they must have been standing between one and two thousand years.

The 7th Division marched to Penamacor, a large city north of the Tagus and about five leagues from the City of Castle Branco. This is our winter's quarters.

The 85th Regiment, or more properly speaking the skeleton, has marched for England. They are replaced by the 68th Light Infantry. The 85th has never been able to recover the rough handling they met with at Fuentes d'Onor, and at Fort San Cristobal.

Colonel Mitchel having exchanged with Colonel Mainwaring has arrived and taken the command of our regiment. I have frequently given you anecdotes of Colonel Mainwaring in which I displayed the fair side of his picture, hiding the dark shades in the back ground. Allow me for the last time in parting with the old man to remark, sometimes his fits of passion would lead or drive him into acts of violence that I am sure must give him pain when his better judgement had resumed her proper seat. For instance at Stenning he saw a man with a pair of shoes; he called to him and accused him with going to sell them, the man was intoxicated and having lost some of his teeth, some of his spittle flew on the colonel—his passion instantly rose, the regiment was ordered out, a drum head court martial took place, the man was tried for spitting in the colonel's face and sentenced to receive 300 lashes, and received the punishment.

In Carapina camp, when we were almost starved for want of provisions, some of our men sold their blankets, to purchase some biscuits. The colonel soon discovered by the size of the knapsack what had taken place, and several men were punished. My comrade had sold his for a dollar, which he paid away for one biscuit about three quarters of a pound weight, but we managed to cheat the old boy. My blanket was made into two, and to make it appear a proper size we had folded up some fern in it; this answered the purpose until the Battle of Fuentes d'Onor when of course we supplied ourselves with good ones.

I could record many instances of petty tyranny, such as giving a man a dozen or two without trial, but I shall let it pass and fill the remainder of this sheet with something rather whimsical, but perhaps I have troubled you with it before. If so I must ask pardon. The latter end of 1810, we lay at Stenning Barracks; one night a deserter escaped from the guard room. The next morning the officer was put on arrest and the serjeant, corporal and sentinel was confined.

On parade, a drumhead court martial was assembled, the colonel was as mad as a march hare. He vowed that if the court did not award severe punishment he would not approve of the sentence. He ordered the bearers to be brought from the hospital, that the men might be carried off the ground after punishment. The sentinel was married and his wife came over to the square, crying. As soon as the colonel saw her, he shouted 'bring her in, and tie her up'—'I will breach her while her husband is being tried.' The poor woman ran off.

At length the court martial was handed to the colonel, he

pointed to a deserter, saying, try him now, or he will escape to-night. The court martial was read the serjeant and corporal was to be reduced and receive 300 lashes each, and the private 500.

The serjeant was stripped, the colonel looked at his back, and said 'his skin has never been broken neither has the other two,' then tearing the court martial to pieces, he added: 'It never shall be said that Colonel Mainwaring was the first that broke it.'

By this time the deserter's sentence was handed to the colonel. 'Strip, sir' was the word 'tie him up' followed.

The colonel looked at his back, called the doctor, the man had never been punished. 'Take him down I will not break his skin and I hope you will make a good soldier.' This and what I have said in former letters will convince you that if at times he was driven to excess by passion, he was in the whole a humane man. I hope his successor will not turn out worse.

No. 29. Penamacor. 28th December 1811.

I have nothing particular to write as we still remain in our old quarters. The greatest evil attending us at present is we want our new clothing, and a fresh supply of necessaries from England, this we are daily expecting. We have spent our Christmas as comfortable as our situation would permit. The weather is very cold and we have had much snow—the oldest people say they do not remember such a great fall.

The house I am quartered in is neither built for comfort or convenience, it is large and might be placed in the second class of buildings. The ground floor, as is the case with all the houses here, is set apart for horses, mules etc. The two next stories are for the accommodation of the inmates, the garrets or cocklofts (for there is no ceiling) is set apart for the servants, in one of these garrets the cooking is performed. A broad thick stone is placed in the corner on which the fire is made, no chimney to convey away the smoke, the only chance it has to escape is through a hole in the corner made by removing a couple of tiles. Generally, the place is so full of smoke you cannot see across the room, and as the fires are made of wood this is very disagreeable to the eyes.

This fire was always occupied by the female part of the family. The mistress, an old shrivelled hag who has been smoke dried some sixty winters and would be a fit character for one of the witches in *Macbeth,* places herself on the right. Next to her are seated her three lovely daughters, real brunettes, with eyes as black as sloes. Then the servants, one of whom seems to be a sister of the old weird hag in the opposite corner, and three others about the same age as the young ladies, but far from disagreeable, complete the group.

Thus huddled together, each having their string of beads and crosses to charm the devil from them, they relate some horrid tale of slaughtered friend by the enemy, or of some headless ghost, till their fears are worked to such a pitch that the least noise frightens them out of what little sense they have. Then they count their beads, crosses themselves and repeat their *Ave Maria* till their fears are lulled to rest.

On one of these occasions I forced myself into their company. Their remarks soon convinced me I was an unwelcome guest, I was a heretic, and they had began to consign me body and soul to the devil. I began to rake the embers for a cinder to light my pipe, but this was not my real intention. I had prepared a devil with the powder of three cartridges and had placed it unperceived on the hearth. My comrade had got another in the other room, ready to start if wanted. I applied the fire to mine, up jumped the party, calling on Jesu, Maria and Joseph and all the holy saints they could think up.

The devil burnt beautifully, it was a complete Mount Etna in miniature. Away went the women into the other room as we had anticipated. There they found another devil ready to receive them. From this they retreated down stairs, leaving the place strewed with beads crosses and slippers. Every night after this we were left in full possession of the fire, the ladies having provided themselves with charcoal fires in their own apartments.

It is astonishing how the term 'heretic' sticks to the English. No good office can wipe out the foul stain, if you wish to come on terms of friendship you must pass for an Irishman. You then are considered as one of themselves, a good Christian.

No. 30. Penamacor. 30th January, 1812.

On the 2nd inst. the 7th. Division marched to the mountains of Sierra de Gatta, in the neighbourhood of Ciudad Rodrigo. We were quartered in the village of Pio, this place contains a few miserable dwellings. We were stationed here to prevent the enemy from rendering assistance to the garrison while the siege was going on. Our duty was very severe, it consisting in furnishing piquets in the passes of the mountains, the nearest to Pio being about two leagues.

The country all round was covered with snow. To shelter ourselves from the keen frosty air that continued during our stay in this part, we dug a large hole in the snow; in the centre, we kept a good fire, round which sat the men on duty; our fuel consisted of furze and fern. Of this we had abundance from places where the snow had drifted, but in collecting it we wanted snow pattern, for often we would sink over our heads, into some hole or burrow, when we expected we had firm footing.

One night, as the relief was returning to the piquet, one of the men popped into a place over head and ears, and others of the party was near paying him a visit. How to get him out was a question, no one could answer. He was therefore obliged to remain there until daylight, when we went to release him from his imprisonment. In a short time we found a way into his apartment. He had had a very comfortable night.

Close to the spot was a shepherds hut with plenty of fern in it, about the hut the furze was very high and bushy on the top, the snow had formed a roof over the furze; he had found the hut, wrapped himself in his blanket, and slept soundly until we awoke him. The men on sentry were not only exposed to the cold winds but were much annoyed by the frequent visits of wolves; this I think for the short time it lasted it has been the severest duty we have yet performed.

We were on duty every other night, our clothes worn thin

and wrecked by the fatigues of the former campaign. It was difficult to tell to what regiment we belonged, for each man's coat was like Joseph's 'a coat of many colours.' We could hear the roaring of the guns at Rodrigo, and we heartily wished the place reduced; the night of the 19th the assault was made and the place carried by storm. This was welcome news to us. A few days after we returned to Penamacor. Here we found our new clothing and a supply of necessaries had arrived; these being issued we were made comparatively comfortable.

To fill up the remainder of this letter for the want of something better I shall give you an account of the manner I have slept this winter. In one corner of the room I have, collected a quantity of dry fern, this forms my bed, it being necessary to strip to keep free from vermin. Every night the contents of my haversack is transferred to my knapsack. This forms my pillow, at the same time secures my kit and provisions from midnight marauders.

The haversack is then converted into a night cap. Being stripped, my legs are thrust into the sleeves of an old watch coat, carefully tied at the cuffs to keep out the cold. The other part of the coat wrapped round my body served for under blanket and sheet. Next my trousers are drawn on my legs over the sleeves of the coat, my red jacket has the distinguished place of covering my seat of honour and lastly my blanket covers all. In this manner I have slept as comfortable as a prince. No idle dreams disturb my rest.

I am in possession of that inestimable treasure, health and a lively flow of spirits. Nothing gives me trouble. I am as well off as my comrades and I am convinced we all are provided for as well as the nature of the service will allow.

Since our return to Penamacor we have been employed in assisting the battering train from Saba Gal to Castala Branco. I understand the train is on the road to Elvas. If so, Badajoz is the next place to be reduced. We expect to march soon. Probably my next will be from that place. It is time we moved from this place for we have nearly glutted the houses, of all the wood we could rip up for fuel. I am getting tired of this dreary abode. The sooner the campaign opens the better. It is true we shall have to encounter great dangers and fatigues. What of that, it is the very life and soul of a soldier to keep moving. If we do suffer privations, at times, we have some sunshiny days, and dame fortune often leads us out of difficulty and puts us into possession of all the luxuries of life.

No. 31. Villa Franca. 19th March, 1812.

We left Penamacor the middle of February cross the Tagus at Villa Velha and continued our march to Burbo, a neat clean little town between four and five leagues from Elvas. When we were on our march from Villa Mayor to Badajoz last May we passed through Portalegra; this time we struck off at Nera to our right. This part appear not to have been visited much by the contending parties, at least not by the enemy. About two leagues from Nera we were astonished to find ourselves, all at one transported into a country abounding with neat clean villages, beautiful vineyards and orange groves, all in a state of high cultivation, which bespoke the industry of the Pisana.

In marching through Villa Rosa, I noticed that the houses were whitewashed inside and well furnished, plenty of pigs and poultry running about while the people were everywhere employed, neat and clean in their persons and their cheerful faces at once shewed that the cruel blast of war had not spread its destroying hand near them. What a blessing to these people that the Tagus separated them from the line of the enemy's retreat and that it lay outside of the usual line of march of their friends.

Burbo is a neat little town, surrounded with gardens, well stocked with fruit etc. Oranges are ripe and in great abundance, these trees have a most pleasing appearance, they are as common in the gardens as apple trees are in England. Here we remained in this delightful little paradise (for such it appeared to us, after passing a dreary winter in the desolated city of Penamacor) about a fortnight; then marched and encamped under the guns of Elvas, close under Fort Elmor. This fort commands everything round it.

The 13th inst, the 1st, 6th, and 7th Divisions, and Heavy Cavalry under the command of Sir Thomas Graham entered Spain by crossing the river below Badajoz. We continued marching without meeting any remarkable occurence until the 17th March when we fell in with the enemy's advance, and made prisoners a corporal and private of dragoons. The next day we halted at Villa Franca.

This being my first trip into Spain I could not but remark that the conduct of the enemy was quite different towards the Spaniards than to the Portuguese. The people seemed very comfortable. In the house I and my comrade were quartered mine host shewed us a bed for our use. However I preferred my old way of sleeping on the floor. We were near the enemy and I should not like to turn out in my shirt. My comrade was of a different opinion—he would sleep on the bed come what would, perhaps he might never get another opportunity. I stretched myself on the floor, and one nap brought the morning.

My comrade had not been so fortunate. He awoke me by cursing the bed. He said he had never had such a night before. He soon dropped off asleep when Queen Mab began her pranks with him, he was soon at home surrounded with his friends, the girl of his heart was close by his side, he was in the act of imprinting a kiss on her lovely rosy cheek when the well known voice of Colonel Mainwaring shouted 'Prepare to receive cavalry.'

This changed the scene, in a moment he was in solid square, the cavalry were sweeping down like a torrent, and a park of guns was tearing the square to pieces, but all at once he was seated by the fireside of our landlord at Burbo, with his little bewitching, beautiful black eyed daughter, with the beads in his hand and the *patrenostre* in his mouth, telling her he was from sweet Ireland and was a good Christian. But just as he was in the act of crossing himself, by the way of confirming the truth of his declaration, the funny queen to punish him for his apostasy introduced the lovely rosy cheeked maid, the pride of Jack's heart. This was worse than all. His Satanic Majesty would have been a more welcome visitor, at that moment. But before he had time to frame an excuse, he found himself on the top of a high fortification that had been surprised by the enemy.

I must cut my story short, suffice it to say, he had been courting, crying, singing, dancing, drinking and smoking, fighting, marching and counter-marching, from the time he lay down until morning when he was roused by a mule who was tuning his pipes in front of our door. The cause of all this confusion arose partly from his sleeping on the bed, for we had not seen such a thing since we left Chichester the night before we left England—except we might reckon the beds on board the *Revenge*—and part arose occasioned by an hour's chat we had over a glass of wine and a pipe, when home with all its sweets became the subject of our conversation.

As we were near the enemy, it brought to our recollection a treaty of friendship had passed between us, this lead to an enquiry and a search to see if we were in possession of the articles of that treaty, which was as follows. Brown had your address and I had his father's, so that if any accident should happen to either of us, the other might write. After we found all right, we finished another bottle over the details of some hard fought battle. This, coupled with the soft bed, had been the cause of all Jack's trouble. It has cured him of sleeping in beds again. He vows he will never get on another if he keeps his health until he returns to England.

No. 32. Albuera Camp. 8th April, 1812.

We had not been many days at Villa Franca when our corps, with two companies of the King's German Light Infantry and a squadron of the 3rd Prince of Wales' Dragoon Guards set off on a secret expedition, to surprise a party of the enemy who were feasting on the good things in the city of Llerena. We marched about three leagues, then halted 'til dark, when we set off again. As the greatest part of our march lay across fields, and over walls, hedges and ditches, we were tumbling about like drunken men.

Besides it rained all night, so that in the morning we looked more like navigators than soldiers. The haze prevented us seeing the town, so that we were close to it before we could discern the proud and lofty steeple of the great church. Not a soul was to be seen, all was silent as death, except the great bell which was calling the lazy monks from their slumbers to their morning prayers. We dashed into town exalting in the thought that we should surprise the frog eating rascals in their beds. But we were deceived, there was not a Frenchman in the town. Whether they had moved from accident or intelligence of our approach I cannot say.

We halted in the market place, and it was laughable to see the surprise and joy of the people on seeing their city in possession of the English, for when they went to rest it was in other hands. They brought out wine, bread, cheese, and many other good things that were very agreeable to our stomachs as we had nothing to do. We were billeted in the town, all now was sunshine, we had forgot the fatigues of the night and had given up ourselves to the service of the jolly god, thinking of course we should have plenty of time at night to fetch up the 'lee way' as the sailor would say, but in this we were deceived—for about dusk our buglers were sounding to fall in, in double quick time and the trumpeters sounding for the dragoons to boot and saddle. The enemy were returning in great force, so we were obliged to be off in our turn as quick as we could, we marched until 2 o'clock in the morning. I never remember in my life to be so tired, I would have given the world only to lie down one minute. At 2 o'clock we turned into a field. I was down in a moment and fast asleep, fully accoutred. After a few hours' rest we returned to Villa Franca.

Two days after this our whole force marched on Llerena again, rested as before in the evening, then moved on towards the city. We were formed in the following order, on the main road the 7th Division with the 6th Division in reserve, on our right the 1st Division, between us a brigade of guns, the cavalry was on our left. The advance guard was composed of two Companies

51st, two of the German legions and two of the Brunswick-ers, with some cavalry. On our march we had collected a great number of dogs. When we neared the town our advance was called in and we moved forward very slow, but an unfortunate affair happened that caused much confusion and was fatal to one of our officers.

It originated in the following manner, our division was in contiguous column of route, several officers who should have been with their companies were at the head of the column, and as our advance was very slow they had imperceptibly gained several paces—or more properly speaking we had lost ground. They had got up unperceived near to one of the enemy's pickets, this caused them to fall back on the column. It being very dark this caused some confusion at the head of the regiment which soon spread through the whole division. The *chasseurs* followed us, and began firing, our paymaster and an hospital assistant who was in the rear of our regiment received the fire of the *chasseurs*. The hospital assistant was killed and our paymaster was severely wounded in the shoulder. Add to this the barking of about 200 dogs, and you will be able to form some sort of a notion what kind of a bother we were in.

Order was soon restored and we pushed forward at a rapid pace. We now could discern something in front like a regular line drawn up to oppose us. Two or three guns were opened on the supposed line but it turned out to be nothing but a long wall. The enemy walked away pursued by some of our light troops, a few shots were exchanged, but we had made a miss of it. After this we kept marching and counter marching near the enemy until the 5th inst. without anything worthy of notice except now and then the enemy would reconnoitre our outposts, which as a matter of course would at times cause an exchange of shots.

On the 5th we encamped on the plain of Albuhera where the battle of that name had recently been fought, here we remained ready to go into position should the enemy think proper to come on. Badajoz was carried by storm last night. It being still, we could hear the roaring of the guns, and concluded the place had been taken. This morning an orderly dragoon, eased our doubts by arriving with the welcome intelligence.

Albuhera still presents visible traces of the late bloody conflict between the army under Marshal Beresford and Soult. In some places large fires had been made, no doubt to burn the dead, again in other places are long ridges or Burrows where some have been buried—of this there can be no doubt for here and there is visible an arm or leg projecting out of the earth. The place is completely strewed with broken shells, breast plates, pouches, scabbards and caps, both of French and English.

No. 33. Camp near Salamanca, 24th June, 1812.

My letter from Castle Banco last month only informed you I was well. I had then no time to write particulars, so I shall in this resume the subject from my letter from Albuhera. The day after I wrote, which I believe was the 8th or 9th April, we broke up from our position and advanced one day's march, but the next day we retired and continued so to do until we recrossed the river below Badajoz, proceeded by easy marches to Villa Velha, recrossed the Tagus and marched on Castle Banco, here we halted a fortnight, then advanced by easy marches until we came into the neighbourhood of Salamanca. The enemy had retreated from this place leaving a strong garrison in the works they had constructed on the site of some convents in the city, these works were of a very formidable nature.

The 6th Division are besieging these works, and we are encamped a short distance from the town, on a delightful spot. The Spaniards have established a good market amongst us, stored with everything our hearts could desire, the weather is beautiful and every afternoon the people pour out of the city by thousands to enjoy themselves with song and dance, so that our camp every evening presents one of the liveliest scenes imaginable, until the pipes and drums and bugles warns both them and us, it is time to retire to rest. Thus our time pass on in one continued round of pleasure, and but for the roaring of the guns at the forts, we should have forgotten that the enemy was near us. But this was too good to last forever. For on the 21st inst the enemy had collected all his force and was advancing to the relief of the besieged. We got the order to advance and soon came under fire, this was at a long ridge (San Cristoval) that overlooked a plain of several miles in extent on which we had a full view of the enemy.

On the descent from the ridge, the Light Companies of the Guards were engaged with the enemy's skirmishers. We had brought our light guns with us, a few rounds from them and the sight of us caused the enemy to fall back and establish their pickets. Our regiment then extended to our right along the ridge for the night. In the morning we were relieved by the Portuguese, we then fell back some distance, piled our arms, and was cleaning our firelocks etc. In about an hour the rum was brought, but in the midst of serving it Sir Thomas Graham rode down and ordered us to fall in, and advance. We were soon on the move, and soon under fire. I was not best pleased for I had not got my rum.

As we advanced the shot whistled brisker, Sir Thomas was in front, he wheeled round his horse, and ordered us to deploy on the 1st Division. Sir Thomas sat with his back to the enemy shading his eyes with his cocked hat, watching the companies deploy. He expressed his satisfaction at the manner we had performed the movement. As our line passed him he said 'my lads you shall give them a taste of your steel directly.' We was soon within point blank distance of their line. Sir Thomas then gave the word double quick, in a moment thirty buglers was sounding the charge and off we dashed in double quick time with three cheers, and away went the enemy to the right about. We had now gained the ridge without discharging a single musket, our bugles sounded the 'halt' and 'fire'.

Two of our guns, on our right, opened on them, at the same time about a dozen of our cavalry shewed themselves. The sight of the cavalry induced the enemy to form square, what a glorious opportunity this gave us to pepper them. There they were about 150 yards from us in a cluster like bees descending the hill. What between our fire and the fire of our guns they were knocked about like nine pins.

Having now gained our object Sir Thomas ordered us to fall back a few paces and lay down to cover ourselves from a battery of fourteen guns they had opened on us. We were now comparatively safe. The square behaved very well under so sharp a fire, although their punishment was great they retired in good order. I now began to look about me to see who had carried the camp-kettle with the rum. Serjeant Botley was serving it out when we got the order to fall in and advance. It could not be in better hands, he had stuck to it during the whole affair and was now sitting up serving the men who had not received theirs.

I crawled over to him. He said to me 'It's an ill wind that blows nobody good, I have just drank Westerman's allowance, there he lies poor fellow' pointing to the spot where he laid dead. 'And there are three more laying there who have not had their allowance, I am going to put it into my canteen —don't I deserve it, think you, for taking care of the kettle all this time.'

'You do' said I 'but give me mine first, for fear you should have the trouble to bottle off mine with the rest.'

'Here take this' said he 'and drink it, and I will give thee another to put into the calabash.'

He was setting with his back to the enemy, and as I was drinking a musket ball struck him in the back of the head. It had fortunately first struck the brow and was much spent, but he was obliged to be taken to the rear.

In this affair Major Rice's favourite Pye Bald Tom was shot under him. We are all sorry for poor Tom, as he was the major's pet. The major is beloved by every man in the corps, so when he is in trouble we share it with him. Tom was as fat as a mole. The *chasseurs* had stripped every bit of flesh off his bones. The major had Tom's hoofs taken off, they are to be converted into snuff boxes.

I have not been able to ascertain the exact loss of our regiment Captain Smillie was wounded and so was our serjeant major; exclusive of these I can reckon fifty-two killed and wounded; we remain still on the ground we fought on. It is beautiful to look down on the enemy at night, the whole plain is covered with fires. The position we occupy is of vast importance, the enemy cannot see a single man of our army, except those who go up to the brow out of curiosity.

No. 34. *Medena del Campo, 14th July, 1812.*

My last letter left us in position near Salamanca. You will see by this that we have had a move. The day I wrote last the enemy shewed much anxiety to obtain a peep at us. For this purpose their commander, escorted by a large body of cavalry, ascended a hill a considerable distance to the left of their position. But it was no go, he was still in the dark. On the night of the 25th June a division of the enemy marched to their left and crossed the Tormas by a ford below Salamanca.

This occasioned us to fall back on Salamanca and cross the river by the ford near the town. This was not a pleasant job, for although the days are excessively hot, the nights are very cold. The river at the ford was up to our waists. We had anticipated the enemy in this movement, for at day light they found to their mortification the 7th ready for them. They had now no other alternative but to retreat or fight. They chose the former and retraced their steps back into their old position, so we had to walk through the river again to get back into our old position. The next night they tried their luck again, but in the morning they found us ready to dispute their right of possession, and on a movement made by a few companies of our corps, Monsieur thought it advisable to sneek back again. This movement treated us with another bathe in the Tormas.

After this the enemy remained quiet, amusing theirselves now and then by firing a few shot into our position but they done no harm, excepting one. This one caused a bit of fun through the regiment. Colonel Mitchell ordered his servant to fry a beef steak for his dinner, the pan was hissing away in fine stile and the cook was peeling some onions to complete the mess, when as the devil would have it bang comes a six pound shot, and sent fire, frying pan and its contents flying. Thus the colonel was deprived of his dinner, and the servant frightened out of a year's growth.

The 6th Division carried all the works in Salamanca by storm, and on the 27th the French army retired on the Doura. We followed until we came to the city of Medina del Campo where we are at present encamped.

Medina del Campo is a large place, it has like other cities in this country a great number of Convents and churches. One of these convents has been completely gutted by us. There being no wood growing in this part we march into town every day and bring a load of wood from this building. On one occasion I was lead by curiosity into a large place set apart for burying the holy brotherhood. The bodies had been put in coffins and all round the walls these coffins were pushed into places left for the purpose. But either the enemy or our men could not let the dead rest, for most of the coffins were dragged out and broken, and their inmates lay scattered about on the ground.

I cannot give you any intelligence of the enemy, I suppose it will not be long so, for two such armies cannot long remain near each other without doing something.

No. 35. Camp. San Il de Fonso. 3rd August, 1812.

No doubt you must have heard before the date of this, of the defeat of Marmont before Salamanca. I am safe and in good health.

Before I say anything of the battle of Salamanca I must go back to Medena del Campo. I had not an opportunity of sending off my last before we advanced. We kept manoeuvring until the 18th July, this day we fell back, and at night encamped on the great plain of Vallisa, here we rested for the night with orders to make no fires etc. At daylight how was I astonished to see the whole of our army formed in three lines, and our brigade on the right of the front line, I must repeat I was astonished on looking around me to see cavalry, infantry and artillery formed in order of battle, when we had not the most distant idea that a single man was near us except our own division.

How powerful must be the genius of that man who can thus conduct so great a force with secrecy to its own members. Here we were all ready formed as if by magic, my eyes was ravished at the sight, I never looked on any scene with such delight. About a furlong to our front the plain terminated in a gentle descent into a woody country, here was the whole force of the enemy. After waiting some time, two of our guns advanced to the edge of the plain and fired several rounds, the enemy then broke into divisions of companies and marched off to their left. We also broke into column of companies right in front and marched with the enemy on our pivot flank.

The enemy ascended a hill along which they marched the greatest part of the day. At times there were some sharp cannonading from both sides. This was the first opportunity they had of seeing the whole of our force.

After midday the enemy had arrived at the termination of the ridge they had been marching on, and halted. We continued our march and did not see any more of them until we went into position at Salamanca. This was on the night of the 21st July. The thunder and lightning with much rain continued until about 3 o'clock in the morning.

I shall never forget this night. We were in a forest of old oak trees under which we sat for shelter from the storm. I had just left the tree where I had been standing some time to go to one of my comrades for a light. During my absence a flash of lightening struck the tree and clave it in two. This was a lucky pipe of tobacco.

The next morning, the 22nd we took up position on the left of the front line. The 68th Regiment was soon after ordered to the front, we soon lost sight of them amongst the trees. They were soon engaged and from the great number of wounded brought to the rear in wagons it was clear they had dropped in for a hot breakfast. The skirmishing having terminated they rejoined the brigade. There was much skirmishing and heavy cannonading at intervals 'til after midday, but from the thickness of the forest we could not see what was going on.

In the afternoon we broke into open column of divisions right in front and marched up the rear of our enemy. This was not a very agreeable job as the enemy were cannonading the whole length of their line, and our route lay within range of their guns. The fire at length became so furious that it were expedient to form grand division, thus leaving an interval of double the space for their shot to pass through.

Our support being required on the right of the line we now moved on in double quick time. This raised such a dust that together with the heat of the day we were almost suffocated. The want of water now began to be severely felt, those who had some in their canteens were as bad off as those that had none, for what with the heat of the sun and the shaking it got it was completely spoiled. Those who drank of it immediately threw it up.

As we proceeded the fire increased. We were wet with sweat as if we had been in the Tormas, and so great was the quantity of dust that settled on our faces and clothes that we scarce knew each other. In fact we more resembled an army of sweeps or dustmen than any one thing I can conceive. Almost fagged to death we arrived at our position on the right of our line; in our front was a hill on which was posted the enemy's left. They welcomed us opening about 16 guns and several howitzers. We found some water near us but it was so bad we could not drink it, however it served to rinse our mouths and wash the dust off our faces, this refreshed us much.

Lord Wellington rode up to us, and entered into conversation with Colonel Mitchell. He waited some time anxiously looking towards the hill, as the enemy's fire was very brisk. Colonel Mitchell said to Lord Wellington that he should like to advance and drive them from the hill, but his Lordship looked as serious as a judge going to pass sentence of death, shook his head and said it is not time yet.

At length he called out '7th Division, Advance'; spurred his horse, rode to our left and in a few minutes was lost in dust and smoke. We had not advanced far before the fire slackened and then ceased altogether.

We afterwards learnt that the hill had been charged by the heavy cavalry, the whole of the enemy was in full retreat. We kept advancing but could not come up with them. About 9 we halted for the night and everything seemed quiet, but at 10 o'clock a smart fire of musketry was heard, it continued about a quarter of an hour then all was quiet for the night.

Having examined a few dead Frenchmen for money etc. we collected what dead bodies were near and made a kind of wall with them. We did this to break the wind which was very cutting as we were very damp with sweat. Under this shelter we slept very sound until morning.

No. 36. Camp Majalahonda. 8th August, 1812.

The morning of the 23rd July we marched in pursuit of the enemy. Our loss in this battle scarcely deserves mentioning, only having ten killed and six wounded. The *chasseurs* dropped in for it pretty tidy. The 68th, like us, escaped without much loss from the cannonade, but they had had enough in the morning, so you see, it is all a lottery.

I consider the loss of the Chasseurs Brittanique Regiment was occasioned by their being in the centre of the brigade, for when we were changing our position from left to right of the line, we being at the head of the column, and as the enemy's fire were directed by the cloud of dust we kicked up, it was most likely that we had in a great measure passed most of the danger before the enemy could point their guns.

I have not been able to learn what the enemy's loss was. It must have been severe in killed and wounded and I believe a great many prisoners were taken. It is reported that Marmont is killed but other reports say he is badly wounded. I believe the enemy has succeeded in saving most of their guns.

On the 24th we entered a village crowded with the enemy, prisoners of war. They were all wounded, more or less about the head, arms and thighs by sabre wounds. On ascending a hill in advance we came on a level, at this place their rear guard had been attacked by the German cavalry. It must have been a most spirited and dashing affair.

I have heard that the enemy's rear, consisting chiefly of infantry, was formed into solid square at this place, and that the German cavalry succeeded in breaking the square, the consequence was that the whole, about 2,000, were killed, wounded and made prisoners. The number of wounded in the village seems to confirm the report, particularly as the place is covered with firelocks, belts, pouches, caps and knapsacks. The charge is represented to be one of the most glorious ever performed.

From this place to Il de Fonso we met with nothing worthy remark, only that the smell from a few dead bodies was very offensive. It is a matter of surprise amongst those who are more experienced in warfare than myself that the French has made so clean a retreat. The road has not much the appearance that a defeated army has retreated on it, with the exception of a few men and horses here and there lying by the side of the road nothing more is to be seen.

Thus far, have I written at Il de Fonso to be prepared for the next mail.

On the 4th we advanced in company with the cavalry. Nothing particular occurred until we came to Majalahonda, here another dashing affair took place between the German cavalry and the enemy's rear.

The Portuguese cavalry under General D'Urban had relieved the heavy German Brigade, but as soon as Monsieur had discovered that the Portuguese had the advance, they advanced on them, and the cowardly rascals not only refused to charge the enemy but they actually rode off, leaving two guns belonging to the light brigade of our division in the hands of the enemy. Luckily the Germans were at hand and drove back the enemy and retook the guns. Our brigade advanced to their support but before we had arrived, the Germans had made clean work of it without our assistance.

The enemy evacuated Madrid on the night of the 11th inst. leaving a garrison in the works at the Retiro.

The morning of the 12th, a remarkable day being the Prince of Wales's birthday, we took possession of the capital. Our division marched right in front, and as our regiment is on the right of the division we were the first regiment that entered Madrid. I never before witnessed such a scene. At the distance of five miles from the gates we were met by the inhabitants, each had brought out something, *viz.* laurel, flowers, bread, wine, grapes, lemonade, *aquedente*, tobacco, sweetmeats etc. etc. etc.

The road represented a moving forest, from the great multitude of people carrying boughs. The intervals of our subdivisions soon became filled up with men, women and children. In one place would be a brawny Spaniard with a pigskin of wine, filling vessels for us to drink, then another with a basket full of bread distributing it around, then a pretty pale-faced black-eyed maid would modestly offer a nosegay or sprig of parma or of olive, while others of the sex more bold would dash into our ranks take off our caps and place a sprig of laurel, then without ceremony seize our arm and sing some martial air to the memory of some immortal patriot who had fallen in the good cause. The immortal names of Crawford and others would also sound in Spanish song.

Thus we slowly moved on, amidst the sweet voices of thousands of the most bewitching and interesting little devils I had ever seen, at least I then thought so. But as we approached the city the crowd increased, the people were mad with joy. They called us 'their *deliverours*, their saviours.' And by a thousand other names. The poor Virgin Mary was forgotten, at least for that day.

The air was rent with the deafening shouts of '*Vivi* Wellington, *Vivi les Angolese, Vivi les Ilandos*' and by ten thousand other *Vivis*, I cannot think on. Wellington was at the head of the column. When we entered the city the shouting increased tenfold, every bell that had got a clapper was set ringing, the windows were ornamented with rich drapery embroidered with gold and silver, such as is only used on great festivals when the Host is carried.

The whole of the windows and tops of the houses were crowded with Spanish beauty, waving white handkerchiefs. The people endeavoured to drag us into their houses. Suffice it to say, that we were several hours going to the convent where we were to be quartered, that under ordinary circumstances might have been walked in fifteen minutes. But amidst all this pleasure and happiness we were obliged to submit to a custom so un-English that I cannot but feel disgust now I am writing. It was to be kissed by the men. What made it still worse, their breath was so highly seasoned with garlic, then their huge mustaches well stiffened with sweat, dust and snuff, it was like having a hair broom pushed into ones face that had been daubed in a dirty gutter.

On our way to the convent chance threw me in the way of an English gentleman who had been settled in Madrid seventeen years and was married to a Spanish lady. He said the news of the battle of Salamanca had reached Madrid the 25th. It was that our army had been defeated with the loss of all our cannon, and so well was the deception managed that it was generally believed for some time. But the extraordinary bustle amongst the French troops began to open the people's eyes, and the truth of the report began to be suspected.

The afternoon of the 11th August he said, he was walking with some French officers when the report of cannon was heard. It was like a stroke of electricity. The Spaniards caught fire at the sound and insulted the French officers and soldiers in the streets. On hearing the report of the guns he said to the officer next him 'Ha, Major, I thought you had beaten my countrymen and taken all their cannon.'

The reply was by a shrug of the shoulders and taking a pinch of snuff, 'That account answered our purpose very well, but we must be off tonight.'

I happened to have a few old newspapers, these I offered to him. He was much pleased, saying that there was much difficulty to get at the truth of what was passing around them. He took my name and company and said he would call on me as soon as the battle was over. He kept his word, for the day after the works at Tetero was given up to us I spent the greater part of a day with his family consisting of himself, wife and two daughters. I was received with a hearty welcome. After regaling myself with a good dinner and a few glasses of wine I entertained the family with an account of the movements of our army etc.

In the midst of our conversation the servant entered and announced Father Kelly, and in walked a holy friar. At first I was not well pleased with our new guest for I dislike the whole fraternity. He was about thirty years of age and stood about six feet. He had a good open countenance, which in spite of my prejudice to the order I could not but think him a good free hearted fellow. I was not deceived. I soon found he was possessed of all that generosity of soul so common to his country. He was from the 'Green Isle.' He took off his shovel hat and seated himself. In a few minutes we were as well acquainted as if we had known one another before.

As I proceeded with the account of the campaigns he seemed to enter into the very spirit of what I was saying. His remarks was so much to the purpose that I could not help observing that he would look well at the head of a grenadier company. He said 'he had always a great inclination to be a soldier, but it was not everyone that could follow the bent of their own inclinations.'

I must close by saying I was well entertained and was obliged to promise to spend another afternoon with the same party. An illumination and public rejoicing continued three successive nights after our arrival.

No. 38. Madrid. 23rd August, 1812.

I had so much to say in my last that I had not room to give you an account of the siege of the Retiro, it must form the subject of this letter. As soon as we had dined on the 13th inst. the division paraded to witness the sentence of several court martials carried into execution. After passing three hours at this disagreeable work we marched and besieged the works at the Retiro.

As soon as it was dark we entered the Royal Gardens under a smart fire of musketry that done us no harm. We soon got under cover of a long wall close under the forts. Through this wall the *chasseurs* were employed in making a breach which they had completed by daylight, sufficient for a subdivision to march through. The noise in making this breach drew a sharp fire from the enemy that continued all night without doing much mischief, as the wall protected us.

About 12 at night many of us had laid down and some of us had dropped off asleep. A man who had volunteered with me from the Surrey Militia was lying at my back, when he received a severe wound in the thick part of his thigh. The ball entered behind, struck the bone and lodged in the thigh. The poor fellow being asleep at the time he screamed out and said he was wounded. Everyone thought it was impossible that a ball could hit anyone, so we endeavoured to persuade him it was the cramp from the awkward position he had been lying. He insisted that the ball had entered the bottom of his foot and had ran up to his a——. We had no light so I put my hand to his thigh and found it was no dream, for the poor fellow was bleeding very much. He was of course removed. This was the only accident that happened.

Daylight shewed us the forts and we were expecting every moment to march through the breach in the wall to storm the works, but the enemy surrendered and before noon the whole of the forts were in our possession.

We now became possessed of a large quantity of stores of every description *viz.* cannon, ammunition, firelocks, provisions and clothing. The 68th was fortunate enough to fall in with the clothing and well stocked themselves with new shorts, stockings and shoes. While the capitulation was being agreed on we turned our attention to the delicious fruit with which the garden abounded. We soon provided ourselves with some of the choicest luxuries that were intended to grace the table of King Joseph. After enjoying a good breakfast we amused ourselves by catching gold and silver fish, some of our men cooked some, but they were not so pleasant to the stomach as they were to the eye, for it made them sick.

These are the most beautiful gardens I ever saw. The walks are completely arched over with vines but the grapes are not ripe. There is every sort of fruit that will grow in this country but what pleased me best was I strolled into a summer house and was agreeably surprised to find a quantity of books, Spanish, French and English. I secured all I could find in my own tongue but as I have not the means of carrying them I distributed them amongst my comrades who I know are fond of reading. I was not a little surprised to find the *Bath Guide* written by Counsellor Anstie of Marlboro' Buildings.

In my last I told you I had spent a day with my new acquaintance. Since then I have passed another day with this hospitable family and Father Kelly in company with three other Holy Friars and two lay gentlemen. Although I found them agreeable companions I cannot but feel a great degree of prejudice against the priesthood of the church of Rome. I have read the history of (what is called) 'The Holy Inquisition' and what is daily passing before my eyes strengthens me in my opinion that the priests only want the power to establish this infernal court again. Thanks to Napoleon for abolishing it; he has done Spain much harm, but this one mighty act has in a great measure, counterbalanced all the mischief he has done.

You must excuse this digression, I was led into it unawares, but to return let it suffice that I spent a very comfortable day, everything that was good was plentiful, the glass went round 'til night and when I took my leave my kind host gave me six dollars, as he said for the purpose of recruiting my knapsack.

I took my farewell of my kind friends, returned to my quarters as happy as a prince and as read as a roost cock. We are now allowed to go out of our quarters by a pass, so I have taken advantage of the indulgence and have had a stroll through some parts of the city.

The buildings are generally good and in some of the squares

are some beautiful fountains, but as we had many pressing invitations to regale ourselves most of our time was spent in the coffee shops, therefore I can say but little about the city. Tom Hooker, the man who was wounded in the garden of the Retiro, remained several days in his quarters, it is astonishing what attention the inhabitants paid him. He had a constant succession of visitors until he was removed.

No. 39. Escurial. 3rd September, 1812.

We took leave of our good friends the 28th August and marched for the Palace of the Escurial about seven leagues from Madrid. The Palace is a beautiful piece of building. I think the noblest I ever saw, the outside is adorned with large statutes not only of the apostles but of some of the principle of the Old Testament saints. Round the Palace are several streets well built for the reception of visitors when the Court resides here. Our division occupies some of these buildings, and we find ourselves in very comfortable quarters. The 1st Division occupies the Palace. Corporal Golton of the 3rd Guards is here, and well. By visiting him I have contrived to see part of the interior of the Palace, but I am indebted to my old acquaintance Father Kelly for a stroll over the whole of the interior. He had come here on some business connected with the church, he soon found me out.

I told him I wished to see the Palace and hoped he would introduce me to some of the holy brotherhood residing here, this he done regretting much that he had not time to go round with me. As none of the monks could spake English, he recommended me to an old monk who was as eager to shew me round the place as I was to see. This old fellow was as I was given to understand a very pious man.

If mortifying the body will take a man to heaven, the old boy was travelling at a rapid rate, his feet was bare and next his skin he wore a horse hair shirt. Age had stripped, or rather old Father Time had mown all the hair off his head, which was also minus a, hat, his skin was shrivelled and resembled parchment and so full of wrinkles that if at any time of his life it had been stretched out to its full extent he must have resembled a butt. His nose and chin almost met when he spoke. Teeth he had none, and from the appearance of his body he could have no use for any, for he appeared to have left of eating at least half a century.

Such is the outlines of my ghostly father who was to shew me round this wonder of wonders; we passed through several splendid apartments containing beautiful oil paintings, mostly from scripture all at once we came into the cooking kitchen, here were a couple of the brotherhood preparing dinner, one of the cooks was as fat and greasy as a bladder of lard, and as dirty as a chimney sweep, it would take a couple of pounds of soap to get any way near his skin. His appearance at once told me he was fond of the good things of this world, he was very condescending, he took much pains in shewing me the different dishes he was preparing, presented me with his snuff box at least a dozen times. He was a thirsty soul but this is excusable in a cook. He brought forward a large flagon and treated himself and myself with some excellent wine.

His assistant was a surly looking fellow, his eyes were not fellows, very small and sank a long way into his head, his whole physog was as disagreeable as can well be imagined. I could not but help thinking he must have been got by envy out of malice. In short he was the most disagreeable mortal I ever saw, and would have made an excellent familiar to the Inquisition. Having tasted some soup and eaten a fish fried in oil, I parted with these pair of worthies and followed the old man my guide about the palace until I was tired.

It will be impossible for me to give you anything like a description of what I saw. That must remain until I am seated by your fireside, some future evening when the toil of war has ceased and our swords and guns are made into ploughshares and reap hooks. But I shall finish this by giving you an account of a saint that lay in a coffin in one of the vaults. From what I could gather from the old man this was the famous Saint Christopher, and as I have somewhere read a story of a Saint Christopher, I will give it you. It appears that this saint was converted to Christianity in the early ages, and being a tall robust man he stationed himself by a ford where poor pilgrims used to cross to go to some shrine to worship. Here he used to conduct the pilgrims through the river.

One day a little boy requested to be carried across, so the pious old man took him on his shoulder but when he got into the middle of the stream the waters began to rise so rapid and the boy got so heavy that the poor saint had a very narrow escape from drowning. However he arrived safe to the opposite side and set this little fellow down, remarking that he was the heaviest person he had ever carried. When the little gentleman condescended to inform him who he was, the saint could not believe that he had carried his master, when to ease his doubts the boy ordered him to stick his staff into the ground. The next morning it had produced as many dates as would stock all the grocers in Bath. Such is the tale I had read of a Saint Christopher, and as this saint appeared at least seven feet in height, I suppose I might venture to say he is the very identical person.

No. 40. Camp near Almos. 9th October, 1812.

What a chequered life is a soldier's on active service. One moment seeking the bubble reputation at the cannon's mouth. The next courting some fair unknown damsel, sometimes scorched alive with heat, then almost frozen to death on some snowy mountain, at one time the inmate of a palace, then for months, the sky is his only covering. Hunting the enemy like a greyhound, and in return as often hunted by the enemy. These thoughts naturally arise when from the midst of ease and plenty, we find ourselves transported as it were by magic, close to the enemy in another part of the country, at a distance of three hundred miles. Such is our case at present.

I had not many days got my last off my hands when we commenced our march for Vallidolid, the advanced post of the enemy. On our arrival they retired on Burgos and we followed them. Our route lay through a country abounding in vineyards, every night we encamped in some vineyard, and as the grapes were ripe for the harvest we had our fill. A days march from Burgos the road ran between two hills, this caused some skirmishing. On the hills the enemy had some cannon, but before they had done any mischief the appearance of our division soon made them withdraw the guns; at Burgos the enemy left a garrison in the castle. The 1st Division and General Pack's Portuguese Brigade are besieging it, we are encamped within sight.

Burgos has turned a tougher job than was first expected. The castle is an old Moorish building, strong by nature and much improved by art; a breach was made in the wall and on the 4th. inst. an attempt to carry the place by storm was tried, but I am sorry to say, was a failure. The several attacks were conducted with great spirit. I never before witnessed such a scene without sharing in it. We were encamped about a league from the castle and could see the whole; you might talk of your grand galas at Sidney Gardens, the greatest body of fire ever discharged there is no more to be compared to this night's storm then a rushlight is to the sun.

After this we marched and passed Burgos, encamped near Almos, about two leagues in advance of Burgos; we have several times been visited by the enemy's *fedets* (*vedettes*) but nothing of importance has occurred. The bombardment is kept up night and day in good earnest. A few days since I have been prevailed on by the captain to take charge of the battery mule but as I never had anything to do with horses I do not expect I shall keep this situation long, the more particularly as I do not like it.

No. 41. Salamanca. November, 1812.

The middle of October, we advanced to Monistaria. Here we had to furnish the outposts in company with the Light Cavalry. Burgos still holds out after repulsing another attack. The troops composing the garrison is an honour to France. On the 18th October the enemy surprised and made prisoners a picquet of the Duke of Brunswick's Oels Light Infantry consisting of an officer and sixteen men. Two days after this the enemy advanced.

This day there were some sharp skirmishing, at night we fell back on Almos, followed by their advance. Here was another sharp skirmish in which the enemy were worsted and fell back now, our brigade were put into a large church for the night.

About midnight when all were fast asleep someone called out 'The enemy, the enemy. Fall in.' You can easily conceive what a confused scene followed, the place was dark as possible, as full as it would hold of soldiers laying down fully accoutred with their firelocks between their legs. All were up in a moment, shouting out 'Where are they? where is the door? fix your bayonets' some were cursing and swearing. The Chasseurs Brittanique Regiment, composed of men from every country in Europe, were each calling out in their own native tongue. Add to this the noise occasioned by fixing bayonets. Everyone of course were seeking the door but no one could find it, at length some got out and discovered it was a false alarm. The word was soon passed and after some time the panic subsided.

All the material of war being removed from Burgos, and the army on the move we pushed on by forced marches for Vallidolid. Having arrived and taken possession of the bridge, got it ready for blowing up, we waited the arrival of the enemy who were advancing on the opposite side of the river. On the morning of the 28th October the enemy brought some guns and fired into the camp. The first round they fired killed Serjeant Maibee's wife, her husband had just gone to the bridge on duty and had left her to prepare his breakfast, she was in the act of taking some chocolate off the fire when the shot carried away her right arm and breast.

I was in the town with the mule getting forage, as soon as we heard the guns we mounted and rode away for camp. John Gilpin could not have looked more ludicrous than I did. I will draw the picture as near to life as possible. Mounted on a refractory mule, a red worsted night cap hanging half way down my back containing several little articles, *viz.* chocolate, tobacco etc. half a dozen canteens full of wine, some upside down and the stoppers coming out, two haversacks full of bread, slung across my shoulder, and a monstrous large loaf under my arm, the mule in a gallop, the tail of my watch coat waving in the wind, and your humble servant a shocking bad rider, how I kept my seat I am puzzled to tell, but keep it I did. In this plight I and old Betty entered the camp.

Here was confusion. The regiment had marched to defend the bridge until the army and baggage were on the move. The enemy were amusing themselves by firing at the baggage animals and at the men who were loading them. Fortunately for me, Old Betty stood fire well and I got her loaded without much trouble. Some others were not so fortunate, their animals ran about half loaded. Some animals would be knocked down then a shot would dab in amongst a heap of boxes and scatter their contents around the place. I was moving off speaking very kindly to old Betty, then cursing the French, and the day I had undertaken the care of the battery mule, wishing the baggage to the D—— and myself with my comrades at the bridge, for there I should have the satisfaction of giving pop for pop, when a shot dropped in front of my mule and set her a kicking and away went load saddle and all between her legs. But I ought not to grumble at this misfortune great as it was, it was as nothing to compare with some that were happening to others around me. I righted my load as quick as I could and proceeded about a league farther when we got out of the range of their guns. I now met with the captain's servant, with the captain's and subaltern's baggage safe.

The regiment defended the bridge until everything was cleared and the army was on the move then blew it up and retired. The loss of the regiment at the bridge was Lieutenant Hickey severely wounded, his right arm amputated and one bugler, and thirteen rank and file wounded.

Two days brought us to Fordeselles. Here we found the Brunswick Light Infantry in possession of the bridge and ready for blowing it up. We encamped on the heights between Rueda and Fordeselles, halted a few days then continued our retreat to Salamanca, where we were joined by Sir Rowland Hill's army from Madrid. We are in hopes to remain here the winter.

No. 42. Moimento. 10th December 1812.

Our stay at Salamanca was but short. The enemy having assembled the whole of his force, advanced, leaving no alternative for us but to fight or run. Accordingly we mustered on the heights of San Cristoval. On the 12th November we were posted at Alba, the day was very hazy, the weather had been very unfavourable ever since we left Monistaro. Nothing now was thought of but a general engagement, and so eager were our men to fight that I have no doubt but we should have given them a hearty drubbing. There was some heavy cannonading, and a movement took place to our right. This continued all day. It was not until the evening that we were acquainted with our situation, and but for the superior skill of our great commander our communication with Portugal would have been cut off.

The enemy had moved part of his force to get possession of the great road from Salamanca to Ciudad Rodrigo, but fortunately we arrived before them. Now the race and bad weather set in in earnest. The fatigue and distress of this retreat will long be remembered by those who shared in it.

Cold rain continued all the way, at night our camp represented scenes so distressing it would be folly in me to attempt to describe. Some notion of it might be formed if you take into consideration that we had endured a long and laborious campaign under a scorching sun, that our clothes were much worn, and by no means fit to protect us from such weather. Our camp or resting place would soon be reduced to mud, ankle deep, on which we must lie or sit for the night. Our blankets were so wet that each morning before we could put them into our knapsacks they were obliged to be wrung. The roads were so cut up that it was with the greatest difficulty the hardiest soldier could march. Provisions were scarce, shoes failed and many were barefoot. But amidst all these difficulties no one murmured, or if there were any discontent, it was because we were not allowed to give them battle.

At Salamanca on the 16th November our regiment was sharply engaged near a river (the cork wood of the village, St. Munos). Captain McCabe was killed and many men wounded. We had now entered a forest of oaks. This place swarmed with pigs feeding on the acorns. The work of destruction soon commenced amongst the swine, so we were soon stocked with pork. But we had neither salt or bread. We soon found the acorns were a good substitute for when roasted they eat much like chestnuts. It must be observed that they were highly seasoned with hunger, that you know is the best sauce. The acorns were very large together with the oaks, are a different sort from any I had ever seen in England.

This day, some of the enemy's cavalry flanked us, and made sad havoc amongst our baggage. Much was destroyed and many men and women were made prisoners. However I had the good fortune to escape, somehow I was overlooked in all this bustle. Seeing the dragoons returning by the way they came, I began to congratulate myself on my good fortune and was returning in order to get nearer to my regiment, giving old Betty many sugary promises etc., when I espied six dragoons, galloping towards us.

There were eight of us in company, each having a loaded musket, so we determined to try our strength, and to reserve our fire until they came so close that each of us could not miss our mark. They had arrived within twenty yards, when some shots from the wood dropped four horses, another moment and we fired. This settled the business, there was not one left to return and tell the tale. We found that the party in the wood, like ourselves, had been overlooked and had resolved to remain under cover of the brushwood until they found all safe, and to fire upon any stragglers of the enemy that should come within reach.

We joined them, then went to inspect our prey. We found a rich booty, six hundred and thirty two dollars. This being distributed amongst us gave each thirty five dollars there being eighteen of us. In a quarter of an hour we were on the march again. The women were returned to our army the next day. After this, the enemy gave us no more trouble. On the 20th November we arrived and encamped under the walls of Ciudad Rodrigo. The enemy returned to Salamanca and we proceeded to Moimento, which is the Head quarters of our division.

Thus ended a campaign that opened on the 2nd January, and closed the latter end of November. The number of miles marched over in this time, if averaged at eight miles *per diem*, 2328. This is not over-rating it. Portugal had been walked over from north to south and back again, three times. Spain, from Badajoz to within two or three days march of Truxillo and back to Badajoz again. Then from Rodrigo to Salamanca and on to Madrid, and from Madrid to Vallidolid, Burgos and Monistaro, and lastly from Monistaro down to Ciudad Rodrigo. Besides the counter marching, when near the enemy. If I had averaged ten miles *per diem* I think I should not have over rated it. Two garrisons of great importance has been taken from the enemy. The Battle of Salamanca caused them to raise the siege of Cadiz, besides the importance of having had possession of Madrid and taking the Retiro, with so much stores of every description, not forgetting the formidable works at Salamanca, so gallantly carried by the 6th Division. I hope our retreating to Portugal will not damp the ardour of the Spaniards.

No. 43. Moimento. 13th January, 1813.

We had not long taken up our abode at this place when a fever of rather an alarming nature broke out amongst us, the natural consequence of the fatigues endured in the late campaign. Above half our men are in hospital, and from the number of deaths our burying ground begins to have the appearance of a ploughed field.

I have got rid of my situation of bat man and am again at my duty. It was with the greatest reluctance that I first undertook it and the longer I continued the more my dislike increased. I had frequently applied to join my company but was always refused. I therefore determined to obtain by stratagem what I could not by force. One day after being absent two days for forage, the captain asked me if I had ever seen any nearer. I told him I knew where there were a few load of *pacca* about two leagues distant. I knew he would order me to fetch it, although it was contrary to the orders for anyone to forage except belonging to the foraging party under the command of an officer.

Early the next morning I started, managed to get my load and returned just as the regiment was on parade. Colonel Mitchell stopped me and ordered me to the guard room. My comrades trembled for me. I was in their opinion booked for 300 lashes. My scheme was now partly accomplished. This was the first time I had ever been confined. Everything worked as I had anticipated for as soon as I acquainted the colonel that I had been sent by the captain's order I was released, and at my request was allowed to go to my duty.

We have spent a very comfortable Christmas, you know I am one of these sort of mortals that do not stand to niceties. Youth and health with a moderate share of the good things of this world always satisfies me. I have often spent many happy hours, when on the outlying picquet, when sitting by the fire smoking my pipe and listening to the marvellous tales of my comrades. But here we are a distance from the enemy, we get our rations regular and we can purchase every eatable very cheap, wine is both good and cheap, so is tobacco. I mention this because I know you will be pleased that we have it in our power to make ourselves comfortable after so arduous a campaign as our last was.

Lord Wellington has issued an order to the army from which he does not seem any way pleased with the conduct of the army on the Burgos retreat. I must confess that although there are some severe remarks embodied in the orders, yet I cannot say they are uncalled for. It is impossible for any army to have given themselves up to more dissipation and everything that is bad, as did our army.

The conduct of some men would have disgraced savages, drunkenness had prevailed to such a frightful extent that I have often wondered how it was that a great part of our army were not cut off. It was no unfrequent thing to see a long string of mules carrying drunken soldiers to prevent them falling into the hands of the enemy.

It would not be fair in me to mention any particular corps, all partook in some degree a share of the disgrace. At Vallidolid, the —— was punishing several hours, the sides of the roads were strewed with soldiers as if dead, not so much by fatigue as by wine. But there is some excuse, from Burgos to Salamanca is chiefly a wine country and as there had been a good harvest, and the new wine was in tanks particularly about Vallidolid the soldiers ran mad.

I remember seeing a soldier fully accoutred with his knapsack on in a large tank, he had either fell in or had been pushed in by his comrades, there he lay dead. I saw a dragoon fire his pistol into a large vat containing several thousands of gallons, in a few minutes we were up to our knees in wine fighting like tigers for it.

No. 44. Mont Gaulda Pro Semo, 30th March, 1813.

The company to which I belong is removed to the above village, distant from Moimento about a mile. Colonel Mitchell has left for England on leave; we are now commanded by Major Roberts, he lost his right hand on General Moor's Retreat.

I must give you an anecdote of the major. At Lugo the regiment was engaged in a sharp skirmish with the enemy when the major received his wound, he was retiring when one of our men observed to him that it was Chelsea as dead as H—l. The major wheeled round and galloped up to a French skirmisher and with his pistol shot him dead. Returning he observed to the man who had made the observation about Chelsea. 'And that's H—l as dead as Chelsea.' He is reported to be a lion in the field. This is the first time I ever saw him, he having been employed on the staff at Bristol. I do not know what to make of him. He seems to be very fond of using the cats, and if he continues as he has begun it will not be long before every one will get a taste.

A few days since we expected one of our men to catch it for robbing an old woman's shop of a few eggs. I will trouble you with the account. Seeing some eggs in a shop and only an old woman to serve, Barnett shuts one eye, walked in and began pricing some articles. When he comes to the eggs, he took them out of the basket and walked away without paying for them.

The woman ran to the major and told him that one of his men who was '*Falta una Olie*' (or in English, a man with one eye) had robbed her shop of some eggs. It being near parade time, to satisfy the old woman she was ordered to attend. When the parade was formed she was at her post; now a laughable scene took place between the major and the old woman. The old woman insisting that the man who robbed her was '*Falta una Olie*' and the major insisting he had no man in his regiment '*Falta una Olie*.'

The argument continued as they passed down the ranks, and the major seemed highly delighted with the joke. At length the old woman made a dead stop in front of Barnett, looked stead-fastly in his face and exclaimed 'Jesu Maria Joseph'—'I never saw two more alike, only the man who stole my eggs was *Falta una Olie*.'

The consequence was she was puzzled and the major was so tickled with the fun he passed on, and the old woman went away grumbling something about '*Falta una Olie*.' After she was gone the major gave Barnett some advice, recommending him not to try the trick again for if he had ordered him to shut one eye the old woman would have identified him.

The beginning of last month, I was taken ill of a fever, the complaint that has been raging amongst us ever since we have been here. I was in hospital nearly six weeks. I am now perfectly recovered and at my duty. I ought not to be dissatisfied, it is the first sickness I ever had and this was comparatively light com-pared to most cases.

An alteration has taken place in our division, the Light Ger-man Infantry are removed to the 1st Division so that our left brigade are now composed of the Duke of Brunswick's Light Infantry, the 6th Regiment and a provisional battalion com-posed of part of the 24th and 58th Regiment. The 82nd has joined our brigade.

I expect it will not be long before the campaign will open, the sooner the better, we are getting tired of lousy Portugal. If fortune favours me I hope to entertain you with something that will give you pleasure. We have received our new clothes, and draughts from our depot to fill up the casualties occasioned by sickness and death. I also hear that large reinforcements has arrived and are still arriving, consisting of cavalry, infantry and artillery. Of the enemy I can say nothing you must know from the papers more about them then I do.

I have had together with the whole of our Regimental Guard a narrow escape of being smothered in an old house used as our guard room. Someone remarked that the whole of the upper part of this old building was supported by a piece of quarter which if a drunken man should fall against might endanger all our lives. We were determined to see if our fears had any foundation, so we shifted into the street and began pelting the prop, when in a few minutes it was knocked down and down came all the inside in a moment.

No. 45. Moimento. 28th April, 1813.

Since I wrote last the hussars has passed through this town, the men and horses looks well. This brigade consist of the 10th, 15th and 18th Hussars. I am sorry to say we have had a serjeant, corporal and private punished by sentence of a division court martial for what the Earl of Dalhousie considers a great crime, and I must myself confess that in a military point of view the private could scarcely be guilty of a greater. I shall relate the story to you, then you will be able to form your own opinion on it.

It being fine weather the general had some tents pitched in a field belonging to the house he was staying in. A mail had just arrived from England and the general and his staff were looking over the newspapers. One of our men, sentry at the tent having got some rum had drank so much that he was quite intoxicated. Seeing the papers he began to be anxious to know how things were going on in England, so without any ceremony he walks up to the tent door, but unfortunately the tent peg or cords caught his toe and in he bolted head foremost and lay prostrate at the Earl's feet, and not having the benefit of a polite education without making an apology for his abrupt intrusion with much *sang froid* asked the general 'What news from England?'

It is easy to guess what followed, the man with the serjeant and corporal of the guard were confined, a division court martial followed. The serjeant was tried for passing the man, the corporal for planting him on sentry, and the man for being drunk on duty. As a matter of course they were all found guilty. The serjeant and corporal to be reduced to the ranks and receive 300 lashes and the private 500.

These sentences were carried into execution in presence of as many troops of the division as could be conveniently assembled. Here you see the Earl of Dalhousie ordering a court martial, himself or some of his staff witnesses, then he approves of the finding of the court and sees the sentences carried into execution. I do not deny but the crime was very great, and most unsoldierlike and for the benefit of the service deserved exemplary punishment, but how could the serjeant and corporal be answerable for this man. They declared he was sober when planted on sentry, and there was no evidence to the contrary. The man himself declared the same, he also added that he had procured a pint and a half of rum about five minutes before the relief turned out, that at the time he drank some and continued to sip when on sentry. Some rum in his canteen seemed to correspond with this statement.

It cannot be long before we shall take the field. I expect we shall find ourselves more comfortable when we do, as we have tents issued, this will shelter us from bad weather. You have often hinted in your letters that I ought to endeavour to get promoted. I have no desire, if I had I might have been promoted to corporal two years ago and perhaps to serjeant before this. I have always declined every offer made to me, simply on this ground. I am young and I have so far kept out of trouble. I always endeavour to perform my duty in the best way I am able. I have therefore nothing to fear. But should I be intrusted with a guard perhaps I might get into a scrape through their neglect. There is time enough after the razor has passed round my chin some hundred times more before I think about accepting of any responsible situation.

No. 46. Camp Miranda. 27th May, 1813.

On the 4th May the division was inspected by the Earl of Dalhousie in the neighbourhood of Moimento. On the 11th we began our advance in search of the enemy. Part of the army by the great road to Salamanca. Our division kept more to the left, crossed the Doura near Villa Nova. The reason of our making this circuitous rout was to get round the right flank of the enemy, they having entrenched themselves in a strong position where it would not only be attended with difficulty to attack them but with great loss on our part, besides the risk of being foiled in the attempt. This movement seems to have had the desired effect for I hear that the enemy has retired.

After we had crossed the Doura the face of the country altered. We now continued to advance through a pleasant country well studded with large cities, towns and pretty villages, without seeing the enemy or meeting with any remarkable occurrence. Having plenty of provisions and sport to beguile our time on the road we were continually starting hares, the country being generally level and being provided with some good greyhounds, the fatigue of marching was much enlivened. So great was the quantity of game through which we have marched that it was no uncommon thing to have half a dozen up at once, some of which would be running through the intervals of our column.

On the 24th. we encamped on the plains of Miranda and find a great difference already in having tents. The Spaniards are lost in admiration at the sight, I know of nothing more surprising to the eye of a stranger then to see our canvas towns rise in a moment. Indeed I was not aware myself of the effect it has on the mind until one day I was at some distance from our camp talking to some Spaniards that inhabited a small village near us.

We were in full view of our division but the tents were not pitched. I heard the bugle sound to stand by the tents. I managed to draw the people's attention into an opposite direction from the camp till the bugle sounded again, this was in about a minute. I then pointed to the camp, how were they surprised. A minute before nothing was to be seen but the soldiers, now the whole camp was studded with several hundred bell tents as white as snow and as regularly placed as if it had been the work of much labour and time. To a people so naturally superstitious as the Spaniards are it must appear like magic. I am inclined to think they looked on it in no other light for they express their astonishment in a volley of '*Caravos*,' then they devoutly crossed themselves exclaiming 'Jesu Maria—these English are the Devil.'

General Sir Thomas Graham has inspected us and from the secrecy of our movements the enemy cannot be far off, so you may expect if I continue in health and escape the battle field to hear something that will prove interesting. So far we are in excellent health and spirits and have no doubts about the approaching contest.

No. 47. Camp near Zamora. 1st June, 1813.

We continued to advance from Miranda to the Eslar. On the 30th May our regiment with the Brunswick Light Infantry encamped about a league from that river. The enemy's advance was at Valdeperdiccas, a village on the opposite bank of the Eslar. At this place there was a ford (Almendra). In the night we moved to the ford in company with the Hussar Brigade. When we came to the river we halted, took off our pouches and placed them on our knapsacks, the belt hanging down in our front, then marched into the river in column of subdivisions.

It was soon evident that we had either missed the ford or that the water was risen by the rain. Whichever was the cause, we soon found the water was too deep and the stream so rapid that in a very short time the whole of the infantry was upset.

Some sank to the bottom borne down by the weight of the fire-lock and knapsack, to say nothing of the pouch containing sixty rounds of ball cartridges.

This proved to be the awkwardest companion of the whole for as soon as we were upset the pouch would slip off the knap-sack and hang suspended round the neck, thus placing us in a very critical situation and was of itself sufficient to drown a man without the other encumbrance. But for the Hussars I should not be alive to tell the tale, they flew to our assistance and picked up as many as they could. It will be much easier for you to conceive the confusion we were in when I tell you the river is divided at the ford in to three parts by two islands, each part is about the breadth of the Avon. There were three regiments of cavalry and two of infantry plunging about in it and so dark we could scarce see each other, besides expecting every moment to receive a volley from the enemy.

The manner in which we crossed after order was in a meas-ure restored was as follows. The hussars each took a firelock the infantry soldier having hold of the stirrup. A serjeant of the 15th Hussars conveyed two of us across in the following manner. I held hold of the stirrup, the other man held fast by the horses tail, the serjeant carrying each of our firelocks.

When we had safely landed on terra firma, the road ascended up a steep hill to the village. It had now become twilight and we could perceive the enemy forming on the plain beyond the vil-lage. They appeared in much confusion and was evidently taken by surprise. The hussars formed as they came up and was soon in sufficient force to advance. Their horses showed much mettle and soon closed with the enemy.

I shall now leave the cavalry dealing death and confusion amongst their enemies and say something about the infantry. Fortunately our assistance was not required. The enemy's force consisting of cavalry and in number inferior to ours. If we had been wanting we could render no help, for there was not a single round of ball cartridge but was sodden with wet, so we began searching for wood to make fires to dry ourselves so as to be ready to advance as soon as we could get our pouches renewed with fresh ammunition.

We picked up many prisoners in the village, some in bed, others half dressed. In a house I with two of my comrades found an officer and a Spanish woman in bed. It was laughable to see him rub his eyes and stare at our red jackets. Having scoured the village well we soon made good fires and began cooking some bacon etc. we found in the houses. By this time the hussars were bringing in a goodly number of prisoners, all very much cut about the head, arms and thighs.

One in particular was said to be an Irishman, he had left Ireland when I boy with his father at the time of the rebellion, he fought like a devil and would not surrender as long as he was able to lift his arm. He said they were deceived by the hussars' horses' swish tails. Their commander took them for Spaniards, this was the reason he waited the charge. The prisoners brought in belonged to the 16th Imperial Dragoons. As we could not muster about half our regiment, and as my comrade was missing, some of us went to the river. How was we surprised to see below the place we had crossed about twenty small islands, covered with our men and the Brunswickers. Some hours after the stragglers came up and my comrade with them, he was doubly welcome for I was doubtful whether he was alive or not besides he had all the biscuits.

It was reported that Lieutenant Mainwaring was drowned. This cast a gloom over the regiment for he was a great favourite and beloved by every man of the corps. He is the nephew of the old colonel of that name. He had been brought up to the profession of arms from his cradle. He was with the regiment on the first expedition to Spain under General Moore and was at Flushing likewise. At both these places he was only a boy in jacket and trousers.

The word was soon passed that young Mainwaring was safe, in a few minutes he appeared amongst us bareheaded, he lost his cap in the river. One simultaneous burst of applause rent the air which shewed how deeply he was beloved. The loss in crossing the Eslar was 15th Hussars, four men, three horses drowned, 51st ten rank and file; Brunswickers, one officer and twenty-seven rank and file.

No. 48. Camp —— 19th June, 1813.

I had intended in my last to give you a description of a pontoon bridge and the reason we forded the Eslar. The enemy's advance being on this river it was necessary to throw over some troops to cover the engineers in the work of throwing the bridge across. I have already given you the particulars of crossing the river on the 31st May and shall now proceed to state what took place directly after it was found that we had driven the enemy and had possession of their ground. The work of laying down the bridge began, large flat bottomed iron boats were launched, their heads anchored towards the current, their sterns also made fast by anchors. A sufficient number of boats are placed side by side at a short distance from each other until the opposite bank is gained, when the whole is made fast to each other and strongly secured by cables and chains to the banks. Planks being laid on the boats, the bridge is ready and capable to bear cavalry, infantry, guns etc.

You might form some notion with what dispatch such bridges are completed when I inform you that the whole of our army, baggage and stores were transported across, the bridge broken up and placed on the wagons by four o'clock in the afternoon. I have called the vehicles wagons because in their construction they resemble timber carriages, these carriages are drawn by from eight to sixteen bullocks according to the nature of the roads.

We remained in camp near the river for the night. Next morning, 1st June, we advanced to Zamora. Near the town we saw several of the hussars with their horses lying dead.

On the 16th June we crossed the Ebro. I shall never forget the beauty of the valley through which this river runs, I had never before seen anything to equal it. About three miles from the bridge by which we crossed, on the top of a mountain, all on a sudden, the valley opened to our view, at one glance many miles of the river were visible, its rich banks ornamented with vineyards. Trees, villages, bridges, all in miniature, as we descended, the beauty of the scene increased as distant objects became more clear.

From the Ebro we continued to advance, we are now two or three days march from Vittoria where, I understand, the enemy are assembling all his force. The country about us is well stocked with pease and all kinds of vegetables. Fortunately for us it is so, for we are getting badly off for rations. Major Roberts commands the regiment, and a better commander we could not have. He allows us to fill our haversacks with what we can get on the roads, often he has said to us when we have halted for a quarter of an hour's rest 'Why don't you fill your haversacks.'

If any of the men seemed unwilling to move he would say 'Be off into the field and stock yourself with field rations, you know the commissariat has none.'

I thought ere this I should have been able to have given you some account of the enemy. I am deceived, for we have not seen a French soldier since we crossed the Eslar, except some few prisoners of war. I understand the enemy has destroyed Burgos, or rather the fortifications. It is now nine days since we had any bread issued to us, but as a substitute we get wheat or rye. This is but of little service as we have neither time or inclination to boil it sufficiently. Meat we get every day, but the fatigue of marching has reduced the bullocks to skin and bone. Wine or liquor we get regular. In the valley where we are halted there is a good stream and several water mills. We have a chance to grind our corn, my comrade is just come from one of the mills with his haversack full of flour and as the mail closes in a short time I shall close my letter and assist Jack in making some dough boys.

No. 49. Camp near Pampaluna. 1st July, 1813.

On the 20th June we encamped near Vittoria. In the afternoon Major Roberts, as he was wont to do, came round our camp to take a peep at the camp kettles. I with some of my comrades were smoking a pipe in our tent when the major peeped in saying very good humouredly 'Well my boys have you any bread to give away?'

We answered we had no bread but if old Bob, meaning his favourite horse, wanted corn we could supply him with plenty.

He smiling replied 'Never mind my lads there is plenty of bread there' pointing with his stump towards Vittoria. 'And by this time tomorrow we shall have plenty.'

The major's prophesy proved true. In twenty four hours after the soldiers of the 'Great Nation,' Napoleon's Invincibles, were totally defeated with the loss of all their cannon, ammunition, baggage, money and stores of every description by a half starved army of British and Portuguese. The enemy, to use their own words, had decoyed us to Vittoria to give us a good drubbing and a dance in double quick time back into Portugal again. Such was King Joseph's confidence that he had caused scaffolding to be erected for the people to see him beat the English. The tops of all the churches and lofty buildings were crowded with spectators to witness our disgrace. Grand dinners were provided and wine in abundance to drink to the health of the conquering French. Long before dark on the 21st June the fairy vision had fled and we were regaling ourselves at their expense.

On the morning of the 21st June we advanced. We had not proceeded far when the company to which I belonged to was ordered out to scour a wood on our right flank. We extended and marched through without falling in with the enemy, but we fell in with plenty of cattle, sheep and goats. We haversacked a few sheep and ran against an old shepherd, we soon relieved him of all he had, *viz.* a four pound loaf, some cheese and about a quart of wine. The poor old fellow cried. It was no use, we had not seen a bit of bread these eleven days. The old man was not far from home and could get more.

The battle had now began on the right of our army. We got clear of the wood and saw our division crossing a river by a stone bridge, but they had got a long start of us and it was some time as they continued to advance, before we could get up. In passing through a village we found many wounded men, several belonged to our corps, from these men we learned the regiment had been engaged and had taken fourteen guns. After this we soon joined. The brigade were in column, in front of a strong position occupied by the enemy.

After sustaining their fire some time we dashed forward, drove them from their position in such a hurry that they left ten guns behind. This charge was executed so sudden that although they sent us a shower of balls and bullets very few done any harm. Soon after this the entire of the French army broke up, and so precipitate was their flight that they left all their material of war on the field. We continued the pursuit till near dark, passed the city of Vittoria some distance on our right, then halted for the night. Here was a scene of confusion, we were surrounded with guns, wagons, horses, mules and baggage. The dead and dying lay scattered all around us.

As soon as we halted my comrade, a famous hand to look out, proposed to go and see if he could get some money, as several men had come into camp loaded with money. In case we should move I was to carry his firelock and pack. He had not been gone long before I grew impatient so I started after him. I had not proceeded far when I met one of the 68th. Regiment with a handkerchief full of dollars.

He was followed by about a dozen Portuguese soldiers, one of these fellows ran in and cut the handkerchief and down went the dollars, a general scramble followed. As the Portuguese were down on their hands and knees picking up the money, we paid them off in style with the sockets of our bayonets. After this fracas was over I proceeded on until my ear caught the welcome sound of Brown's voice, he was singing his favourite song 'When wild war's deadly blast was blown.' I knew there was luck, for he never sang this song but when he was elevated with the juice of the grape or he had met with good luck. I soon found him, he had been in a flour cask and was as white as a miller.

As soon as he saw me he shouted 'my dear fellow come back to camp, I have enough to last us both as long as we live.' I soon learned that the extent of his treasure was two canteens of brandy, three loaves, two haversacks of flour, one ham and two dollars and a half. I took a good swig of brandy and half a loaf. Brown went home to make dumplings and I started off in the direction I heard most noise, soon came to the place where the money was. After much difficulty I secured a small box of dollars, and was fortunate enough to get back safe to camp.

No. 50. Camp, Heights of Eschellar, (Echalar). 17th July, 1813.

When I returned to camp, how was I surprised at the great change that had taken place during the short time I had been absent. When I left no fires had been lit, now the place was all in a blaze. I knew of nothing to compare it to but an Arab camp after a successful attack on some rich caravan. Wearing apparel of all sorts and description lying about in heaps or trampled underfoot, boxes broken to pieces for fuel. Everyone was in motion, some bringing in loads of different descriptions on their shoulders, others leading or driving horses and mules loaded with baggage, provisions and liquors and something of everything that forms the baggage of an army. Dame Fortune had distributed her gifts in her usual way, to some money, others bread, hams, cherries, tobacco etc. This of necessity soon established a market. Now the camp represented a great fair and the money and goods soon became more equally distributed. 'Who will give fifty dollars for this pipe?'

'Here is a portrait of Napoleon for one hundred dollars.' Then a general's coat would fetch more dollars than it cost *francs*. Wine and brandy would fetch a high price. Cognac from forty to fifty dollars per bottle. The market soon changed into a grand masquerade. British soldiers were soon to be seen in French general's and other officer's uniform covered with stars and military orders, others had attired themselves in female dresses, richly embroidered in gold and silver.

In the midst of all this hurly burly, frolic and fun, the belly was not forgotten. An hundred fires were occupied in preparing food, all our camp-kettles were in requisition and loads of cooking utensils that had been taken from the enemy. The cooking reminds me of seeing one of our men walk into camp having a large table cloth tied by the four corners, it contained dishes, tureens, plates, knives and silver forks. He found it ready laid. The guests were not there so he bundled it up together and walked away with it.

While we were regaling ourselves Major Roberts paid us a visit, he said 'Now my lads you see I am no false prophet, did I not tell you yesterday we should have plenty.' He told us to make ourselves merry, but above all things to keep sober, for the moment was not known but we might move.

What a contrast between this night and the last. Twenty-four hours before we had not enough in the regiment to bait a mouse trap, this night we could scarce move without trampling on all kinds of provisions. Suffice it to say that after eating and drinking, singing and smoking we dropped off asleep, marched the next morning loaded like donkeys, leaving as much provisions in the camp that would serve for a month.

The loss of the regiment in killed was Lieutenant Percey, two sergeants and twenty-two rank and file. Wounded, Lieutenant and Adjutant Jones (severely) one serjeant and fifty-four rank and file.

We continued our march to Pampaluna, meeting with nothing remarkable on the road only that we passed a howitzer upset in a ditch. It is said this was the only piece of ordnance the enemy saved on the 21st June. From Pampaluna we made forced marches on Tudela de Ebro, to cut off a corps of the army under General Clausel. He was not in time for Vittoria. On hearing of the defeat of King Joseph he retired to this place. He done the job well, for before we could come up to him he had crossed the frontiers. We now returned to Pampaluna, gave pickets against the town, then after a halt of two days, ascended the Pyrenees and encamped on the heights above the village of Eschellar, about five miles in front of the village.

We are now stationed about the centre of the Allied army;

on our right are the troops under Sir Rowland Hill guarding the pass of Ronselvalles; our division in the pass of Eschellar. The Light Division on our left watching the Bidasoa and on the left of the whole the troops under Sir Thomas Graham. From our camp we have a very extensive view into France, and of the French army. They are busy erecting huts and intrenching themselves.

No. 51. Camp near Eschellar. 7th August, 1813.

On the 24th July the enemy advanced and attacked Sir Rowland Hill's position at Bastia. We watched the contending parties all the afternoon and could plainly perceive that our right were falling back. About dusk we broke up our camp and retired. We continued retreating until the 29th when we went into position on the left of the front line, having Pampaluna a short distance in our rear. On the 30th the Invincibles got another drubbing. In our front was a lofty mountain on which was posted the enemy's right. This was the key to their position, it being almost impregnable and commanded their whole line. It fell to our lot to drive them from it. Major General Inglis commanded our brigade.

The attack was made as follows. The brigade marched to its left some distance, when the 51st turned to the right and under the cover of brush wood and trees began to ascend the steep front of the mountain. The 82nd and Chasseurs Brittanique Regiments ascended on the enemy's right. The 68th advanced farther round the hill before they began to ascend, so that we were marching to the attack in their front on their right and in their rear.

The part of the mountain by which we advanced was very steep, something similar to Beachenclif and full ten times higher. The wood completely covered us and helped us in climbing, some places were so difficult that we were obliged to assist each other. I understand the 68th met with the same difficulties on their side. The 82nd and Chasseurs Brittanique Regiment met with less difficulty and advanced in good order in two lines. It was in their direction the enemy expected the attack and were formed ready to receive them. Fortunately we all arrived at our different points of attack at the same time.

The enemy allowed the 82nd and Chasseurs Brittanique's to come nearer them in their usual custom, before they opened their fire, at length the enemy fired a volley which was instantly returned by the 82nd. We then slapped a volley into them that seemed to say 'well done 82nd'. Before the noise was well subsided bang goes the 68th, which spoke as plain as possible 'well done the whole. Now fifty buglers were sounding the charge, and the drums of the 82nd and Chasseurs Brittanique's were beating time to the music. A general rush was made by the whole brigade, accompanied by three tremendous British cheers.

The concert was to powerful for the nerves of *Monsieur*, who without ceremony changed the concert into a ball, and off they danced, the Devil take the hindmost, down the hill to our right, the only way they had to escape. We followed them close to their heels and soon got them on a small level, here they soon got huddled together like a flock of sheep. This place was well studded with thick bushes of underwood, and here and there a cork tree. As we were galling them with a sharp fire, they summed up resolution to turn on us and threatened us with a taste of their steel.

As soon as their intention was perceived our bugles sounded the charge and in a moment we were on the level with them. Now the tug of war began. As they could only get away by a few at a time, not only were the bayonets used but many were the fractured sculls by the butts of firelocks. Every bush were soon turned into a citadel, and in many instances the same bush was occupied by each party. Serjeant Major Davis had equipped himself with a French musket and pouch, and when in the act of firing a French grenadier jumped up from behind the same bush and levelled his piece at him. The serjeant major struck the muzzle of the piece with his hand just at the moment the piece was discharged. The charge passed through his hand but he seized the grenadier, and being an active man tripped him up, disarmed him and took him to the rear a prisoner. The enemy was soon thinned by some getting away and by their loss in killed and wounded, the remainder we made prisoners.

We then returned back to the top of the hill and received a lecture from General Inglis for following the enemy down the hill, contrary to the sound of the field bugle. He informed us that had we remained on the hill and fired, the end would have been gained with less loss to us, for the remainder of the division were posted to gall them by cross fire. He said he could not but admire our ardour but hoped we should be more attentive in future. Courage, if not controlled by discipline was often the cause of much disaster etc. The general is a good old soul, and although he endeavoured to look mighty angry we could see he was not so much displeased as he pretended.

We now had a view of both armies, they were hot at it, but from the nature of the ground nothing extraordinary was done. Two howitzers in our line were served well and were seldom fired without dealing destruction. In the afternoon we perceived a movement in the enemy's line. In a short time after their whole army retreated, we then descended into the valley and by a cross fire annoyed them for some time. Here I found my comrade, he had with a few more followed the enemy from the level. In this valley we lay down for the night and slept well without rocking.

No. 52. Camp near Eschellar. 17th August, 1813.

The valley we halted in for the night I have since learnt is called the pass of Donna Maria. In the morning we rose with the lark, put our firelocks in some sort of order, then advanced. On our march we fell in with a large body of the enemy in column at the village of St. Steven. We ascended a rocky ridge to our right. This ridge formed a natural breast work. Over this ridge Major Roberts looked and said 'There they are my lads, pepper them well.' And there they were sure enough as the Cornishman would have said, in one dense black column, occupying about as much ground as the houses in Queen's Square. We had nothing to do but to fire down on their heads, or hurl down rocks.

We amused ourselves some time in this way while some troops of our brigade were firing at them from the valley we had left. We soon made the place so hot that they soon fled to the mountains. We then pushed along the ridge, the extremity of which joined to the mountain they were retreating up. Here we had another opportunity of peppering them again, but we had not now all the fun to ourselves for the enemy threw out his Voltigeurs, and taking all things into consideration they covered their retreat well. We kept pushing them on until our ammunition was expended, when we were relieved by the Highlanders of Sir R. Hill's division. We then fell back and remained near to the village of St. Steven for the night.

The next morning continued our march along the valley, this day we did not fall in with the enemy. The only remarkable thing that struck my observation was a French soldier of the 148th Regiment. He was sitting on the side of the road on a bit of a stump, amidst some hundred of pick axes and shovels. He looked like 'grief on a monument'—making an ugly face at us as we passed him.

This night we halted and I went on the quarter guard. In our front was a large field of potatoes. Several of our men, amongst whom was my comrade, was filling their haversacks. The Provost popped amongst them and seized Jack, he brought him to the quarter guard while he went in pursuit of others. In the mean time I took Jack to the rear. On passing Major Roberts's tent my comrade told him that the Provost was going to flog him for taking a few potatoes, and that he was then prisoner in the quarter guard. 'Take him back' said the major, 'and when the Provost comes tell him he is in my custody and I will punish him and send the potatoes to me.'

Shortly after the Provost arrived and demanded his prisoner. The serjeant followed the orders of the major, and the Provost was obliged to go away without breeching Jack as he intended. The major then came up and gave Jack a good lecture for being so stupid as to be caught. He ordered him to be released, saying 'go to my servant and get your "Murphys" I have only taken a few for my own dinner.'

The next morning we ascended the mountains. Our left brigade was sharply engaged this afternoon and but for a dense fog that came on we should have assisted them, but so dense was this fog that we could not identify the man next us. The whole brigade was soon intermixed. As we proceeded the fog became so thick we could not see the ground, the confusion was beyond everything, men calling to each other, in every direction. The Chasseurs Brittanique Regiment were bawling in the French language, so that we were not certain if we were not intermixed with the enemy. At last our bugles sounded the halt and to lie down. I wrapped myself in my blanket and slept very comfortably until daylight when I awoke, looked round me (for the fog was gone) saw the brigade scattered about like a large flock of sheep. I have taken the liberty of calling this mountain 'Babal' Mountain, for such a confusion of tongues I never before heard.

This day we marched for the village of Eschellar where we are now encamped in a large apple orchard, the trees of which are loaded. The remainder of the division are encamped on the heights. The loss of our regiment on the 30th and 31st July was killed, three serjeants, one bugler and thirty-five rank and file; Wounded, two serjeants, two buglers, and eighty-one rank and file. It is most extraordinary and singular fact that we had not a single officer killed or wounded either day.

No. 53. Passages. 2nd September, 1813.

We remained encamped in the apple orchard enjoying ourselves under the cooling shade of the trees until the 30th August, then marched and encamped near the town or village of Lezaca, the headquarters of the army. In the morning we marched through the town and ascended the mountains in advance. At Lezaca we were joined by Lieutenant Dodd and thirty men from England. The men were distributed through the regiment. One of them was ordered to fall in on my right, this separated me from a man who had stood next to me in many fights and was not relished by either of us. The man saw we did not wish to be separated, offered to change places, this I accepted and he took my left.

We then advanced. The enemy had crossed the Bidasoa in three divisions at the fords near Salim, to relieve St. Sebastian. We soon came under their fire. They outnumbered us greatly, the nature of the ground prevented us from bringing many men into action, only a few companies could engage. I was in reserve the first two hours and witness many noble achievements performed by private soldiers, that if properly related would deserve a conspicuous place in the proud history of Britain. Before we had sent out our skirmishers, and by the first fire of the enemy, the stranger on my left was struck in the forehead and fell dead. He having just arrived from England had a good kit. Exchange is no robbery so I slung off my light knapsack and took possession of his.

The enemy kept reinforcing their skirmishers, so that the fire that was at first slack now began to be very brisk, and in a short time they began to advance on our line, but not with that firmness one should expect from their superiority in numbers. Our skirmishers stood firm, but the fire being too hot for their liking they rushed forward on the enemy, who gave way—and in a few minutes our line had possession of their ground. This charge drove the enemy into a forest on their reserve.

Their fire was now tremendous and our line fell back to draw them out on open ground. The hill now swarmed again with the enemy, and a stationary fire was kept up a long time. General English had ridden to the front to become better acquainted with the ground, when by some unforeseen accident he became separated from his men and would have been made prisoner but for the little band who at a great disadvantage rescued him. Captain Frederick saw the danger his general was in, ordered his bugler to sound the charge, the sound was answered by three cheers, and off his company went accompanied by Lieutenant Bayley's company and one company of the Chasseurs Brittanique Regiment. In a moment they were mixed with the enemy and down the hill they went together, *pel mel*, into the wood. The general was rescued.

Our company was now ordered to the front, we soon got into action but as the enemy had joined their reserves and the large trees completely covered them, we fell back on our reserves. This soon drew them out from cover and brought us all together by the ears. I never remember to be under so sharp a fire in an affair of this kind before. My comrade Brown was wounded in the right leg near the knee and was obliged to go to the rear. Shortly after a ball glanced the inside of my right knee, it deadened the leg for some time and caused some pain.

We were now obliged to give way to superior force. By dusk we had lost nearly a league of ground, without allowing the enemy to gain any other advantage. I think it was the dearest league they had ever purchased. I believe a few such bargains and they would be bankrupt. Night put an end to the affair.

Our brigade lay on our arms all night, although it rained much during the night I slept well. The Earl of Dalhousie arrived with the remainder of the division before daylight. This put us in high spirits for we were now confident we should give them a good thrashing. A deserter came over to us in the night. From him we learnt that we had been engaged all day with the 3rd Battalion 51st Regiment, just arrived from France, and was at the commencement 1400 strong, while our strength including the detachment from England was only 304 rank and file. This I know to be correct, we were in eight divisions of nineteen file each. Our loss was severe having killed: Captain Douglas, Lieutenant Dodd, one sergeant, four buglers and thirty rank and file. Wounded, Major Roberts (severely), Captains Keyts (severely) Kelly (severely) Fredrick (severely) John Ross and Jas. Ross (slightly) Lieutenants Bayley (severely) left arm amputated, Minchin, Thurston and Brook (slightly) thirteen serjeants, four buglers and 167 rank and file. Colonel Mitchell commanded the regiment. He had one of his spurs shot away. It is worthy of notice that Lieutenant Dodd and every man of his party were either killed or wounded.

No. 54. Camp, Heights of Eschellar.
8th September, 1813.

In my last you have an account of the smart affair near Lezaca. I had intended to have said something about some of our officers who were wounded that day, I shall begin with Major Roberts. He received two wounds, one in the right shoulder, the other in the stump. When he was being carried to the rear, he said 'See my lads, they cannot let my stump alone, I am sorry to leave you, I hope you will stick to the rascals'; we have lost in him a good, kind, brave and generous officer.

The name of Douglas and courage are so closely connected in British history, it will only be necessary to say, he stood high as a brave soldier, but he was in possession of another virtue, rarely to be met with to so great a degree in any man—it was a noble generosity and good will that he extended to all about him. He had acquired the appellation of 'Father' by his company, by whom he was almost idolized. By the regiment at large he was highly beloved and respected. Notwithstanding he was a strict disciplinarian, but somehow, he never had any trouble in keeping his men in order, as a look or a word from him had more effect then 500 lashes would from some officers. Our regret for his loss can be much easier imagined then described.

In the night the enemy fell back and began to recross the Bidasoa. Daylight broke upon them before they had well began to recross the river. Now their trouble began, some guns that had been planted in the night now opened on them. The sharp-shooters of the Light Division pushed them close, beside all the disposable force that could be brought into action. It will be sufficient to say that they sustained a very great loss. The rain in the night had swollen the river, the fords were very dangerous, and hundreds in the confusion were washed down with the stream never to rise again. It was the intention of the enemy to relieve St. Sebastian but this place was carried by storm yesterday at the same moment we were engaged.

We now turned our attention to the wounded who were collected in a convent in our rear. A party consisting of our paymaster and thirty men were ordered to proceed to Passages with the wounded officers, who were carried on bearers (I was one of this party). On the road we had a full view of St. Sebastian. The town was in flames but the enemy's flag was still flying on the castle. A heavy fire from our ships of war was kept up on this place. We at length arrived at Passages, from this place I wrote my last letter. We halted two days at Passages then marched to join our regiment.

We passed the place where we had been engaged, curiosity prompted us to walk over the ground. The eagle and other birds of prey had began their work on the bodies of such as had not been buried. A Spaniard had been led to the field out of curiosity or for the sake of plunder. He pointed to the mountain on our left, saying there had been a great battle fought there the 31st August. Our time was our own, so we determined on exploring the place. Off we started taking the old boy for a guide, two hours brought us to the spot. We found what the old man had said was true, it appeared to have been fought between the French and Spaniards, and a desperate job it must have been and no mistake about it, for the contending parties lay dead bayonet to bayonet. I saw several pairs with the bayonet in each other. As night was approaching we wended our way into the valley, took up our quarters in a church, where we slept comfortable for the night. The next evening we joined the regiment who were again encamped on the heights in advance of Eschellar.

No. 55. Camp. Heights of Eschellar.
1st October, 1813.

We have not had a move since I wrote last. Your letter I received yesterday expressed so much anxiety for my safety, has caused me to write this to satisfy you that I am in possession of the best of health and spirits. I am afraid for the first time I shall be compelled to send you a short letter, for everything remains exactly as when I wrote last. I must therefore charge my recollection and see if I have not omitted something in my former letters that might be amusing. If I should fail, you must excuse me for really I am in much the same situation as the Children of Israel in Egypt when they were obliged to 'make bricks without straw.'

To begin I shall relate something that happened some time ago when the orchards were loaded with apples. You must know that in our turn we give picquets, near to the Puerto de Eschellar. On one of these occasions I was on the advance post. An orchard that lay between ours and the enemy's advance sentries was loaded with fruit. It being forbidden ground, of course these apples were coveted by both parties, although the whole place consisted of scarce anything else but apple orchards.

At length some daring souls of each army entered the orchard. At first each party confined themselves to their own side, but growing more bold, they by degrees advanced to the centre, and shortly our men and the enemy were completely mixed. Indeed it was no uncommon sight to see a British and French soldier picking apples from the same tree, with as much unconcern as if they were belonging to the same service.

On the right of this orchard was a lane that ran into the enemy's lines. At the bottom of this lane ran a stream of water. About twenty paces from this water was the spot we pushed forward our advance sentries for the night, about the same distance on the other side of the brook was the enemy's advance. These two outposts were guarded by a corporal and file who were relieved every hour. At daylight each party withdrew to their respective picquets. The officer commanding our picquet asked me if I had any objection to take charge of the outpost the last hour before daylight as he considered the duty too hard for the corporals, who besides performing this duty had to plant the other sentries.

To be selected for this post roused my ambition and I accepted the proposal with delight. When I got to my post, the corporal pointed to two figures about the common height of men, and in a direct line to the spot occupied by the enemy's advance, and about half-way between us. He said they had been walking about all the time, he had been posted, did not know what to make of them etc. He then crawled back to the picquet leaving us to keep a sharp lookout on the two strange gentlemen who kept walking about. Sometimes they seemed almost close to us then, as if doubtful, they would retire. We were ready cocked but they might be deserters, besides to fire on two when there were three of us would not look well, and it would perhaps set both sides a popping and create an unnecessary alarm.

At length daylight shewed us who these two gentlemen were. It was nothing but two bushes, now and then bending up and down by the wind that ever and anon swept through the valley. It was now time to crawl back, we found the corporal had made his report of the two strangers and that the whole picquet were on the alert. When I unravelled the mystery, it caused a hearty laugh. It frequently happens such trifles will cause a sharp skirmish, that do not always end without mischief.

The enemy are still employed in intrenching themselves and building batteries along the whole front of their line, they are likewise bestowing much labour on their huts. I suppose it is their intention to remain where they are all the winter, if we do not put them out of it. This we shall be very apt to do soon, for we have nearly completed the roads we have been making across the mountains to convey our light guns etc.

No. 56. Camp, Heights of Eschellar.
13th October, 1813.

Early on the morning of the 7th inst we struck our tents and went into position on the heights that commands the valley running to the Puerto de Eschellar. The enemy had strongly fortified this pass by trenches, forts and a half moon battery, that ran across the valley. It was over the left of this battery we were stationed, on a high mountain called The Hermitage. On the right the battery was occupied by the enemy. The formidable appearance of the enemy's position promised a hard day's work to the troops who should be employed against it. The Spaniards were to be employed, it is said they had volunteered their service to have the honour of driving the enemy into France.

We had taken our ground some time before they had arrived, so we had the pleasure of seeing them pass to the front. A sudden burst of laughter announced their arrival, and we all placed ourselves so as to see them march by. Their advance column was headed by a friar that more resembled a wool-pack than anything I can think of, in his right hand he displayed a crucifix, his head was bare so was his feet, that spread like a camel's. The sweat poured down his bald head and face like melted butter.

If holiness is estimated by weight, this man had enough and plenty to spare, but if an opinion is to be formed from the horrid curses he continued to utter against the French I should be led to suppose he had applied himself more to the practice of swearing than to praying. By his side stalked a tall meagre figure in holy orders, he would not have made a bad rammer to a long nine pounder. In his left hand he carried a sort of basket containing holy water and in his right a brush to sprinkle it with. He said nothing, his eye was fixed on the enemy's position, fear was visible in his countenance, and if it were possible to dive into his thoughts I am mistaken if he would not have preferred being shut up snug in his convent, meditating over a good breakfast then be employed as he was.

The column that followed these two holy personages had the appearance of anything but soldiers. 'Sir John Falstaff's ragged regiment' were kings to them. We did not expect much from such a rum lot. We made sure that we should soon see them in full retreat and that we should have to finish the job for them, but in this we were deceived, they fought well. By dark they had cleared the mountain. Between three and four o'clock in the afternoon someone called out 'Fall in.' We were looking at the half moon battery expecting every moment to be led against it, we ran to our arms with a hurrah and away ran the enemy out of the battery. Our left brigade soon took possession and followed the enemy, some skirmishing took place but as night came on the firing ceased, the next morning we joined our left brigade and opened a fire on the enemy's advance who retired from their breast works. This finished the affair.

After remaining in their camp a few hours, destroying their huts etc. we once more returned to our old camp on the heights. The Puerto de Eschellar is now in our possession, our roads is complete, so that I expect in a very short time we shall advance into France. It is a delightful looking country and from the number of towns and villages is likely to afford us good winter's quarters. But before we can get to them we shall have hot work, for the enemy is strongly entrenched, not only on the ground they occupy, but for many miles to their rear.

No. 57. Camp. Heights of Eschellar.
3rd November, 1813.

We are getting heartily tired of remaining so long here, the weather is cold and foggy and we have had some very sharp frosts, but our tents protects us much better than could be expected. I have always endeavoured to give you the leading particulars of every event I thought would be interesting. I am now about to relate a tale, the recollection of which causes a tear to the memory of an unfortunate comrade, generally beloved by everyone in the corps, who has been shot by the sentence of a general court martial. It was poor Serjeant Roach. 'The bravest of the brave,' the kind hearted honest affectionate Roach.

Serjeants McCormack and Roach in an evil hour were drinking at a wine shop in the village of Eschellar. After indulging too much with the wine, and had become pretty mellow, McCormack missed his money. After searching in vain for some time he at length told Roach that he had lost guineas to the amount of £65, and that he had taken it. This brought on a war of words which rose so high that an officer was sent for, who, on hearing the cause of the dispute ordered Roach to the guard room. (As they were both drunk he should have ordered both into confinement.) Roach being warm with wine, and fired with indignation at being suspected a thief, struck the officer. A general court martial was the consequence. He was tried on two charges. *Viz.* first for the robbery of which he was acquitted, the second was for striking his superior officer in the execution of his duty; on this charge he was found guilty and sentenced to be 'Shot to Death.'

From the aggravating circumstances attending the case, everyone thought the sentence would have been commuted, particularly as Roach had always borne a good character, and the officers had interested themselves in his behalf. But his time was come. Poor Roach who had faced death in a thousand shapes—he had shared in all the toils of the regiment from his birth, having been born in the corps, was never suspected before of a single dishonest action, in short he who had never wilfully before this time offended any one—was brought out in front of the 7th. Division of the army, and, to use his own words was 'Shot like a dog.'

After willing over his effects to his comrade Douglas, of whom he begged to conceal the disgraceful manner of his death from his parents and friends, he offered up a short prayer, then called out '51st farewell,' and said in a firm voice 'I'm ready.' The provost marshal gave the signal, he fell to the earth pierced by about a dozen balls, his mangled corpse presented a sad spectacle, his head was literally blown to pieces. It is almost needless to add there was not a dry eye in the regiment for as I said before, he was generally beloved. He was buried on the spot and we have raised a pile of rude stones on his grave, not only to mark the spot but to prevent the wolfs from scratching up his body. He is now no more, let us hope he has obtained that mercy in another world that was denied him in this.

Since my last I have been promoted to corporal, I never undertook anything with so much distrust and misgiving, it has been completely forced on me. Our pay serjeant was killed at Lezaca and our captain wounded, the men's accompts were left in a very confused state. Our paymaster recommended me to set the books to rights. I was in the officers' tent, just finishing the debt and credit roll, when the officer commanding the company brought in our adjutant. The adjutant told me I was 'a D——d fool,' I might have had a serjeant's coat before this. He said I should have my choice of two things, that was, I should be put in

orders that day for corporal, and I might do the duty, either with, or without pay. I had no alternative. If I refused, then I should be appointed lance corporal, that is I should have to perform the duty on private's pay. Of course I consented to the wishes of my friends, and a few hours after I was appointed.

No. 58. General Hospital, St. Jean De Luz.
20th November, 1813.

There is an old saying 'That the pitcher never goes to the well so often but it gets broken.' My pitcher is not broken, it is only cracked and I am in hopes it will soon get patched up so that I shall be able to take it to the well again. Don't be alarmed, I am wounded, not dangerously. I suppose if I was a colonel or general it would be (severely), but according to my humble rank I shall call it slightly. I have already said enough to satisfy you that my spirits have not been hurt. I have much to write, have patients and I will tell you the whole.

But before I say anything of the battle I am inclined to pay a compliment to the brave garrison of Pampaluna. I am not one who wish to claim all the merit on our own side, no, while I endeavour to record the gallantry of the British I cannot in justice to a brave enemy be silent in their praise. Pampaluna held out until the 31st October.

A considerable time before they surrendered the garrison was reduced to the greatest privation, not an animal of any description escaped the butcher save the Governor's horse. Dogs, cats and rats were all devoured, and when they marched out with the honours of war, so ghastly were the appearance of the men that one would have supposed they had all risen from their graves. I was told, by some who witnessed the sight that the men could scarcely stand, they had held out until completely starved. What more could be expected from them. They are an honour to the Imperial Army and to their country.

I shall have plenty of time on my hands, and if I am not troubled with my wounds more than at present I shall write often and be particular in detailing all that came under my notice on this eventful day.

On the 7th Nov. we received a party from England. Hooker, the man who was wounded at the Retiro, joined with it having lost my old comrade Brown, and as Hooker volunteered with me from the Surrey, he has taken Brown's place. I mention this because I shall have something to say about Tom either in this or some future letter. The weather had for some time become unpleasant, frosty nights, rain, and sleet made us wish to drive the enemy from their more comfortable camp.

On the night of the 9th. inst. we struck our tents and marched to the Puerto de Eschellar, here we rested on our arms 'til morning, then advanced. The attack was made along the whole line of the enemy's works. The enemy shewed but little opposition until we came to the village of Sara. Behind this place there is a long range of hills, strongly fortified. Here they had determined to stand, and it fell to our lot to attack that part of their position directly in rear of the village. We soon came under their fire.

As we advanced Hooker had been relating to me some part of the unpleasant history of his family affairs, it seemed to weigh heavy on his mind. On the contrary my spirits was as light as a feather, I did all I could to enliven him it was but of little purpose. After passing Sara we entered a field of Indian corn, I remarked to him as the balls were striking the stalks that I had never seen them fire so low, and that if they continued the practice some of us would get broken shins. He made no reply, he seemed full of thought.

We now arrived at a wall that ran across our front. We halted here to collect our stragglers and to get into order, for we had become much scattered owing to the irregularity of the ground. A fat pig running down our front was soon shot and in a minute several of us began cutting him up, one of the men thus employed received a shot through his hand. I had got a nice piece of pork and wished Tom to have part. 'It will be of no use to me' said he 'look at poor Webster there, that is the way I shall have my wind knocked out of me directly.'

That moment Serjeant Webster was shot dead by a ball entering about an inch below his breast plate. Had I not known Tom Hooker I should have taken him for the greatest coward in the army, but Tom was no coward, he was as brave a soldier as ever drew a trigger. As soon as our stragglers had formed we advanced, drove the enemy from behind a hedge and was soon over after them, and they, by being reinforced, tried to drive us back again. In this they were deceived, we allowed them to come within a very short distance of us, then we poured a volley into their faces and before they had well got over their surprise we were upon them with our bayonets. Here was a fearful slaughter on the part of the enemy, nearly every shot told and their dead and wounded covered the place. All that could, scampered back and we after them.

No. 59. General Hospital, St. Jean de Luz. 21st Nov. 1813.

On the top of the hill they had a reserve, these came forward and gave us a crack. Now a brisk fire was kept up on both sides, as I was in the act of pulling my trigger I received a wound in both legs, the ball glanced or scraped the skin just above the outside ankle of the left foot and passed through the gristle behind the ankle of the right just missing the bone, down I fell. I endeavoured to rise but found I could not stand and that my shoe was full of blood. 'The Devil's luck to ye' said Ned Eagan, 'For a fool, now can't ye be easy and lay quiet for a minute or so 'til we give them another charge, and send them in double quick over the hill.'

At this moment Hooker came to me and said 'I hope Bill you are not much hurt, take some of this rum.'

'Arrh Tom' says Eagan 'now you would be the best fellow alive and so you would if you would just be after letting me wet my trottle with a drop of the crature.'

Hooker gave him his canteen saying 'you are welcome Ned.'

Ned wetted his 'trottle,' gave Tom the canteen shouting 'Och my jewels, then bad luck to me if one of ye don't get this ledden pill through ye, then you may say that old Eagan's son is the biggest liar in all Ireland.'

So saying he put in the cartridge. Hooker was employed in empting some of the rum into my canteen, and Eagan was busy in sending down the charge, when down he came on top of us. They did not give him time to fulfil his promise, he was shot through the body and in a moment was a corpse.

Hooker shook my hand saying, 'Cover yourself behind Ned, I must set to work, can I do anything more for you.'

On leaving me he said 'I know I shall not see this day out, as soon as you get intelligence of my fate write to my mother.'

Now the battle raged with double fury, fresh troops poured up to reinforce each side and soon our men moved forward, but it was not many paces before our buglers sounded the retreat and the enemy advanced, but was soon driven back. My comrades this time nearly gained the top of the hill, but there they found the enemy had been reinforced, and was again obliged to retire. I soon became in rear of the enemy's line and exposed to the fire of our men. This was not of long duration, for ours drove them back to their old ground. I observed fresh troops pouring down to join the enemy, who again advanced and passed me some distance. Now the fire was very hot and our balls passed and dropped about like hail.

A French soldier came and took what money I had in my pockets, and was in the act of taking my knapsack when our men cheered and charged. I caught fire at the noise and as soon as the enemy had passed me I put my hand on poor Ned's fire-lock, for my own was not loaded. I had not taken my eye off the fellow who had robbed me, I took a deadly aim at him and down he fell. I was so overjoyed at seeing the rascal fall, and so animated was the moment, at the thought of being released from so perilous a situation, that forgetting the danger I exposed myself to, I sat up with my cap on the muzzle of my firelock and cheered my comrades as they passed me. Hooker was in the throng, he smiled and said something to me as he rushed by, but I could not catch the words.

Our adjutant rode up to me and said 'Corporal Wheeler I

hope your wound is not severe, I shall remember your conduct, and recommend you for promotion.'

This time the hill was taken. I looked around me, the combatants had disappeared, nothing was to be seen now but the killed and wounded. I crawled to the fellow that had robbed me, got my own and more money in to the bargain, he was shot in the small of the back just under his knapsack. I had been long enough in this place so I managed to get down the hill to the hedge, here I found Dr. Fitzpatrick, got my wounds dressed.

While the action was in its hottest fury I was several times struck with admiration at the heroic bravery of the officers and non-commissioned officers of the enemy. I shall select one out of many instances of zeal and self devotion displayed by these brave soldiers. A young officer about twenty was in front of his men leading them on. The men were several times stopped by our fire yet this brave young fellow kept in their front, waving his sword, calling and entreating them to come on.

At length he returned to his men and with the flat of his sword drove them or rather some of them on, but his men had lost all confidence. Finding he could not prevail on them to advance, he ran towards us some distance and halted, here he continued to wave his sword in hopes to inspire them with courage, when one of our men shot him through the body and he fell dead.

I could relate many acts of bravery performed by our men, let the following suffice until I see you, or shall have more room. One of our regiment was struggling with a French soldier for the possession of a musket. After much wrestling our man got the other down, twisted the firelock from him and gave him several smart blows on his head.

P.S. I forgot to mention that in this evening I found two musket balls in my knapsack, one was lodged in the blanket.

No. 60. General Hospital, 23rd November, 1813.

As soon has my wounds were dressed I managed to crawl to a farm house, not far distant from the spot I had left. Here I learnt the fate of poor Hooker, he was shot through the body on the top of the hill a few minutes after he had left me. From what I have said of him you will suppose he was a coward, if so, I must correct you. Hooker was one of the bravest soldiers in the regiment. No one has had more opportunities of witnessing his conduct in action then I have, from the time we volunteered, we had shared in all the ups and downs, so common to a soldier employed on active service, up to the time he received his wound, the night we besieged the Retiro. To say he was a good soldier, in the common acceptance of the word would not be doing Tom justice. He was pre-eminently courageous, and would in any other service, but the British, have ranked as an officer.

A short time before the battle of Salamanca he was very much troubled with a flux. I tried to persuade him that as we were much harassed by manoeuvring close to the enemy, it would be much better for him to report himself to the doctor, his reply was 'What would you have me crying to Doctor Webster, when we are close to the enemy and expecting every hour to be engaged, no, no I will wait a bit longer and try my hand at shooting at a few Frenchmen first, afterwards I will give up but not before, I would die on the road first.'

In the course of a fatiguing march he could not keep up, and that day we were retiring we had made sure he had fell into their hands. The next day there was some skirmishing, we were not engaged. Tom had lost us, he had joined the skirmishers and was engaged several hours, he joined us two days after, and brought a letter from the officer commanding the regiment he had voluntarily joined speaking highly of his conduct. It was singular that this skirmish cured Tom's flux, he often told me after that when he went into action he felt a sudden change in his body, his natural vigour returned and he felt no more inconvenience from the disorder. I could relate many interesting anecdotes about him. I must reserve that for some other time. Poor Tom is no more, he died a hero on the 10th day of November 1813.

I will now endeavour to give you some description of the farm and what was going on, but in this I am certain I shall fall

126

short, for it would require the genius of Hogarth to perform the task. You must have seen to believe, even then you would not credit your own eyes. You must know that this farm had been used by the enemy for their commissariat stores. Outside the buildings were a great many wounded soldiers, some drinking and smoking, others rolling about, some half and others mad drunk, while a great many lay stretched out as if dead. Women too who had followed up the rear of the army had forgot they had come up in the laudable pursuit of seeking their husbands, had freely partaken of the damnable poison until they had transformed themselves into something more like fiends than angels of mercy. But for the honour of the sex there were many exceptions.

In one place you would see a lovely young woman, supporting the head of her dying husband on her bosom, anxiously watching the last gasp for life, then again your eye would meet with one in bitter anguish, bewailing her loss, fondly clinging to the cold remains of all that was dear to her, and many were seen running about mad, unconscious of where they were going or what they were doing, these had received the news of their husband's deaths in some distant part of the field. But let me draw a veil over this melancholy picture, I have not yet taken you to the inside of the barn where the stores were kept. Before I can, I must relate something more. My thoughts are so much occupied with the misery and misfortune of so many of my comrades and their wives I cannot get into any other strain.

I was resting myself on a wall or rather a bank, thinking to what trouble and misery many lovely young women of respectable connections had brought themselves into by marrying soldiers who but a few years since I had seen in old England in the full enjoyment of health etc. when I was roused from my reverie by a well known voice saying 'Then you have caught it at last, Corporal.'

I looked up and there stood Marshall who I had once saved from a watery grave, his arm was in a sling. I was about to spake to him when I was interrupted by a female voice in a trembling accent, 'Oh Wheeler have you seen my husband or can you give me any account of him.' I shook my head.

'Oh it is too true, your silence confirms what I have just been told, he is dead.' She then ran away towards the hill where the severe conflict had taken place.

'Ah Marshall' said I 'her fears are but too true, he is dead indeed, he fell not many yards from where I lay.'

'Who the D——— is she?' said Marshall 'I did not see her to notice her.'

'Not know her' said I 'it was Mrs. Foster.'

'Oh Damn it' said he, 'was it, I am sorry for her, but you know there is so many of these damned women running and blubbering about, enquiring after their husbands. Why the D———l don't they stop at home where they ought to be. This is no place for them. Come let us go in and get something to drink, not stop here to be pestered to death by a parcel of women. Come make haste, here comes Cousins' wife, snivelling as if she was a big girl going to school without her breakfast.'

'She has reason to snivel as you calls it' said I 'she is the most unfortunate creature in the army.'

'Unfortunate indeed' said Marshall 'why I think she is devilish lucky in getting husbands, she has had a dozen this campaign.' Marshall was drunk and had rather stretched the number. This unfortunate woman was now a widow for the third time since the battle of Vittoria.

No. 61. General Hospital, St. Jean de Luz. 24th Nov. 1813.

I got rid of my troublesome acquaintance Marshall, and being weary and faint I thought I would see if I could find some place inside to rest for the night, for it threatened much for rain. By the help of my firelock I managed to get into the barn. Here was a scene that baffles all description. The enemy in their retreat had not time to remove or destroy their stores. You can judge of my astonishment, I found the place full of wounded men as comfortable to appearance as if they had been at home with their friends. The brandy had made them forget their trouble. Those who had received wounds in the legs or thighs were setting down smoking and drinking and either listening or joining in chorus to some war song. Others who had the use of their legs, some of whom with their heads wrapped in bandages and some with their arms in slings, were footing it to the merry dance.

The musician was a piper of the 83rd Regiment and was wounded in the thigh. I had seen enough to convince me that I could not expect to find any spot where to rest in this place. I was about to return and seek some other when Douglass (poor Roach's comrade) came to me with a large jug of brandy, 'Come' said he 'drink hearty, this is the best antidote for wounds that can be, it will stop the pain, keep away mortification and drive away the blue devils. Ain't we a lucky set of fellows to drop into such good quarters, drink again man, why the Devil are you afraid of it, here take a draw out of my pipe and give me your canteen and haversack and I will stock you well with brandy and biscuit.'

As soon as Douglass was gone I heard a great shout. I hobbled out to learn the reason, it was a dragoon had brought the pleasing intelligence that the enemy were completely beaten and were in full retreat. He was going to the rear to order up the baggage. I felt no inclination to go into the store again, so I took up my old position on the bank, I got my canteen and haversack. Douglass had fulfilled his promise, they were both full, this was about 3 o'clock, my right foot and leg was very stiff so I made up my mind for to sleep where I was.

Shortly after, the old man belonging to the farm made his appearance and came direct to me. I saw he was in trouble, I asked him if any of my comrades had robbed him or done him any injury, he said 'No,' but he was grieved at the thoughtlessness of our men who he said were 'killing themselves by drinking so much brandy.' He likewise said that in the height of their madness, they might accidentally set fire to the place, when he would not only be ruined but many would be burnt to death.

I asked him where he had kept himself during the battle, he

said he had remained at home to protect what little property his own countrymen had left him; he was afraid of the Spaniards and Portuguese not of the British. He was aware that the 'Grand Marshal,' meaning 'Nosey' I suppose, would protect the lives and property of the French who were not in arms, and he knew enough of the British from their conduct in Spain that so far as regards us he was safe (I could not help thinking I hope you will not have cause to change your good opinion of us, my old boy).

He was well aware of the depredations committed by the French in the Peninsular, and naturally supposed the Spaniards would on every opportunity retaliate on the French inhabitants. It struck me that I might turn the old man's fears to some account in my own behalf, so I offered him my service to protect his house. I told him I was a cor-po-ral, Frenchifying the word as much as I could by drawing it out as long as my arm or longer.

The old man closed the bargain by taking me on his back, carried me into his house, placed me by a good fire. The first thing I did was to write with chalk on the door in large characters 'Provost Martial.' This was the complete talisman, the house was spellbound against marauders. There were several of our men in the house who had and were still behaving well, the old farmer seemed satisfied, if he was not, I was. After taking a little biscuit, and frizzling some of the pork I got in the morning and washing it down with some brandy and water I settled down and slept 'til morning.

No. 62. General Hospital, St. Jean de Luz.
28th November, 1813.

My last left me sleeping by the fire at the farm, and a comfortable sleep I had. I did not awake until the old man roused me and offered me a cup of coffee, this was about daylight. From enquiry I learnt everything was quiet during the night but now some of the boys were stirring and had commenced a fresh attack on the brandy.

Soon after daylight a party of dragoons came and took charge of the stores, this soon put an embargo on the provisions and spirits. My wound in the right leg was very sore stiff and uneasy if I moved, but when still I felt little or nothing of it. I felt no inconvenience from the other as it was only a scrape. It will be sufficient to say I remained here until the 14th when I was removed on a mule to St. Pedro, this was a painful journey, from St. Pedro I with one of the Brunswickers was conveyed on a car to St. Jean de Luz, and safely and I might say comfortably lodged in the hospital where I am at present.

I have received a letter from my regiment from which I learn our loss on the 10th November at the battle of the Nivelle including all ranks killed and wounded were 117. Our strength on that morning was only 240 rank and file. My old comrade Brown has been sent to England, his leg is much contracted and it is thought he will be discharged.

I have often been tickled in reading the general despatches of the army, when some lord or general or colonel has been killed or wounded. Fame takes her trumpet and sounds it through the world that, Lord A—— fell in the moment of achieving some great exploit, then follows a long lamentation of the serious loss Old England and H.M. Service has sustained. Then General B—— is severely wounded, with a long panegyric of his military virtues and services etc.

Or that Colonel C—— of the General Staff of the army had received a severe wound (scratch, it should have been) that will deprive the army of his valuable service for some time etc. But who shall record the glorious deeds of the soldier whose lot is numbered with the thousands in the ranks who live and fight and die in obscurity.

Be it my lot to record Brown's if not to the world at least to you. We both joined the regiment together. Brown had volunteered from the South Gloster Militia. We were strangers then but soon formed an acquaintance that grew into friendship, that all the misfortunes and hardship of a long war only served to cement. Brown had never missed an action or skirmish from the time he joined until the day he was wounded. I never knew a more cool collected and determined soldier in action than he was. Let the danger be ever so great, if he saw an opportunity of firing to advantage there was no moving him, he was a good shot. When our bugles sounded to advance no one answered or obeyed more cheerfully than Brown. But when the retreat would sound, he could not bear the idea of turning his back to the enemy. On these occasions I have often said 'Come along Jack, don't you see they are closing on us.'

'That is what I want' he would say 'don't you see that fellow, I shall have him within point blank distance directly, let us wait 'til I fetch him down.' I want a comparison and for a better I must compare him to a stubborn donkey beset by a parcel of mischievous boys. He was as mischievous as a monkey himself.

I remember once being on an advance picquet with him. The officer second in command, whose heart rested nearer the seat of his trousers than in its proper place, was ordered to take a patrol and visit our advance chain. Brown said to me 'let us go with him, I will frighten him out of his wits, he stopped my rum the other day.' So we took our arms and went.

It was very dark and Brown pretended to know the ground well, so he was to be our guide. After passing a couple of our sentries he managed to lead us near to one of the enemy. All of a sudden he fell down, and bang goes off his firelock in the direction of the enemy, this was returned with interest. Mr. —— was so alarmed that we lost him.

We saw him when we returned, reporting us to the officer in command. Brown made up a good story, said he stumbled over something and that his piece went off by accident, this took very well and as there was no harm done there was no more about it.

No. 63. St. Andia, 14th December, 1813.

On the 3rd. inst. a party of wounded soldiers with some French prisoners, all wounded, were put on board a Spanish boat. The boat was open except ahead and astern, where there were a sort of false deck not for shelter but for the fishermen to stand on to manage their nets. The crew consisted of the captain and three sailors. The wounded were myself, who was commanding officer, the Brunswicker who rode with me from St. Pedro.

Eleven British belonging to different regiments, a French captain, a corporal and ten men, most of the prisoners were badly wounded. We took three days provisions with us, started with a fair wind expecting to arrive at Andia before night.

The French corporal could speak English well, was about three years older than myself, as light hearted and merry companion as I could wish. He had been five years in the French army, three of which he had served in Spain, such a man was not to be met with every day so I soon formed an acquaintance with him. The Brunswicker was a shrewd fellow, well stored with German anecdotes, could sing well and was what is termed a merry witty good sort of a fellow.

We were creeping along under the land for some time passing our time as a soldier is wont to do, enjoying a pipe and glass seasoned with song and stories, when a thick haze set in accompanied with a stiff breeze that blew every way but the way we wanted. Night came on, the captain said we must make the best of it we could, we wrapped ourselves in our blankets and made ourselves as comfortable as our situation would allow.

The wind still increased and our little bark rode over the waves as if she was drunk. Most of the prisoners were badly wounded and lay or rather sat in the bottom of the boat leaning their backs against the sides. Their sufferings must have been great for the boat shipped much water and it being their first trip made their sufferings still worse. Corporal Pipin, for that is the name of the French corporal, sat aft with me and had share of my blanket like myself, his wound was in his leg, he suffered much from sea sickness.

At length morning came and presented to us a sad spectacle. The wind was still blowing strong, the haze was thicker than it was the night before, the poor fellows in the bottom of the boat were sitting in water a foot deep, moaning in a frightful manner.

They looked more like ghosts than living creatures and to add to our comfort the Spaniards looked as if they had been fairy led.

The captain declared to me that he did not know where he was, at the same time crossing himself. He laid all the blame to me for lighting my pipe at the lamp that was burning in front of the holy virgin. The fact was, near where I was sitting there was a small box containing what he called the blessed virgin and a lamp burning in front of it. I wanted to light my pipe so I opened the door to get one, and was in the act of lighting it when Corporal Pipin shoved my elbow and out went the holy flame. Soon after the bad weather came on.

This occasioned a war of words in which my friend joined by cursing the Spaniards, calling them a cowardly superstitious set of priest ridden slaves, this drew the captain's guns off me on to the French corporal. Some were for making a Jonas of the poor captain. The French captain had been laying quiet, overcame by seasickness, but he stirred himself and fired a volley of oaths and was for sending the captain, his boat and the virgin to boot to the D———. Suffice it to say that after all the curses, in the English, German, French and Spanish languages had been fairly brought into action, the battle ended and we all became friends.

The bad weather continued all this day, the poor Frenchman had given up all hopes of ever seeing land again. The English rather made light of the matter, having their canteens full of brandy when we started. At night we were becalmed and we lay rolling about all night in grand stile. The next day there was not a breath of wind and the fog was so thick we could scarce see the length of the boat.

The Spaniards prayed to the Virgin and to all the saints they could call to mind, not forgetting the famous St. Pedro of Toledo, but none of the holy personages took the least notice of our distress. We again passed a miserable night benumbed with the cold and wet to the skin.

Towards morning a light breeze sprang up, at daylight we found the fog had left us and that we were about twenty miles from the land. We were soon becalmed again. An English gunboat lay between us and the land, from her we got assistance and in the evening of the 6th inst. we dropped anchor in the Bidasoa under the old Moorish fortifications of Fantarabia and in a short time was landed at Andia.

No. 64. St. Andia, 1st January, 1814.

The ill effects of our voyage soon shewed itself in several of the passengers, two of the prisoners died shortly after we landed. We were all put together into a large house, the next morning the French were removed to Fuentarabia, an old Moorish garrison on the bank and near to the mouth of the Bidasoa on the Spanish side. St. Andia is on the French side, the distance is nearly two miles, this space is covered with water when the tide is up. St. Andia is used as a convalescent hospital or receiving depot. I soon got into employment. First the doctor set me to work about his books, the commandant wanted a clerk, and an acting quarter master serjeant was wanted for the depot. All these duties I manage to perform by the help of my crutch and stick.

You will learn from this that I am in a fair way of soon recovering from my wound and shall soon be able to join my regiment again, but I am afraid I am going too fast for one who is obliged to hobble about with a crutch. To tell you the truth it is doubtful if ever I shall have the proper use of my right foot again, the heel is much contracted and I cannot bear an ounce weight on the forepart of my foot. The doctor has told me it will be a long time before I shall be able to throw aside my crutch, and only that I fill a situation and am found useful I should be sent to England.

As much as I desire to see my dear native land, my home and all my dear relations, old playmates and neighbours, I would much rather rejoin my regiment again and take my chance with it. Then, when this long protracted war is over, if fortune should favour me I should have the proud satisfaction of landing on my native shores with many a brave and gallant comrade, with whom I have braved the dangers of many a hard fought battle. This is the first time of my being absent from my regiment since I entered into it and I hope it will not be long before I should hear the sound of its soul stirring bugles again. I must not complain for when I look back and consider how fortunate I have been to escape as I have done, I am lost in astonishment.

When you write do fill your letters as full as you can with news from our army, this might seem a curious request but as I am situated it is impossible to know what is going on. Every day we get reports but there is no reliance on them. I have not heard but once from my regiment since I left it. The letter contained an anecdote that happened on the 10th of November, it is not of a pleasant nature but it will serve to fill the remainder of this letter.

A man of the regiment named Higgins, of a very indifferent character and thought but little of by his comrades, and one of the Brunswick Light Infantry entered a house in which were two females, whom they attempted to violate. The cries of the women attracted the attention of the mounted staff, a species of *gendarmes* formed by cavalry soldiers, who are on the lookout for marauders. The two ruffians were made prisoners and taken to the division just at the time Wellington was with the division congratulating the officers on the success of the day.

The report being made to 'Nosey,' he said 'I will pardon the man of the 51st for their gallant conduct and good service this day, on condition that he hang the Brunswicker this moment on that tree.' A rope was procured and in a few seconds the Brunswicker was suspended by the neck to the old cork tree, and there hung until he was dead.

No. 65. Fuentarabia. 20th April, 1814.

My wound has broken out and I am sent to the general hospital at Fuentarabia. It was about a week after I wrote you last, I am happy to say it is doing very well. I have met with my newly acquired friend the French corporal, we are together in the same ward, his wound is almost healed. I now begin to find the value of his acquaintance, he spends several hours every day by my bedside reading some amusing history or tale, or relating to me the history of his campaigns in Spain, he was wounded at the battle of Albuera, was with the army that drove us from Burgos, saw the confusion amongst the baggage at Vallidolid, had a narrow escape at Vittoria, taken prisoner at the battle of the Pyrenees, but contrived to escape, in short he has seen much service. He speaks highly of the British as soldiers, particularly of our infantry, but of the Spaniards and Portuguese he seems to think but little, indeed he holds them in contempt.

The reason of his being so perfect in the English language is that his mother is of English extraction and his father is very much attached to our nation. His father's brother was an officer in the French navy and was made prisoner at the battle of the Nile, had received much kindness from the British. This has had such an effect on Corporal Pipin's father that when he writes to his son he always reminds him to behave well to any of our army that the chances of war might throw in to his power.

The corporal had written to his father as soon as he found he was to remain at Fuentarabia, he has received an answer with an order to draw 100 dollars on a merchant at Bordeaux. I shall never forget his kindness to me for as soon as he got the money he brought me half, saying he should never be able to compensate me for my kind attention to him.

But I refused on the ground that I was richer than himself, for I have plenty left out of the spoil at Vittoria. I now found out that his father is in independent circumstances and so are the whole of his family for he has a brother a physician and he himself was intended for an advocate, but Cupid interfered and in a great measure was the cause of his becoming a soldier in the ranks.

I will be as brief as I can and tell you the history of his love affair. Corporal Pipin, as was natural for a person of his age, saw and loved to use his own words, as beautiful a young lady as ever the sun shone on and she in return loved him. They were never happy but in each other's company, they had sworn to be constant to each other and as soon as he had finished his studies they were to be made one at the altar of Hyman after two years courtship.

The young lady fancied herself slighted and out of revenge began to flirt with one of his companions. This was too much for Pipin. The green eyed monster took possession of his brain, he left home and all that was dear to him, went by the diligence to Paris, here he entered the army as a volunteer, his father knew nothing of him until he was wounded at Albuhera. He then wrote and in answer learnt the frolic had almost cost his darlings life. She was recovered from a long illness and had entered a convent determined to end her days there if her Pipin should not return.

Time and the fatigues of war had not worn out the first impressions of love. He is looking forward with joy in anticipation of once more embracing and imprinting the kiss of love and reconciliation on the lips of the most beautiful of women, for such my friend in his enthusiasm describes her. Nothing now seems to disturb him but my wound, it is not mending and he is afraid it will get worse, his whole study seems directed to anything that will please and make me comfortable.

The other day I observed he was very busy, at length he came to me with a camp kettle containing a delicious stew cooked by himself in real French style, he had not spared expense to make it good. 'Here' said he 'is something that will do you good, taste it.'

'It smells excellent' said I, and I soon found the taste was better than the smell. I had taken a pretty good portion of it when I asked what the rabbit cost, I never saw so fat a one before.

'It's no rabbit' said he 'it's the tabby cat that often comes in this ward. I gave old Wright a half dollar to kill and skin it for me, knowing it would with a trifling expense make us a good treat.'

'The Devil you did' said I, but recollecting myself, for I knew he had reckoned what a treat it would be, I forced down a few more spoonfuls, then gave it over saying I had quite sufficient. 'I will put this by until evening it will do for supper or for dinner tomorrow.'

The next day I excused myself by saying I was afraid it was too highly seasoned for my wound, so he gave the stewed cat, after eating some himself, to a comrade of his who swallowed it down as greedy as if he had been fasting a week. For my own part I never eat anything more nice but when I found out it was cat I was done. For fear he should cook another cat I told him in a day or two afterwards that the English never eat such food, that we looked upon it with abhorrence. He said that before he had joined the army he could not himself, but he had learned to eat many things since he had became a soldier.

No. 66. General Hospital Fuentarabia, 14th June, 1814.

It is now nearly two months since I wrote last. I have had a severe time of it. Banish your fears about my safety, I am fast recovering. It was in the afternoon of the 3rd. May that I felt a beating in my wound as if anyone was tapping the place with their finger, in the night the beating increased attended with pain, the next morning when the doctor opened it, it was declared to be sluffed. I was then ordered upstairs to what we call the incurable ward, none of the other patients in the hospital are allowed to enter this ward as the sluff is infectious, so that it is a kind of senetar.

My wound continued to get worse, I had every attendance that could possibly be given and all the remedies applied to prevent mortification, at length my leg and thigh was reduced so small that I could span it with my hand, but the wounded part and foot were swollen to an enormous size, and the wound was as large over as a tea saucer. It was at length agreed to amputate my leg, this I joyfully agreed to being heartily tired of such a frightful troublesome member.

Twice were I removed to the surgery to undergo the operation, but each time the little Spanish doctor, who had charge of me, overruled it and I was taken back to my bed, I understood my doctor wished to try something else, then if that failed the leg was to come off. He brought from his home a small bottle filled with something like pepper and salt mixed, with this he covered the wound on which he put lint, bandaged it up, crossed himself, muttered something to himself and left me. Several times that day he visited me and my answers to his questions seemed to perplex him much.

The next morning my answers seemed to please him, he took off the bandage in good spirits—when all the sluff excepting two spots, one about the size of a sixpence, the other smaller, came off with the lint. My wound now was changed from a nasty sickly white-brown colour to a bright red. He capered about like a mad fellow, called the other doctors who all seemed surprised, he put some more stuff out of the bottle on the spots and the next morning I was removed down stairs. This was on the 9th inst. Since then my wound improves surprisingly.

The French corporal is removed to the convalescent hospital, his wound is nearly well, he took the first opportunity to visit me and testified his joy at my happy escape from the grave.

The ward I had left upstairs was one continued scene of misery and woe, the dreadful sufferings of the patients is beyond description. During the five weeks I was in it, what numbers have I seen die under the most writhing torture, and their places filled again by others, who only come to pass a few days in misery, and then to be taken to their last home.

The beds next mine were occupied by six different soldiers, five died, the sixth I left in a hopeless state. One of those men I knew, he was a serjeant of the 82nd Regiment, his wife was nurse to the ward, she pricked her finger with a pin left in one of the bandages, caught the infection, her finger was first amputated, then her hand, the sluff appeared again in the stump, she refused to undergo another operation, the consequence was she soon died. In this house of misery how many fine brave young fellows have died without the assistance of a friend, mother, sister or wife to soothe their agony in their last moment. No minister of religion to cheer the dying sinner.

The people of England little think how her soldiers are neglected respecting spiritual aid, or I believe it would not be so. If they could but hear or see the agony of the dying, their prayers, their despair and the horrid oaths uttered by some in their exit from this world, I am sure this most of wants would be attended to. It is true there are chaplains with the army who sometimes perform divine service, but of what use are they, the service they perform has no effect, for their mode of living do not agree with the doctrine they preach.

I have often heard the remark 'That a chaplain is of no more use to the army than a town pump without a handle.' If these reverend gentlemen were stationed at the sick depots and made to attend to the hospitals, they would be much more usefully employed than following the army with their brace of dogs and gun, running down hares and shooting partridges etc. In winter quarters these men once on a Sunday (weather permitting), perform divine service, but when the campaign opens, it is seldom or ever an opportunity offers, every day then is the same, few trouble themselves about days or anything else. It is only on the eve of a battle that any enquiry is made, what day is it.

No. 67. Fuentarabia Convalescent Hospital. 11th July, 1814.

I am in hopes soon to sit by your fireside and enjoy a pipe, while I relate to you a thousand things that will be interesting, that for the want of room I am obliged to omit in the short space of a letter. I have heard that some of the most effective regiments are sent, or are going to America. If so the Yankees will find some rum customers to deal with, for the troops that has been employed under Lord Wellington from long practice are become fire proof.

I was discharged from the general hospital the beginning of this month, my wound is quite healed and I am daily gaining strength, but my heel is much contracted and it is a question if ever I shall be able to walk again without the help of a stick, at present I hops about with a crutch and stick. The convalescent hospital is situated about a mile from Fuentarabia on the main road to Irun.

This is a very delightful place, the grounds belonging to the convent are pleasantly laid out in shady walks, the gardens abound with grapes etc. so that we are compensated in a measure for the fatigue we have endured. The weather is beautiful, and having nothing to do we enjoy ourselves by strolling about the gardens talking to the Good Old Fathers of the convent, who are very kind to us, or by taking a walk into town, to feast our eyes by gazing on the sweet faces of the pretty dark eyed maids of Fuentarabia.

On one of these excursions the other day I accidentally fell in with George Davis of the 10th Hussars. You cannot conceive the thousandth part of the pleasure one feels on falling in with an old schoolmate in this country. In meeting George the treat was great for I had no knowledge of his being a soldier much more of his being employed in the same service, he is servant to a doctor and is quite well. I have lost my French comrade, since the peace the whole of the prisoners of war capable of being removed have been sent to Bayonne.

A few nights since several of us were enjoying ourselves with a pipe and some wine under a beautiful shade composed of vines, listening to the monks at their evening vespers, relating and listening to anecdotes of many a brave comrade who had fell in action or had been sent home, when on a sudden we heard a confounded noise proceed from Fuentarabia. It sounded as if all the inhabitants were shouting accompanied with the ringing of the church bells. As the noise continued we determined to go to the town to discover the cause of such a clatter, as we proceeded we soon met droves of people loaded with furniture etc., all that we could learn from them was that the place was on fire.

Shortly after we met one of our, comrades returning to the convent, 'Come back with me' said he 'if you go forward you will' (as he expressed himself) 'all be blown to the D———l.' As we were not inclined to pay his Satanic Majesty a visit we returned, when we learned that a house near the old castle was on fire, and rumour with her hundred tongues had told a hundred stories. The most correct is as follows, the fire was in the vicinity of the hospital I was in, close to which is a fever hospital.

It appears from the following circumstances that it must have been done for the purpose of destroying the hospitals, for from the house that was on fire a train was laid of combustible matter to the castle. In this place was deposited a great quantity of powder etc. so that if the fire had communicated it must have blown up. The consequence would have been not only the two hospitals but a quantity of stores of various descriptions would have been destroyed and great part of the town. The soldiers by their exertions soon got the better of the fire and wet blankets were placed on the door of the magazine so that the diabolical intentions of the persons concerned were frustrated.

No. 68. Irun, 15th August, 1814.

We have moved a few miles towards Passages in order to embark for old England. When we left the convent one of the 'Fathers' who was much attached to us gave us some sweetmeats and his blessing, saying most fervently 'he hoped the blessed Virgin would conduct us home safe to the land of our fathers.' It was a charitable wish of the good old man, but as I do not entertain exactly so high an opinion of the powers of her Ladyship I could not help thinking that if our seamen did not understand the management of a ship better than the Virgin, we should be apt to remain in Spain forever. However we are progressing homewards and ere long I hope we shall be safely landed in merry old England.

Irun is a small town about a league from Passages, the place is all bustle and confusion, occasioned by the transporting of stores etc. to Passages for embarkation. I have nothing particular to amuse you with except a description of a bull bait. It being so different from anything of the kind in England, and the first I have ever witnessed in this country, I shall venture to trouble you with it. The joyful news of peace has driven the Spaniards mad, so they had determined to devout a whole week to their favourite diversion of bull baiting.

The large towns in Spain has all their bull rings but this one is more properly speaking a square. The sport commenced on a Sunday above all other days, the people were summonsed to the sport by about a dozen ragged barelegged fellows parading the streets with drums. I of course went to see the fun, and got a good place near the grand stand, round the square were places fitted up for the spectators. The stand occupied by the municipal authorities and grandees was most superbly decorated, the others varied in appearance downward agreeable to the circumstances of the people, the whole having something the appearance of an amphitheatre with a space in the centre of about two hundred paces.

In this space were four men in silk dresses, each dress varying in colour, the men had each two spears about sixteen inches long, and a loose cloke hung carelessly on the shoulder, hussar fashion. Upon a signal a door was thrown open and out rushed a bull. The cheers given by the people at first puzzled him, he made a dead halt, eyed the people some time pawing the ground, and roaring stoutly, at length his eye caught one of the men upon which he made a rush. The man stood still with his arms uplifted until the bull's horns was close to his thighs, when in a moment and as quick as lightening he, the man, darted the two spears one behind each of the bull's ears, stepped on one side with as much coolness as if nothing had happened.

The bull is now at the top of his rage, he first attacks one then the other, but what enrages the poor creature most is the people, who are all well provided with short darts, do as often as opportunity offers, shower them down upon him, so that in a short time he is covered with them. When any of the men sticks the darts in the right place he is greeted with cheers and a shower of dollars. After the bull is worn out with passion and fatigue he is allowed to return into the stable. About a quarter of an hour is then devoted to drinking and smoking, while the combatants rest themselves, then another is let out.

The sport varies but little through the whole day except some of the bulls might be said to shew more courage and to act more fierce than others. Then the men are often apparently in great danger but somehow they managed to escape unhurt. The whole of the bulls being baited in their turn, this finishes the days sport and the good Christians of this most catholic country return to their homes full of glee, spends the evening in dancing and singing until bed time, then offers a prayer to the Virgin or some favourite saint and sinks into the arms of Morphus.

The first days description must answer for the whole week. Fortunately the whole went off without any accident except a few broken shins etc. This was on the third day, one of the stands gave way from the great number of people on it, down they came into the ring helter skelter all together, it happened just at the time the door was opened for the bull to run in so the people was not troubled by his presence amongst them.

I never laughed so much in my life, there were men and women rolling over each other in the greatest confusion, every one expecting the bull would be giving them a poke with his horns. In some parts of Spain they bait the bulls on horseback. This is the only thing of the sort I ever witnessed.

No. 69. Portsmouth, 25th September, 1814.

The long looked for day has at last arrived and I am safely landed once more in the land of my birth in health and spirits, and but for this game leg of mine a better man than when I left it. My regiment is stationed here, so that on our arrival we were welcomed by our old comrades in arms. It was a joyful meeting but when I look around me and see so many strange faces, I am a wonder to myself, scarcely four years has rolled over, ere, at this place I embarked with about 900 of my comrades.

Where are they now? I could not muster one company out of the whole number. The battlefield, fatigue, privations and sickness has made sad havoc in the ranks of as fine a set of young fellows as ever belonged to the service. The blanks are filled up and the regiment is fit for any service the country should require of them but I must not include myself.

It will be some time before I shall be again fit for duty although it is now nearly eleven months since I received my wound. You might expect me soon. I am measured for my new clothing and shall as soon as it is ready come home on a two months furlough. Our adjutant has promised me, and he further said if I had not gained the use of my foot in that time I was to write to him and my leave should be extended. I have about £20 back pay to receive so I shall be able to enjoy myself without being a burden to you.

In the meantime I shall by way of filling up this letter give you the outlines of our voyage home. It was on the 9th inst., we embarked at Passages on board the *Anne* Transport, sailed the same evening in company with about an hundred other ships conveying troops and laden with stores, convoyed by two sloops of war. We sailed all night with light breezes, the next morning the Pyrenees were in sight and continued so until noon when they disappeared. For several days we made but little way, at length the wind freshened and we began to send it to the tune of seven knots an hour.

We were going at this rate on the 13th when the cry of a man overboard was heard, the helm was soon down, and 'bout we went, the boat was lowered and after much difficulty succeeded in picking up the man. The person was a commissariat belonging to the army, and our men were not long in assigning the cause of his throwing himself over board to the gnawings of an evil conscience in having cheated many a soldier out of his rations and that now he was going home he would have to render an account.

Be this as it may, it was somewhat singular that at the moment he committed the rash act the rum was about to be served out and the men were loud in their complaints, saying that the rum had been watered by the steward. That he should say 'It's a lie by G—d' and jumped over the side, what saved him was the boat cloak he had on, it gathered the wind so that he could not sink. When we had him on board again he was guarded by a sentinel the remainder of the voyage, to prevent anything of the sort again occurring.

The only other incident worth mentioning that happened was that we fell in with a large frigate, she was at first taken for an American. Our two gun brigs bore up to her with their guns ready for action but she turned out to be a French, ship. Everything being all right we were wafted over the waves by gentle breezes, sometimes becalmed, until the 21st inst. then anchored at Spithead, in a few hours we landed at Common Hard, here we were welcomed by many a well known face, the evening was spent with song and glass, and after drowning all our cares in some good old English October (ale made in that month) we retired to rest to dream of home and all its sweets.

No. 70. Brussels, 8th April, 1815.

The news, so prevalent in Bath the day before I left, of the Emperor Napoleon's escape from Elba, was confirmed beyond doubt when I arrived at Portsmouth. I found the regiment undergoing an inspection by Lord Howard of Effingham, the Major General in command of this garrison. I reported myself and party to Colonel Mitchel, the prisoner was pardoned and we took our places in the ranks.

The regiment were returned fit for service and on the 23rd March embarked and sailed, once more for the Downs, amidst the hearty cheering of thousands of the inhabitants. At the Downs we were removed from the transports into small cutters and sailed for Ostend.

From this we proceeded in boats up the canal to Bruges, landed, went into good quarters, plenty of good grub, gin and tobacco, and as the Flemish man says 'all for nix.' Being old campaigners we made the most of the good things fortune threw in our way, knowing from past experience that her ladyship is a fickle dame. In the evening we embarked again, well provided with what makes a soldiers heart glad, and proceeded for Ghent, our passage to this place was very pleasant.

A beautiful country each side the canal, the people cheering us as we passed. On board the boat it more resembled a party of pleasure than soldiers going in search of the enemy, the social glass and song went round 'til midnight, all was mirth and festivity, then sleep put an end to our carousals. About noon the following day brought us to Ghent, here we landed and was quartered in the town two days, we dropped in for good billets again. Our next move was to Brussels, we had now left the canals and was obliged to march. At Brussels we were quartered in a convent, everything is very cheap and good, and there is excellent accommodation in the public houses.

The Prince of Orange is in command of the army. There can be no doubt but the Prince is well experienced in war, having served on the Duke of Wellington's staff during the Peninsular War but he is not the man for us. None but Wellington or Hill, or some one of the generals who have served with us in the late campaigns can have our confidence.

The Emperor will most assuredly command the French army, and it will require a general of uncommon skill to withstand so powerful a genus. Wellington's the man that must lead us on, he who has baffled the skill of most of the French martials, and lead his army victoriously from the Tagus to the Pyrenees, and then into the heart of France. He is looked to by the remnant of the old Peninsular army, an hundred times a day, the question is asked, 'Where is Wellington? surely we shall not be led to battle by that boy,' meaning the Prince.

The established religion of Flanders is of the Church of Rome, but there is a wide difference between these people and the people of the Peninsular. They do not appear to be so priest ridden, the houses are well built, well furnished and kept very clean, and the inhabitants are very neat and clean in their persons neither do they appear to be so priest ridden. Many words in their language very much resemble our own. Brussels is all alive, the storm is gathering fast, and ere long you must expect to hear that the blow has been struck.

No. 71. Grammont, 29th May, 1815.

The 13th of April (Wylly's account says 9th) we marched from Brussels to Grammont. Before we left we were delighted by a General Order issued by H.R.H. the Prince of Orange, in which order he 'Surrenders the command of the army into the more able hands of His Grace the Duke of Wellington.' I never remember anything that caused such joy, our men were almost frantic, every soldier you met told the joyful news.

I happened to be out in the city when the order was delivered. I met some dozen soldiers as I was returning to the convent. I was accosted by everyone, thus, 'Serjeant Wheeler have you seen the order?'

My answer was invariably 'No.'

The reply would be 'Glorious news, Nosey has got the command, won't we give them a drubbing now?'

When I arrived at the convent I had a bottle of gin thrust up to my mouth, and twenty voices shouting 'drink hearty to the health of our old commander, we don' care a d———n for all France, supposing everyone was a Napoleon etc.' Let it suffice to say that it caused a general fuddle, the evening was spent by reminding each other of the glorious deeds done in the Peninsular, mingled with song and dance, good Hollands and tobacco.

Grammont is General Hill's head quarters, he commands the 2nd Corps of the army, it is also the head quarters of our brigade. The brigade consists of the 14th Foot, 23rd Welsh Fusiliers and the 51st Light Infantry, commanded by Colonel Mitchel, 51st, and is the 4th Brigade of the army. We are put to the 4th Division of the army, which is commanded by Lieutenant General Sir Charles Colville. The division is composed of the 4th British (right) 4th Hanoverians (centre) and the 6th British (left) brigades.

We are in excellent health and spirits, and have the best of quarters. The people are remarkably kind to us. I with one man are quartered at a tobacconists, so we do not want for that article, we eat and drink with the landlord and family, coffee stands ready for use all day long, when we get our rations we give it to the mistress of the house, except our gin, this we takes care of ourselves.

We never see a bit of the bread after, if the meat should be good, it is cooked, if not, it is given with the bread to the beggars. I will tell you the manner we live. As soon as we rise a cup or two of good coffee. Eight o'clock breakfast on bread and butter eggs and coffee. Dinner meat and vegetables, dressed various ways, with beer, afterwards a glass of Hollands grog and tobacco, evening, salad, coffee, etc. then the whole is washed down by way of a settler with Hollands grog, or beer with a pipe or two, then off to bed.

There are some very pretty young women here, some of them are got very much attached to our men, and I doubt not when we move there will be an augmentation in the number of women. I must here observe that your humble servant does not intend to get entangled with any of them. It might be all very fine in its way and no doubt there are many sweets in having a pretty lovely young woman for a comrade, but then, I know from observation that there is an infinite number of bitters attending it, a soldier should always be able to say when his cap is on, his family is covered, then he is free as air.

I cannot give you any certain account of the enemy, you will be better informed about them from the newspaper, than from anything I can say about them, there is no doubt but they are assembling a great force. This does not trouble us, we are commanded by Wellington, we have plenty of the good things of this life, so the best way is to enjoy ourselves while we can, it will be time to bid the D———l good morning when we meet him. But when the time arrives no doubt there will be hot work but we have no fears as to the result for Wellington is at our head.

No. 72. Grammont, 13th June 1815.

Yours of the 8th inst. I received yesterday.

I am sorry I cannot give you any information respecting young Towers. I have not seen any of the army excepting our own brigade and the Hussars Brigade since the army has been formed. I cannot even tell you to what brigade the 82nd belongs or if they are in this country, the whole army is very much extended for the sake of cantonments.

If chance should throw me across the 82nd I will enquire and let you know for Mrs. Tower's information. You see we are still living with the good people of Grammont, and what is extraordinary they do not appear to be the least tired of us, we cannot be more comfortably situated.

You might form some opinion of the friendship existing between the inhabitants and us, when you read what follows. A short time ago, the duke fixed on Grammont for his head quarters to review the whole of the cavalry, to make room we were obliged to turn out and seek quarters some distance from the town.

We were away about a week then returned, according to custom the quartermaster procured billets from the mayor. At a miles distance from the town, the people had come out to welcome us back, such cheering and shaking of hands, my landlord gave me a new pipe and some tobacco telling me he had a good dinner provided and a bottle of gin, happiness beamed from every face on our entering the town, the merry church bells struck up a quick march.

We formed in the square opposite the Guildhall, and the men were getting their billets, when the people, finding they would not have the same men again, they gathered round Colonel Mitchell, begging him to let us all return to our own quarters. Some men had got their new billets and were moving away, when the buglers sounded the assembly, in a few minutes the disperse was sounded, so we all returned to our old quarters as if we had only been to a parade.

The remainder of the day was passed as a holiday such feasting and rejoicing followed that a stranger would have thought we had been raised in the town and had just returned from a long campaign.

Since we have been here I have not heard of a single fall out between any of our men and the people, but I am sorry that a few of our officers one night in a drunken frolic gave cause for offence, and the people were not a little vexed at the time. What follows was the cause. In the great square, opposite the Guildhall, there is a fountain, in the middle stands a naked boy, apparently about four years old, his left hand rested on his hip, and with his right he held his little c— out of which the water flowed into the basin or more properly the well, for it is some twelve feet deep.

One night some of our officers had been indulging themselves rather too much, they sallied out in quest of adventures, they managed to get a rope round the neck of the little urchin and pull him off his perch. He being made of lead, down he sank to the bottom of the well.

In the morning the news of the disaster spread amongst the people and they were running about and seemed as much perplexed as the good people of Stratsburgh when the man with the big nose passed through the town. However as the little urchin has regained his position again in two days and looked none the worse for the ducking it was soon forgot.

I can give you no account of the enemy or what they are about. I expected ere this we should at least have had a peep at them.

No. 73. Camp near Nivelles, 19th June, 1815.

The three days fight is over. I am safe, this is sufficient. I shall now and at every opportunity write the details of the great event, that is what came under my own observation. Before you receive this you will have the official dispatches published, it will be a grand treat to John Bull.

To be as concise as possible I shall begin by saying that about 8 o'clock on the morning of the 16th inst, our buglers sounded the alarm. In a very short time we were under arms and marched, accompanied with the tears and prayers of the inhabitants who seemed to take as much interest in our welfare as if we had been their own children.

About ten the hussars brigade passed us, a very friendly connection existed between the hussars and our regiment ever since we crossed the Eslar together. As they passed us we could distinctly hear the roar of cannon. This produced three animating cheers from us, which was returned by the hussars. We marched the whole of the day and at night encamped in a field near to the rifles.

The next morning we continued our march without meeting with anything remarkable until we came to Nivelles, a smart sized town. This place was crowded with heavy cavalry belonging to Belgium, they were in a great hurry to get through the town and as our colonel thought they were changing their position, we halted to let them pass, but we afterwards found they were running away, helter skelter, the devil take the hindmost.

They were fine looking fellows and much resembled our Blues, but this is all can be said of them except that they were the rankest cowards that ever formed part of an army. If they were not covered with mud and sweat. However it is an ill wind that blows nobody good.

One of the pitiful scoundrels in urging his horse through the gate way, by some means upset the horse and in the fall the fellow lost his purse. It was picked up by one of my section. In this section there is a few old campaigners, we had agreed to stick by each other come what would and all plunder was to be equally divided. This was not a bad godsend to begin with.

Outside the town, as well as in, the roads were literally choked up with baggage, and as it began to rain the road soon became very heavy. We continued marching intermixed with cavalry, guns, stores, and baggage of all descriptions a considerable time, when we turned down a byroad to our left and after some time halted in a field of corn, about an hour. The rain increased, the thunder and lightening approached nearer, and with it came the enemy. At this time we were getting our gin, when a smart cannonade began from both sides.

What a sight, even to we old campaigners, but more particularly to the young soldiers. I should like to give you a lively description of it, but it is not in my power. The cavalry retiring in sullen silence as often as opportunity served would wheel round to check the enemy. The rain beating with violence, guns roaring, repeated bright flashes of lightening attended with tremendous volleys of thunder that shook the very earth and seemed to mock us with contempt.

We stood to our arms and retired to the village of Waterloo, here we halted in a corn field for the night. One man in the village was selling brandy and Hollands, the money picked up a few hours before procured us plenty of both, and some bread and cheese, this was very acceptable as most of us had in the hurry of packing up neglected to provide ourselves with food. This neglect was natural enough in the young soldier but unpardonable to we old campaigners.

Night came on, we were wet to the skin, but having plenty of liquor we were to use an expression of one of my old comrades 'wet and comfortable.' The bad weather continued the whole of the night, we had often experienced such weather in the Peninsular on the eve of a battle, for instance the nights before the battles of Fuentes d'Onor, Salamanca and Vittoria were attended with thunder and lightening. It was always the prelude to a victory.

It would be impossible for anyone to form any opinion of what we endured this night. Being close to the enemy we could not use our blankets, the ground was too wet to lie down, we sat on our knapsacks until daylight without fires, there was no shelter against the weather: the water ran in streams from the cuffs of our jackets, in short we were as wet as if we had been plunged over head in a river. We had one consolation, we knew the enemy were in the same plight.

No. 74. Camp Cato Plains 23rd June 1815.

The half days halt at Nivelles enabled me to send you a letter, now that we are going to halt here for some time I shall embrace the opportunity and continue my account of the great battle.

The morning of the 18th June broke upon us and found us drenched with rain, benumbed and shaking with the cold. We stood to our arms and moved to a fresh spot to get out of the mud. You often blamed me for smoking when I was at home last year but I must tell you if I had not had a good stock of tobacco this night I must have given up the ghost.

Near the place we moved to were some houses, these we soon glutted and what by the help of doors, windows, shutters and furniture, we soon made some good fires. About 8 o'clock our brigade went into position on the right of the line, on high ground that commanded the farm of Hougomont. The regiment was commanded by Lieutenant Colonel Rice, Colonel Mitchel having the command of the brigade. Major Keyt commanded the light troops in advance, consisting of Captain Phelps' Company 51st, The Light Companies of the 23rd and 14th Regiment.

About 9 o'clock (reports show after 11 o'clock) three field pieces were discharged from our position and Captain McRoss' company was ordered down to reinforce the advance, who were warmly engaged. A quarter of an hour had not elapsed, before four more of our companies were ordered to the front, the company I belong to was one. We soon saw what was up. Our advance was nearly surrounded by a large body of the enemy's lancers. Fortunately the 15th Hussars was at hand and rendered assistance.

Our appearance altered the state of affairs and ere we could make them a present of three rounds each, the lancers were glad to get off. We were now exposed to a heavy fire of grape, and was obliged to push across a large space of fallow ground to cover ourselves from their fire. Here we found a deep cross road that ran across our front, on the opposite side of this road the rye was as high as our heads. We remained here some time, then retired back to the ground we had advanced from, the 15th Hussars were in column on our left.

I shall here endeavour to describe to you how matters stood where we were. On the hill behind us on which was posted some twenty or thirty guns blazing away over our heads at the enemy. The enemy on their side with a battery of much the same force were returning the compliment, grape and shells were dupping about like hail, this was devilish annoying. As we could not see the enemy, although they were giving us a pretty good sprinkling of musketry, our buglers sounded to lie down.

At this moment a man near me was struck and as I was rising to render assistance I was struck by a spent ball on the inside of my right knee, exactly on the place I was hit at Lezaca. Like that it was a glance and did no harm, only for the moment caused a smart pain. A shell now fell into the column of the 15th. Hussars and burst.

I saw a sword and scabbard fly out from the column. It was now time to shift our ground to a place of shelter, the hussars moved to the left and we advanced again to the cross road under a sharp shower of shells. One of the shells pitched on the breast of a man some little distance on my right, he was knocked to atoms.

We gained the cross road and was then under good shelter, this was my position the remainder of the day. This road was opposite the Observatory where it is said the Emperor with his staff were posted. On our left a main road ran direct into the enemy's lines, on this road was an arch that crossed the deep road we were in. I was ordered to go to this place with a message to Lieutenant Colonel Keyt. I now found our left communicated with about 300 of the Brunswick Light Infantry, and saw that the bridge was blocked up with trees.

A little to the front and to the left stood the farm house of Hougomont, on which the enemy was pouring a destructive fire of shot, shell and musketry. The house was soon on fire and the Battle increased with double fury. Never was a place more fiercely assaulted, nor better defended, it will be a lasting honour and glory to the troops who defended it.

So fierce was the combat that a spectator would imagine a mouse could not live near the spot, but the Guards, who had the honour to be posted there not only kept possession but repulsed the enemy in every attack. The slaughter was dreadful, but I must spake of this when I come to the close of the action.

I was ordered with two men to post ourselves behind a rock or large stone, well studded with brambles. This was somewhat to our right and in advance. About an hour after we were posted we saw an officer of hussars sneaking down to get a peep at our position. One of my men was what we term a dead shot, when he was within point blank distance. I asked him if he could make sure of him.

His reply was 'To be sure I can, but let him come nearer if he will, at all events his death warrant is signed and in my hands, if he should turn back.' By this time he had without perceiving us come up near to us. When Chipping fired, down he fell and in a minute we had his body with the horse in our possession behind the rock.

P.S. I omitted to say that Captain John Ross' company had a very narrow escape of being made prisoners at the commencement.

No. 75. Camp Cato (Le Cateau) plains.
23rd June 1815.

I have finished one letter this morning. I shall get on with this in continuation of the last. We had a rich booty, forty double Napoleons and had just time to strip the lace of the clothing of the dead hussar when we were called in to join the skirmishers. The battle was now raging with double fury. We could see most of the charges made by the cavalry of both armies. I never before witnessed such large masses of cavalry opposed together, such a length of time.

I am at a loss which to admire most, the cool intrepid courage of our squares, exposed as they often were to a destructive fire from the French artillery and at the same time or in less than a minute surrounded on all sides by the enemy's heavy cavalry, who would ride up to the very muzzles of our men's firelocks and cut at them in the squares. But this was of no use, not a single square could they brake, but was always put to the rout, by the steady fire of our troops.

In one of those charges made by the enemy a great many over charged themselves and could not get back without exposing themselves to the deadly fire of the infantry. Not choosing to return by the way they came they took a circuitous route and came down the road on our left. There were nearly one hundred of them, all *cuirassiers*.

Down they rode full gallop, the trees thrown across the bridge on our left stopped them. We saw them coming and was prepared, we opened our fire, the work was done in an instant. By the time we had loaded and the smoke had cleared away, one and only one, solitary individual was seen running over the brow in our front. One other was saved by Captain Jno. Ross from being put to death by some of the Brunswickers.

I went to see what effect our fire had, and never before beheld such a sight in as short a space, as about an hundred men and horses could be huddled together, there they lay. Those who were shot dead were fortunate for the wounded horses in their struggles by plunging and kicking soon finished what we had began. In examining the men we could not find one that would be like to recover, and as we had other business to attend to we were obliged to leave them to their fate.

Either the noise of our fire or the man who escaped informed the enemy of our lurking place, for we were soon informed by a *fedet* that the enemy were marching down on us with cavalry, artillery and infantry. Hougomont had been in flames some time and the tremendous fire of guns and Howitzers on the place seemed to increase. The news brought by the *fedet* caused us to move and form square. In a short time we were obliged to shift more to our left to get out of the range of some cannon the enemy opened on us.

Lord Hill now paid us a visit and asked for water, he was very much fatigued. While his Lordship was drinking out of one of our men's wooden canteens an eight pounder picked out four of our men. We were then ordered to shift our ground a little further. The enemy did not make their appearance.

We remained here until dusk when we discovered a large column of cavalry coming down on us from our rear. Their commander saw we were ready to receive them, rode down to us. When we found they were Prussians, they passed us to the front and we followed. At this time the enemy were in full retreat, we marched into an orchard belonging to the farm where we halted for the night. This place was full of dead and wounded Frenchmen. I went to the farm house, what a sight.

Inside the yard the Guards lay in heaps, many who had been wounded inside or near the building were roasted, some who had endeavoured to crawl out from the fire lay dead with their legs burnt to a cinder. It was now certain the enemy was off in good earnest.

I managed to make up a supper, wrapped myself in my blanket and slept very comfortably until daylight, then marched to Nivelle. Our loss is but trifling considering the heavy fire we were under, but we have to thank the deep road and the field of Rye for it. Killed one bugler and eight rank and file, wounded Captain Beardsley, Lieutenant Tyndale, one serjeant and thirty-four rank and file.

On the 20th we left Nivelle. On the 21st we were joined by the remainder of the division, they had been employed on some particular service and was not at Waterloo. On the 22nd we encamped on the plains of Cato, where we at present remain, it was at this place I believe where the Duke of York was defeated.

No. 76. Camp near Cambray (Cambrai).
25th June, 1815.

On the morning of the 24th inst. we marched on Cambray, about a league from the town we fell in with some cavalry picquets. After passing them we soon came in sight of the town, saw the tricolour flag flying on the citadel. This place had been strongly fortified, but the guns were withdrawn from the works, except the citadel. A great many stragglers were collected here, and these with the national guard belonging to the place seemed to threaten us with some resistance.

Our brigade marched to the opposite side of the town, the remainder of the division halted on the side nearest to Cato. We had collected what ladders and ropes we could find in the farm houses, then we began splicing to enable us to scale the walls if necessary.

A flag of truce was sent to the town but they were fired at, which caused them to return, and a ball had passed through the trumpeter's cap. We were now ready for storming and were only waiting the order to advance. In a short time our field pieces opened when a shell, I believe the first thrown from the howitzer, set a large building on fire. We now pushed on to the works, near the gate, got into the trenches, fixed our ladders and was soon in possession of the top of the wall. The opposition was trifling, the regular soldiers fled to the citadel, and the shopkeepers to their shops.

We soon got possession of the gate and let in the remainder of the brigade, formed and advanced to the great square. We were as was usual, received by the people with *vivas*, many of whom had forgot to wash the powder off their lips caused by biting off the cartridges when they were firing on us from the wall. The remainder of the division entered the town at the same time on the opposite side.

Piquets were established at the citadel, and about dusk the remainder of the division were marched out of the town and encamped. We had picked up some money in the town, or more properly speaking we had made the people hand it over to us to save us the trouble of taking it from them, so we were enabled to provide ourselves with what made us comfortable.

About an hour after we had left the town we heard an explosion and soon learned that a serjeant corporal and four men fell in with a barrel of gunpowder. They being drunk took it for brandy, and Corporal C—— fired into it, as he said to make a bung hole, while the others were waiting with their tin canteens to catch the supposed liquor, but it blew up and all the brandy merchants were dreadfully mutilated.

The loss of the regiment was two rank and file killed, and ten wounded, exclusive of the brandy merchants, who are so dreadfully scorched it is feared that four cannot recover, and the other two will not be fit for service again.

The 25th we halted and His pottle belly Majesty, Louis 18th, marched into the loyal town of Cambray. His Majesty was met by a deputation of his beloved subjects who received their father and their king with tears of joy. Louis blubbered over them like a big girl for her bread and butter, called them his children, told them a long rigmarole of nonsense about France, and his family, about his heart, and about their hearts, how he had always remembered them in his prayers, and I don't know what.

The presence of their good old fat king had a wonderful effect on their tender consciences, the air rent with their acclamations. The loyal and faithful soldiers of the Great Napoleon followed their example and surrendered the citadel to their beloved master Old Bungy Louis.

No doubt the papers will inform you how Louis 18th entered the loyal city of Cambray, how his loyal subjects welcomed their beloved king, how the best of monarchs wept over the sufferings of his beloved people, how the citadel surrendered with acclamations of joy to the best of kings, and how his most Christian Majesty effected all this without being accompanied by a single soldier.

But the papers will not inform you that the 4th Division and a brigade of Hanoverian Hussars (red) were in readiness within half a mile of this faithful city, and if the loyal citizens had insulted their king, how it was very probable we should have bayoneted every Frenchman in the place. The people well knew this, and this will account for the sudden change in their loyalty or allegiance from their idol Napoleon (properly named) the Great, to an old bloated poltroon, the Sir John Falstaff of France.

No. 77. *Camp Bois de Buologne. 7th July 1815.*

We have been two days encamped in this delightful wood. It is within three miles of Paris or at least our camp is. But I must return back to Cambray and inform you that we left that place early on the morning of the 26th leaving old Bungy Louis drinking coffee and going to Mass with his faithful and beloved subjects.

Our advance was as rapid as possible for we had lost two days, one at Cato the other at Cambray. On the road we met with no new adventure, but I could not help noticing that the feeling of the people were strongly in favour of the emperor.

On the 30th we halted near to a Château belonging to Marshal Ney. The Prussian army passed our camp on its march to go into position on the other side the canal, they did not forget to destroy everything they could as they moved on. Ney's country seat was none the better for their visit, everything they could lay their hands on was knocked to pieces. A small town about two miles from us which we marched through was completely sacked, it reminded me of some of the doings of the French in Portugal.

On the morning of the 1st July we marched and went into position in the front of a canal in advance of the town of St. Denis. The enemy was in Paris, and report said they were determined to be buried under its ruins rather than allow foreigners to enter.

We passed three days reckoning on the rich booty we should possess, if we stormed the capital. But on the morning of the 4th we saw some French officers pass over to our side and hold a friendly conversation with our officers, so we took the hint and walked over to the French picquet, and it was not long before we were all well agreed, smoking our pipes and refreshing ourselves with a drop of brandy.

About midday the French picquet retired and we took possession of the bridge. Now the good people of Paris began to pour out of the city and mix amongst us as if nothing had been the matter. As the song says, here was 'Old and young, grave and sad etc.,' refreshments of all descriptions came in to our camp, it was truly astonishing to see what confidence the inhabitants placed in us.

The next day we marched into the Bois de Boulogne and took up our encampment on the road from Newillee (Neuilly) to Buologne about midway from each place.

If we remain here the summer it promises us a delightful resting place, nearly the whole of the British and Hanoverian Army is encamped here, our tents is quite a set off and enlivens the scene. The Parisians flocks out of the city, so that we are amused with thousands of visitors. Some of the young lasses are truly the most engaging little devils I ever saw.

We have a plentiful supply of every kind of vegetable and fruit in season, besides provisions of every description, the brandy is ten-pence a quart, the old campaigners in my section has not been to sleep.

What we scraped together on the 18th and after the storm of Cambray has pretty well lined our pockets so we intend to make ourselves as comfortable as we can, for a soldier's life is full of ups and downs, although the French army has retired some forty leagues from Paris there to wait orders of the French Government, yet they might give us some trouble before the summer is over, for you know the Emperor is a crafty old fox. I believe the Prussians are quartered in Paris. I hope we shall remain where we are, the weather is delightful.

The River Seine runs a short distance in rear of us, we can bathe when we have an inclination. In short I anticipate enjoying the happiest summer I ever had in my life.

No. 78. Camp Bois de Boulogne. 1st August, 1815.

The Bois de Boulogne is a beautiful wood set apart for field sports, thickly planted with oak trees and well stocked with under wood. It is about two miles in diameter, in the centre is a column from which verges out several roads sixteen in number, other roads run across these, so it is admirably laid out for hunting or for taking pleasure in carriages or on horseback, the whole being inclosed by a wall, except the back from Boulogne to Newillee, where the river runs.

The walks on each side the roads are kept in excellent order. It is now become quite a fashionable place of resort for the Parisians, it being crowded every afternoon. A market is formed in our camp, which is over glutted with everything the heart can desire. The weather continues beautiful, every day is quite a fair and as yet has been one continued round of holiday.

Colonel Mitchel has fixed his quarters at Newillee. A few days since I was on guard at this place, shortly after we had been on duty I was surprised to see the inhabitants running about as if mad and shutting up their houses and shops. A few minutes explained the cause of their alarm, a detachment of Prussian infantry marched into the town. I turned out my guard to pay them the customary salute but their commanding officer declined it and told me to dismiss my men, they then halted on the ground in front of the town hall, piled their arms and dispersed.

The officer on command went into the hall to the mayor who was sitting with other magistrates transacting business. The soldiers kept returning to their arms well provided with bread etc. which they had got possession of without either ceremony or payment.

At length the officer came down stairs with the mayor, both seemed out at elbows, the bugle sounded, the men fell in and marched with the mayor at their head between a file of men. I was afterwards informed by one of the *gendarmes* that the officer asked for a guide to conduct them to some place. The mayor was busy and did not at that moment attend to him, so he made the old mayor go himself.

You will say this was hard usage, so do I, but the Prussians tell us if we say anything to them about their pranks 'You English know nothing of the sufferings of war as we do. England has never been overrun by French armies as our country has, or you would act as we do. The French acted a cruel part in Prussia, destroyed our houses, violated our mothers, our wives, our daughters, and sisters, and murdered them afterwards, they taught us a lesson we are now come to France to put into practice.'

The Allied army in and about Paris is composed of all the nations in Europe, the Spaniards and Portuguese excepted. Report says they amount to the almost incalculable number of eleven hundred thousand men. I think the French has drawn a pretty hornet's nest about their ears. It is impossible they can rise with any hope to liberate themselves, such an immense multitude would sweep everything before them like a torrent.

We have made a strange alteration in the appearance of the wood we are encamped in. Not content with our tents we must have huts, so everyone is daily at work cutting down trees. Such is the quantity of wood destroyed already that we can see the river in our rear, although at our first coming we could scarce enter the brake. I have been into Paris several times on duty since my last, it is my intention to have a day soon, then I shall say something about it, perhaps in my next.

No. 79. Camp Bois de Boulogne, 26th August, 1815.

A party consisting of half a dozen of us has been into Paris, the weather was delightful. We had the whole day and never in my life time did I enjoy a more rich treat. I will endeavour to describe it to you; we left camp early in the day, came out of the wood on the great road leading to Palace of Turiliere (Tuileries), about a mile from the entrance of the garden, the road is as straight as a line and wide enough for ten carriages to run abreast, on each side are beautiful walks shaded by large trees. Before you come to the palace you pass through the celebrated Champ de Mars, where Napoleon the Great was crowned.

This is a most delightful spot, the trees are planted with such regularity that in whatever direction you cast your eye they appear in strait lines. This place is well dotted with temples dedicated to the jolly God. Wines and all kinds of liquor are to be procured at a very reasonable price.

The gardens attached to those places are all laid out in the most agreeable manner, here are likewise all kinds of amusement, *viz*. skittles, four corners, the devil among the tailors, ringing the bull, shooting at a mark with the bow and arrow or with the riffle, and numerous other amusements not to be met with in England. Walk in, call for a bottle of beer, wine, punch or coffee, the garden with all its amusements are free, with the exception of ball practice, but this is trifling, you have to pay only five *sous* per round for powder and ball.

The next place we visited was the garden of the Turaliese, this garden abounds with gravel walks and beautiful pieces of sculpture, many ponds having fountains throwing water to a great height. These ponds are full of beautiful gold and silver fishes, and swans swimming on the water who are so tame, they will feed out of your hand. This place is free to the public. The palace is a noble building through which we passed and came to the triumphal arch, dedicated by Napoleon, to the Imperial Army.

This is a stupendous piece of masonry on the top of which are placed the two horses of golden lead, ten feet in height. They are fixed to a golden chariot in which formerly stood the Emperor, the horses are led by two female figures representing victory and fame.

The horses I am told were brought from Venice when that place submitted to the French I must acknowledge, I felt no small degree of self pride as I stood gazing on this stupendous monument raised by such a man to the glory of the army of the grand empire who had never dared to cross bayonets with the British.

Passing from this we next came to the Louvre, here is collected the finest painting of Europe brought from every place the French had conquered. Beneath this beautiful place is a large space set apart for sculptured figures, these have also found their way here under the same circumstances as the paintings upstairs.

After passing an hour at this place we retired to a place of refreshment. On our way we fell in with an old comrade, a serjeant, who had formerly belonged to the Chasseurs Brittanique Regiment. He was discharged and residing in Paris. Our old comrade in arms soon hushed us into a 'café' or, what we would call in England an eating house or cook shop. We were at first struck with the splendour of the place, and thought there was some mistake.

The room is boxed off, each box contains cushioned seats, a marble slab table at the end of which is a large looking glass. In one of these we seated ourselves, when a bill of fare was handed to us out of which we ordered such dishes as suited our inclinations. We soon had a dinner set before us fit for noblemen. This done, we retired to another room, here we regaled ourselves with wine etc. Smoking our cigars, reading the news and chatting to our old friend for an hour. When calling for the bill we were astonished to find that each of us had to pay only the trifling sum of two *francs* and a half, or two shillings and one penny English money.

Our friend learned we had not been to the Place de Vendôme, he conducted us there to see the monument. This monument is dedicated to the French army who under Napoleon subdued Austria, and is built of stone cased with brass, being the cannon taken in the campaign melted down. The shape of this monument resembles our monument in London. The front of the basement has an inscription to the 'Glory of the Grand Army.'

The letter N with the imperial diadem surrounded with laurel is conspicuous on this part. On the four upper corners of the base are Imperial Eagles, each supporting a wreath of laurel, that goes round the base.

On the four compartments are several trophies of war lying prostrate with many standards of Austria, Prussia etc. bearing the initials of their respective sovereigns. The column runs to a great height, this is covered with brass on which is a representation of all the battles of the campaigns beginning at the bottom and winding to the top. At this place is a gallery to which you ascend by a winding flight of steps inside the column. On the top of the whole once stood the Emperor's image or statue, but its place is now occupied by the national flag of the Bourbons.

It now being time to think of returning we retraced our steps to the Champ de Mars, paid another visit to the gardens, took a parting glass with our old companion in arms, returned to camp by eight o'clock, after spending one of the most pleasant days that can be imagined, at the small expense of four *francs* each.

No. 80. Camp Bois de Boulogne. 23rd Sept., 1815.

Since my last I have enjoyed one continued round of holidays, the weather has been beautiful. Our camp continues to be daily crowded by all the rank, fashion and beauty from the capital. Serjeant M———, late of the Chasseurs Brittanique Regiment, has paid us several visits accompanied by several of his friends. I have fell in with young Pillinger, he is servant to the commissariat general.

The day that Pillinger came to camp to enquire after me, he found me with several of my comrades in company with Serjeant M———, his son and daughter and half a dozen of his acquaintance who had come to spend the day in our camp. The large hut we had built for the purpose of receiving company, and which we have named the 'British Hotel,' was full of company, and at the moment Pillinger dropped in upon us we were just beginning dinner, not of soldier's rations but of well dressed joints brought from Paris by the old Chasseur Brittanique. Pillinger found himself a welcome guest.

It is needless to say we spent a pleasant and agreeable afternoon. Wine, liquors and coffee with abundance of *segars*, was the order of the day together with music and songs. In the evening we accompanied our friends to the Champ de Mars, where after spending a half hour we parted and returned to our camp.

Serjeant M——— was one of the many royalists who escaped from Paris at the time of the revolution, he was accompanied by his wife, they resided in London some time, where Madame M——— gave birth to a son. At length he was obliged, through distress, to enter the army, his wife accompanied him. It was shortly after our brigade was formed at Carapina Camp in Portugal that I first became acquainted with him.

He has seen a great deal of service, his wife died shortly after the Battle of Vittoria and left him with a son and daughter, the two who accompanied him to our camp. After his regiment was disbanded he returned to his native place, Paris, where, after an absence of more than twenty years, he had the good fortune to find an uncle, who died six months after his arrival, and left him about £250 *per annum*. He tells us his countrymen are all in the greatest ferment as it has been made known that it is the intention of the Allied powers to strip Paris of all the plunder the French army had brought from the different countries in

Europe.

He says nothing gives him more delight than to sit in a café and listen to the Parisians denouncing the Allies as a set of thieves and robbers. It is evident the French are sadly piqued, for Old Blücher has doubled the guards and planted cannon on the bridges, and in several of the principal streets, but with this we have nothing to do. The French not having the worth of one penny belonging to 'John Bull.'

I have seen Towers of the 82nd Regiment. He has spent a few hours in camp with me and I have again seen him in Paris. Since my last a serious accident has happened in our camp, it was occasioned by the removing of some live shells. By some means one of them burst, which set fire to the remainder, when the whole, a *cassion* full exploded, several men were killed and wounded with some horses. Fortunately the mischief was not so great as might have been expected, the broken pieces of shell spread in every direction, passed over our camp without doing any harm.

We have nearly had a serious row with the Hanoverian brigade belonging to our division, the following was the cause. A lady having ascended in a balloon at Paris, it came in the direction of our camp. When the balloon was over the Bois de Bologne the lady detached herself from the balloon and descended in a parachute in admirable stile, the balloon pitched near us and all hands flew to the spot, when a general scramble took place and in a short time it was torn to rags.

A battle royal instantly took place between the British and Hanoverians. Some of the latter rap to their camp and seized their arms, but fortunately the row was stopped without any serious mischief, a few of the belligerents having black eyes and bloody noses.

No. 81. Camp Bois de Buologne. 20th October, 1815.

I have since my last spent a day in Paris with Pillinger. This time I went by Passay, as soon as we cleared the town we found the road ran alongside the Seine. The first thing that strikes the eye of a stranger is the noble dome of the College of Invalids, it is covered with gilt and when the sun shines on it it has the appearance of burnished gold.

This is the French Chelsea, it stands on the opposite side of the river near to the Pont des Invalids, a new and noble bridge, built by the Emperor, and is like every other national work, erected under the auspices of Napoleon, a credit to France. The bridge was formerly ornamented by imperial eagles but they have been replaced by the Fleur de Lis.

I crossed the bridge, thinking to get a peep at the interior of the college, but I could not gain admittance. The sentry belonged to the National Guard. I soon observed one of the Invalids coming out. The sentinel carried arms and the old soldier returned the compliment by moving his cocked hat. He took the way to the bridge and I followed. I soon overtook him, as I was passing he saluted me with 'Good Morning Serjeant.' This was enough, in a minute we were acquainted.

He was going to take a last look at the trophies of the army to which he had belonged before they were removed. He had shared the dangers and glory of the Armies of Germany, Italy and the Peninsular, was wounded severely in the arm and taken prisoner in Spain, and had passed five years in England, prisoner of war. On his return to France he was admitted an inpensioner of the college, the wound had deprived him the use of his left arm.

Since Napoleon's return he had been honoured with the Cross of the Legion of Honour. I do not wonder that the soldiers of France are so attached to the Emperor, when the same honours are alike open to all ranks, as Corporal Trim said 'from the general to the lowest drum boy.'

He said he had several times seen our army in the Bois de Boulogne but could never see a soldier with any badge of distinction although there must be many in the ranks who had seen much service. I explained to him that only the field officers in command of a regiment at a general action received a medal. He replied that if he was an Englishman, the general and field officers should fight the battles themselves for him if that was the case.

On our road we passed an Austrian soldier on sentry. 'There' said the veteran, 'is an Austrian with four medals and I have observed that most of the soldiers of that nation and of Prussia, are covered with those trumpry bits of brass. Soldiers who we have hunted down like flocks of sheep.'

We had now came to the place of parting, I treated the old soldier to a bottle of wine, then parted, he to mourn over the misfortunes of the French army and I with a light heart went to Rue de Mont Blanc in search of Pillinger not expecting to have such a wild goose chase before me. I knocked at No. 36 but was informed that no such person lived there, neither could I gain intelligence of any one where the commissariat general was quartered.

I then took a coach and ordered the man to drive to the adjutant general's office, thinking to obtain the place of abode of Pillinger's master, but I was directed to the quartermaster general's office. I was now certain I had got the right scent but I was again deceived, for here I was directed to apply at the commissariat general's office. Away we went, I could not help blaming myself for being a thick-headed fool for not first applying at this place.

Having arrived I found I had to return to 66, Rue de Mont Blanc. After riding about five miles and paying a French five *franc* piece I found Pillinger, fortunately. His master was out of town so the day was his own. After dinner we had a ramble over Paris, called on Serjeant M———, then retired to an hotel kept by an Englishman and spent the evening in company with about twenty of our own countrymen. It being too late to return to camp. I slept with Pillinger.

In the morning Pillinger accompanied me to the Champ de Mars, here as we were taking a cup of coffee a Frenchman and Pillinger began quarrelling, when the Frenchman attempted to stab Pillinger with a long knife. Fortunately I saw the move time enough to prevent mischief by striking *Monsieur* on his nasal organ, which floored him.

The landlord sided with us and seized the poor fellow by the hair of his head and dragged him out of doors.

Away he ran towards Paris as if the devil was at his heels. I have not yet informed you that we are daily supplied with a paper, printed in English called Galignancis Messenger, so that we are in possession of all the news interesting to an Englishman.

No. 82. Verriers. 13th November, 1815.

Our delightful summer's abode has at length changed with the season. October came, the nights and mornings was cold and chilly, the leaves began to fall and from frequent rains our camp soon became unpleasant, the gay Parisians visits became less frequent towards the middle of the month, the weather began to set in. At length the welcome news came to brake up camp and go into Winters quarters.

Verriers is the head quarters of the brigade. Here we are stationed, it is about eight miles from Paris. I am quartered on an old couple who are far advanced in years, they have seen better days, seventy winters have passed over their heads and now their life is one continued round of toil and sorrow. Both their united efforts are scarce sufficient to keep the wolf from the door, in their younger days they were in possession of a farm.

Their family consisted of six sons and one daughter, the six young men have been killed or perished in the wars, one in Italy, one in Spain, three on the retreat from Moscow and the last and youngest fell at Waterloo. Their daughter fell a victim to her pretended lover and shortly after died of a broken heart.

When I entered the house with my billet I found the old couple plunged in grief. I soon learned the cause of their trouble. The Russians had been quartered on them for some time, they had marched the day before our arrival to make room for us. Last night the poor old couple had for the first time these three months, slept in their bed, but now we had arrived they would again be obliged to sleep on straw.

I desired the old man to fetch me a bundle of clean straw, this

I shook down in one corner, mine and my comrade's blankets and watch-coats made us a very comfortable bed. I then told the old man that we should sleep there, that we were British soldiers, and rather than deprive two such old people of the only comfort they could enjoy, we would rather sleep on the bare boards.

At such unexpected treatment the poor old man was struck dumb for some time, then clasping his hands together exclaimed '*Mon Dieu*' and being a good Catholic crossed himself. I missed the old man, he had ran out to tell his neighbours the joyful news, it soon spread over the little village. The old man soon returned with a bottle of brandy to treat his good friends and seemed twenty years younger. I should not have thought this incident worth mentioning only for the effect it has on the whole of the inhabitants.

I and my comrades are become the favourites of all the villagers both old and young. I am very comfortable in my humble quarters, the old people studies everything to make us so. I am become so attached to old Lebal and his wife that I would not exchange quarters even to the richest house in the village. The evenings are long, a good fire and brandy punch with tobacco kills time, besides our old host is not a bad singer for an old man. So putting all the good and bad together we shall manage to pass away the winter tolerably well.

Paris begins to feel the ill effects of this second visit of the Allies. The golden horses are gone, their removal disturbed the people more than anything else, it was necessary to have a strong guard round the place while the engineers were employed in removing them. The bare wall in the once beautiful picture gallery looks frightful, the monument at the Place de Vendôme has been stripped of its brass ornaments and everything that has been brought from other countries has been restored to its proper owners.

No. 83. Boulogne Sur Mare, 30th December, 1815.

Part of the British army are ordered home. Our regiment being included in the number we marched from Verriers the 5th.

December, leaving our old landlord and his spouse in tears. Our first days march was to St. Dennis, weather and roads bad. On the 10th. we arrived at Beauvis.

A sharp frost had set in on the evening of the 9th. and so intense was the cold that on the 10th. we could not keep ourselves warm, although performed nearly the whole of the days march in a jog-trot. Here I and my comrade dropped in good quarters, it was a gentleman's house and as liberal a man as I had ever met with.

This being my birthday I had an opportunity of celebrating it with plenty of good cheer. We halted here the 11th., then moved on, the frost still continued but the keen wind had abated. This made the march pleasant.

On the 17th. we marched into Abbeville. When we had formed in the market place amongst the crowd of spectators, I discovered my old friend Corporal Pipin making signs to me. The surprise and joy at our unexpected meeting can be easier imagined than described. As soon as I got my billet we met. the extravagance of Pipin's joy drew a great many of his countrymen about us. Pipin called me his dear friend, his comrade and I don't know what.

The people could not unravel the riddle, some said I must have been in the same regiment with him, others that I had saved him from being murdered when he was wounded, and twenty other different stories got afloat but none knew the right one but ourselves. He looked at my billet, it was for five he said, how fortunate it is but two minutes walk from my house. Then addressing the men, he said follow me.

We soon entered a café, after treating my comrades he gave them a card with his address, saying by this you will find the serjeant at any time he might be wanted. He had written a note to apprise his family of my arrival, he sent it by a man whom he directed to shew my comrades his house and then conduct them to their billet. After I had regaled myself with some coffee and biscuit we started for his dwelling.

When we entered I shall never forget the ceremony of bowing and scraping, five of the family were present, Pipin's father, mother, uncle, brother and his wife, for my friend had got married to the little woman who was the cause of his entering the army. She is a very pretty little woman and is about to present her husband with the first pledge of their love.

While dinner was preparing I went to my billet to see how my comrades were situated and to brush myself up, and returned to dinner. Another brother and a sister of Pipin's had arrived during my absence. After dinner we had enough to do to talk of old times, nothing that had passed on our voyage from St. Jean de Luz, and our stay at Fuentarabia was forgot, even the stewed cat was brought up, this caused a good laugh at Pipin's expense.

I had to fight the battle of Waterloo over again, I was surprised to hear Monsieur Pipin's remarks, but I soon found that the whole family was of decided Republican principals, they did not wish to see either Napoleon or Louis govern France. They were for a pure Republic, where the chief magistrate should be elected by the voice of the people for a limited period and be responsible for his acts.

We had spent about two hours in running over the different battles we had each shared in, in the Peninsular, when our horn sounded for orders and in about an hour afterwards my comrade called to tell me the regiment was to parade tomorrow morning at 10 o'clock and that we were to halt tomorrow.

Pipin rewarded him with a thumping glass of brandy and water and a cigar for the pleasing intelligence. It will be sufficient to say I had a choice of everything I wished for and at 11 o'clock retired to bed, rose early the next morning and prepared for parade, then partook of a sumptuous breakfast.

We were some time on parade and I could not help observing Monsieur Pipin was continually surrounded by groups of gentlemen and ladies to whom he was continually talking, using strange gestures, often pointing to the part of the line I was in.

After parade I joined my friends, when Pipin told me he thought his father would never be tired of talking about us. He had told the story an hundred times over, how that our two regiments had been engaged together and that we had both been wounded, of our meeting together on board the fishing boat, and that if I had not given share of my blanket to his son he must have perished.

In short, every little incident that had happened from our first meeting until we parted, was not forgotten. It will be easy for you to imagine what sort of a day I had, many gentlemen called to pay their respects to Monsieur Pipin or perhaps were lead more out of curiosity to see me. Many of them expressed their regret that my short stay prevented them enjoying the company of Corporal Pipin and his English friend at their own homes. I believe had I stopped at Abbeville three months I should have spent the whole of the time in visiting.

On the 19th the regiment marched, I obtained permission from our adjutant to remain a few hours, when I was to overtake the corps by the diligence. After dinner Corporal Pipin and I mounted the diligence and soon joined the regiment. They had made but a short march, the road in front being blocked up by the troops who had preceded us.

We did not march until late the next day, when I took leave of my old and good friend. I saw him on the diligence, when the coachman cracked his whip he called to me and threw me something wrapped in paper. I picked it up, he had then gone some distance, he was waving his hand. I opened the paper, it contained a double *napoleon*. Nothing worthy of notice took place until we arrived at this place. In a short time we shall be in old England, when I shall write you again the first opportunity.

No. 84. Dover Castle. 3rd January, 1816.

I was quartered on a fisherman at Boulogne. The house is in the old town near the water and is well stored with English earthenware, some of the furniture was English and a beautiful eight day clock made at Canterbury stood in a conspicuous part of his dwelling. The old fisherman was at sea, his wife and two daughters kept house, the two girls were from eighteen to twenty and as fine young women as ever I had seen. It was soon evident we were unwelcome visitors.

The old lady scanned us over with a suspicious eye and made us understand there was no room for us in the house, but she would provide us out. But not liking the quarters I and my comrade returned. I soon found our company was not so disagreeable to the daughters as it was to the mother.

The fisherman returned home about two hours after our arrival, he welcomed us in English, said he had just returned from Folkstone, and with all that frankness so common to a sailor, asked us if we had dined. I said we had not, but was just talking of going over to the eating house opposite. This he would not allow and ordered one of his pretty daughters to fry some beef steaks, saying 'I know you English are fond of beefsteaks.' There being plenty of prime fresh fish, we preferred the latter.

While the fish was hissing in the pan we were treated with some good bottled porter (English). He informed us his wife was anxious to get us away because of his absence, but now he was at home all was right. His daughters had enjoyed themselves at our expense, for they understood and spoke English as well as their own language. Now I and my comrade had been making love to the two devils thinking we were safe. Fortunately we had not uttered one single offensive word, so there was no harm done.

After having our dinner, which by the by was quite a treat, we went to a public house, discussed the news of the day over a bottle of porter. When we returned we found the mother and two daughters smarted off. The sisters looked so bewitching with handkerchiefs tied so neat about their heads that I was almost tumbling head and ears in love with both. We spent a very agreeable evening by a good fire.

In the course of conversation I learned that tomorrow being the last day in the year the two lasses were going to church. Of course I tendered my services to escort them to the Holy Sanctuary and was taken at my word. After breakfast they came into the kitchen saying they were going. They were dressed in their holiday clothes and appeared perfect angels. My comrade was on duty so I had the pleasing task of conducting two as pretty young women to prayers as could be found in France.

The church was in the upper town, I had nothing to do with the saints only to satisfy my curiosity at looking at the images and pictures while the two little beauties were kneeling before the Virgin. They were in close conference about ten minutes, this settled what accounts stood open between them for the year.

After this we walked 'til dinner time, saw everything worth seeing, visited the spot where the Grand Army encamped that was intended to invade England. Our walk gave us a good appetite to our dinner, took another walk in the afternoon, at night the fisherman and I drank the old year out and the new one in, then went to bed, was roused early by the noise in the house occasioned by the neighbours visits to compliment the family, it being the new year, hastened down stairs, was presented by Mariane with an apple, not knowing the custom was rather bothered, thought I could not be far wrong if I purchased the apple by a kiss, happened to be right for once in a way.

Next came Janette with her apple and her sweet smiling face, she was the favourite. Of course she had an extra squeeze, went to breakfast, orders came to march at eleven o'clock, grew peevish wished the order at the Devil, took a glass of brandy to rouse my spirits, it was no use. The bugle sounded the assembly, with a heavy heart took leave of the girls, met the fisherman and his wife at the door returning from prayers, shook hands, joined my company and marched towards Calise.

The white cliffs of Albion was viewed with rapturous delight by my comrades. Could not join with them, halted about half way between Calise and Boulogne, joined a party in the evening to celebrate the new year. Oceans of brandy and cider got drunk. Returning to my quarters must slide on a horse pond, ice broke, let in above my knees, went to bed, dreamt of Janette. Next morning after breakfast played at four corners, lost every game.

Marched at 12, arrived at Calise in the afternoon. Embarked, sailed, arrived at Dover in the night, disembarked the next morning and marched into the Castle Barracks.

No. 85. Blatchington Barracks, 20th January 1816.

I must go back to Calise, having forgotten to mention Jno. Manley. While we were waiting to embark I strolled on the pier, saw a small pillar erected to commemorate the landing of Louis 18th. in 1814, after so long an absence from France, the spot where he first placed his foot on the pier is marked with all due solemnity by cutting the stone to the size of his boot, this is inlaid with brass.

From this place we could see the bold lofty white cliffs of Dover, as I stood gazing on the many vessels passing backwards and forwards I was saluted by a slap on the shoulder followed by a voice exclaiming 'D——n it Bill, how are you, give me your fist, I have been hunting for you this hour.' I turned round and found it was Jack Manley of the 32nd. Regiment. He is living servant to Major General Sir Manley Power, who is stationed here to superintend the embarkation of the troops.

I got permission to get into Calise for an hour with Manley, when I returned I found our colonel surrounded by five young women natives of Grammont, except one who was from Paris, begging permission to embark with the regiment and not to be left friendless on a foreign shore. The colonel called the men to him, who promised they would marry them on the first opportunity that offered when settled in England.

The poor creatures had been decoyed from home by the men they were living with, and as their fidelity to these men were above suspicion, they having conducted themselves with the strictest propriety, they were allowed to proceed to England (last Sunday the whole were married).

Everything being ready we stepped on board, bidding *adieu* to a country from whose inhabitants we had received the greatest kindness and civility. Only six months had passed since we entered France as enemies. Above all other nations we were her most determined foe, we had overthrown their darling Emperor

179

and had made a total wreck of the Imperial Army. Every art was used to prejudice the inhabitants against us.

Notwithstanding all these disadvantages, as we advanced we secured the good will of the people. The strict discipline observed by our army soon convinced the inhabitants, to use the words of Monsieur Pipin, 'If we were terrible in the field, we were harmless when mixed with the people.' I perfectly remember when we left Grammont to go to Waterloo that the general opinion of the Belgians were that we should not be a match against the ferocious troops of France.

But to return, we landed at Dover the 2nd inst., went into barracks at the castle. On the 5th we marched for Portsmouth. At Rye we met with an unexpected treat, the inhabitants had entered into a subscription. The money was set apart to treat the men of every regiment that had been at Waterloo to a quart of eight-penny stout.

The day was stormy, about a mile from the town we met a farmer, 'Cheer up my lads' said he 'there is a pot of stout for every one of ye in town.' The townspeople dropped into the public houses, ours being the first Waterloo Regiment that had marched into Rye. As a matter of course a general fuddle was the consequence. The next day our route was altered, we received orders to proceed to Blatchington Barracks where we are at present stationed.

No. 86. Blatchington Barracks, 25th March, 1816.

When I volunteered from the Militia, Major Frederick advised us to engage for seven years, saying if we did not like the service we could then leave it, or we might go to another regiment at the expiration of our time should we not like the regiment we were in. I was one who volunteered for seven years. Not wishing to throw away nine years service and believing I shall not better myself by changing into any other corps I have determined to follow the fortunes of my old corps as long as I am fit for service. Consequently I have taken on for an unlimited period.

The regiment is at present under the command of Major Thwaites, who has revised a system of Colonel Mainwaring's, that is to allow the men two play days a week, *viz.* Wednesdays and Saturdays. These days are passed as follows. After the morning parade everyone is busy employed in cleaning appointments. This done the day is devoted to athletic exercises, boxing, wrestling, running, picking up a hundred stones, sometimes on foot at others on horseback, cricket, football, running in sacks and any other amusement we might fancy. This produces an excellent feeling between officers and men, for the officers always takes a part in the diversions.

When Colonel Mainwaring commanded, although he was getting in years he was generally foremost in any of the sports, nothing would please him better than to put on the gloves and be matched with a private who would stick well to him. If he found a man timid for instance at football, he would say 'Don't give way to me, we are now all on a level, there is no difference in rank. Jack's as good as his master.'

There would not be a single game going on but he would go round and take share in it and by his presence infuse life into everyone. Such was Colonel Mainwaring, he has left us but he has thrown his mantle over the major, who takes a delight in treading in the colonels steps, so far as it conduces to the health and pleasure of the soldier, this makes duty and drill pass over with ease. I think I might safely say I belong to as good if not the best regiment in the service.

In your letter you say you frequently hear soldiers, some who are still in the service and others who are discharged, speak against the Duke of Wellington for his tyranny in the Peninsular. Whenever I meet such characters I generally treat them with contempt. It is a well known fact that the army of the Peninsular was sent to protect the inhabitants and not to plunder and murder them, each soldier were fully acquainted with the nature of the service and the consequence of a breach of discipline.

The army, composed as it was of men of all grades of character, could not be kept in order so essential to its well being, if some examples had not been made. although it must be painful to see capital punishment carried into execution for comparatively trifling offences yet such punishments were necessary to deter others. Owing to the difficulty of procuring men to keep the army effective, recruiting parties attended the sessions and received men who had committed thefts, who if they had been put to trial would have been transported.

Such men when they joined the army set about their old trades and corrupt men of weak minds. If you knew but the hundredth part of the atrocities committed by men calling themselves British soldiers it would chill your blood.

Respecting privations, soldiers on service must expect them and bare with them. I have been told that men have been hanged or shot for taking a morsel of bread when they had been fasting ten or fourteen days. I do not remember any case of the sort, but I know many have plundered when there has been no excuse, for at the time we had been well supplied. It is true we were sometimes badly off for biscuit, but taking everything into consideration no army could be supplied better.

Indeed it is a mystery to thousands how we were supplied so regular as we were. You never hear any of those grumblers say a word about the comforts provided for the sick and wounded, their favourite talk is of evils for which there could be no remedy.

If England should require the service of her army again, and I should be with it, let me have 'Old Nosey' to command. Our interests would be sure to be looked into, we should never have occasion to fear an enemy. There are two things we should be certain of. First, we should always be as well supplied with rations as the nature of the service would admit. The second is we should be sure to give the enemy a d——d good thrashing. What can a soldier desire more.

No. 87. Brighton. 23rd June, 1816.

The first anniversary of the battle of Waterloo was ushered in with all due form and solemnity. Major Thwaites was determined all ranks should enjoy themselves, roast beef, plumb pudding, with plenty of brown stout was the order of the day. At 11 o'clock the 10th Hussars formed on the Steene. At the same time we marched out of the Barrack yard and formed. After firing a *feu de joi*, the bugle then sounded 'Cavalry in sight.' It seemed to be the intention of the two commanding officers to shew to the numerous spectators, the terrible resistance a square of infantry can offer to a body of cavalry.

Accordingly as soon as the firing was over our bugler sounded 'Cavalry in sight.' In an instant the square was formed and an animating fire as perfect as the roll of a drum was kept up for some time, the bugle then sounded 'cease firing,' when the kneeling ranks, whose fire is always reserved, fired volleys at the retreating cavalry. I was the commanding officers orderly, and being mixed with the spectators, a gentleman remarked it was one of the most sublime sights he ever saw, the square presented on solid mass of steel and fire. The Brightonians testified their delight by three volleys of cheers.

We then marched to barracks, the day was beautifully fine. The tables were placed in the barrack yard, over which were hung festoons of laurel and flowers, at one o'clock the men sat down to a sumptuous dinner, the tables groaned under the weight of roast beef and plumb pudding. A barrel of beer was placed at the end of each table, many ladies and gentlemen accompanied by our officers came and tasted of the dinner and drank our healths, everything passed off in high glee.

After dinner we got up a bit of fun to commence with. The Brighton paper says, and no doubt it will go the round of most the Provincial papers, that after the regiment had dined, the men assembled and carried one of their comrades on their shoulders to the king and queen where they spent the afternoon in fuddling etc., that the man so honoured by his comrades had particularly distinguished himself at Waterloo.

Now the truth of the story was as follows. Corporal Wood, a simple harmless good hearted fellow as ever descended from Old Father Adam, had taken into his simple noddle to chose a comrade for life. The object of his choice was as great a simpleton as himself and held the distinguished post of servant at the 'King and Queen' tap. All the necessary preliminaries being settled between the parties, the auspicious 18th of June was fixed for the nuptial ceremony and while Major Thwaites was amusing the people on the Steine, Corporal Wood was plighting his vows to the fair nymph of the King and Queen tap.

After dinner we seized the poor corporal in order to give him a ride round the barrack yard, with a huge pair of horns on his head, or pay the fine, he chose the latter. The horns were dispensed with and his brows ornamented with laurel. Off we marched with the corporal mounted on a stool, the whole corps of buglers in front playing a quick step, many of our men followed in procession which gave it the appearance of what the editor of the paper represented it to be.

A gentleman who met the cavalcade and learned the cause, was so tickled with the fun, he followed the party to the tap and ordered a pounds worth of beer.

The afternoon was spent on the flat going to the horse barracks by a match of cricket by a party of the 10th Hussars and 51st. The former corps was winners, in the evening the officers gave a dinner ball and supper at the Steine Hotel. The serjeants and wives dined at the King and Queen Inn, a ball took place afterwards that lasted until four in the morning. The corporals put up at the Swan public house where they spent the night and the private soldiers distributed themselves over the town to the different public houses which they were in the habit of using. The expense of the serjeants' Ball amounted to £32.

In the morning as we were returning to our barracks (about 5 o'clock) we met the officers with the band and colours, we had the whole corps of buglers, the two parties joined and marched home together, the band and buglers playing together made such a confounded noise that awoke all the ladies and gentlemen within hearing. It was laughable to see all the windows crowded with heads with nightcaps on.

The 19th. the men that was on duty on the 18th had a day

and on the 20th Major Thwaites put all to rights on the hills near the race course by treating us to a field day that lasted nearly three hours. It is singular and worthy of remark that not a single soldier disgraced himself during the whole holiday.

The men received their Waterloo Medals at Brighton. Colonel Mitchel died when the regiment lay at Chatham in 1817 and Lieutenant Colonel Rice succeeded to the command of the corps. In former letters the writer has often expressed his opinion strongly against soldiers marrying, however it appears he has been caught, having at Plymouth led to the Altar of Hyman a buxom lass some four years younger than himself.

No. 88. Winchester Barracks, 10th December, 1820.

Shortly after the 'bill of pains and penalties' was given up by His Majesty's Ministers, the regiment was inspected on Hampton Court Green by Sir Henry Torrens. Amongst the spectators I saw Sir John Fredrick, Colonel of the 2nd Surrey Militia. As soon as the inspection was over, I mustered the men who had volunteered with Captain Fredrick (there was only six left out of the 128) and went to Sir John, who was in conversation with Colonel Rice and several of our officers.

Colonel Rice asked what we wanted, when Captain Fredrick said 'It is some of my brother's old comrades who want to wish him a good morning.'

I was to be speaker so I expressed the pleasure we felt at seeing our old commanding officer in good health etc. Sir John asked where the remainder were that volunteered with us. Captain Fredrick said 'Six are all that are left out of the whole party, some have been killed, some disabled by wounds, and others worn out and discharged. Not one of these but have been marked in their turn.'

'Yes Sir John' I said 'we have all been wounded, some twice, these two were wounded with your brother in a charge at Lezaca, when we retook our General out of the hands of the soldiers of the 51st French Regiment of the line.'

By this time Sir John could call four of us by name and said 'You all must drink my health, here is two pounds.'

Then addressing Colonel Rice he said 'Rice, I have a favour to ask of you, if it will not interfere with any particular arrangements, might these men have liberty for the day.'

The liberty being granted Sir John wished us well and told us to go and enjoy ourselves. On the 18th November we marched to Winchester Barrack were we are at present stationed.

No. 89. Portsmouth, 5th May, 1821.

In a letter written from camp near Badajoz in June 1811 when I detailed to you the particulars of the two unsuccessful attempts to storm Fort San Cristoval, I believe I noticed the gallant conduct of Ensign Dyas in volunteering on both occasions to lead the forlorn hope. For this service Mr. Dyas never received promotion. It is true that Mr. Dyas got a lieutenancy but it was occasioned by the death of Lieutenant Westropp who was killed on the second night. Mr. Dyas would have received this promotion had he been in England with the depot, he being the senior ensign.

After the inspection at Hampton Court Lieutenant Dyas' conduct came under the notice of Sir H. Torrens, when in looking over the record book he expressed his surprise that Lieutenant Dyas had not been promoted for such distinguished conduct. It appears that on the general's return to London he brought Mr. Dyas's service before the proper authorities and I feel great satisfaction in general with the whole corps, to say that the long neglected and brave sub have at last been rewarded. It has come at the eleventh hour, but better late than never. Before we left Winchester Lieutenant Dyas was gazetted as captain in the 2nd Ceylon Regiment.

Had his gallant conduct been rewarded at the time, that in justice it should have been, he would now, in all probability have had a regiment in place of being a junior captain in a foreign corps. How many striplings, who have entered the service since 1811 have jumped over his head with no other qualification than interest and money. Captain Dyas could not boast of high birth or fortune, but he had a lion's heart.

Ireland never produced a better soldier, nor one more qualified to fill a high station in the army, being in possession of that secret how to govern those under him not through fear but love. We are all rejoiced at his promotion, but sorry for his leaving the regiment.

We have received an order from the Horse Guards that in addition to the honours and distinctions the regiment at present bears, we are in future to bear the title of 'The King's Own Light Infantry Regiment' and that the facings are to be changed from green to blue. We are of course all proud of the distinguished honour, I am afraid it will spoil the appearance of the regiment. Green facings suits a Light Infantry Regiment, it has a much lighter appearance than blue.

No. 90. Albany Barracks, Isle of Wight. 20th July, 1821.

The regiment embarked at point the middle of last month for Malta. I am left home with the depot. At this place there are upwards of fifty depots belonging to regiments on foreign stations. I am already sick of this place and would rather be with my regiment even if they were on the worst station in the world. It shall be no fault of mine if I am not with the old corps the first opportunity that offers.

The whole of the depots are under the command of Colonel Ross (staff). We have sent out several recruiting parties, and I have found some difficulty in remaining here. I am determined if it be possible not to leave the depot, if I do, all chance of going out will be over. It will be some time before any opportunity will present itself, the parties must first get recruits and they must be drilled.

No. 91. Albany Barracks. 7th July, 1822.

I have heard several times from the regiment, the men do not like the place (Corfu). They complain of the very severe discipline in practice. Garrison court martials are almost an everyday occurrence; this is occasioned by the great number of commuted men stationed in the Ionian Islands, these men are distributed through the Ionian Army. Our regiment has upwards of forty attached to them. Commutes are men who have deserted from the army, and bad characters who have committed thefts and other crimes, who, to avoid the punishment due to their offences, volunteer their service, or more properly speaking, commute their service.

This is tantamount to transportation for life, but these men can redeem their characters provided they behave well for seven years. They are then, by recommendation from the colonel commanding, allowed to remain in the corps, and their service, during such good conduct, are allowed them, and when the regiment returns home they are allowed to go with it—while those, who continue to behave ill are not only punished for every offence, but are transferred from one regiment to another.

It is therefore evident that where such men are, crime must be more frequent, consequently strict discipline is rendered necessary. This will account for the dislike our men have for the station. Another complaint is, the men are obliged to work on the roads. It appears since the islands have been in our possession the soldiers are constantly employed in making carriage roads in all the island.

Another, and the worst grievance of all, is that the soldiers are prohibited from purchasing any articles, such as wine, spirits, groceries, etc., except at certain places called canteens. The owners of these places pay a tax to the government for the privilege of selling to the troops, consequently the men pay dearer, and what they buy is inferior in quality to what they could purchase if the shops were all open to them.

If any Greek shop keeper, not being a licensed canteenman, sells to the British soldier he is liable to a fine of ten dollars for the first offence. Notwithstanding all these disadvantages I hope to go out soon, then I shall be able to send you more particulars.

No. 92. *Gibraltar, 13th November, 1822.*

An order from the Horse Guard on the 20th October informed us that the John Richard's merchant ship fitted up for troops, was about to leave the river and would call at Cowes to take our troops and stores to the Mediterranean. She arrived on the 27th. The next day the different detachments for the regiments on that station embarked and I am happy to say, your humble servant is amongst the number. I being the senior serjeant the double duty of acting serjeant major and quarter master serjeant devolved on me. This is no bad situation, particularly as I am never seasick and have always a better appetite at sea than on shore.

We sailed the 29th, wind fresh and favourable. It continued so until we cleared the Lands End, when it suddenly chopped round and increased until it blew a complete gale, this lasted twenty four hours. We rode it out, sustaining no other damage but having our starboard bulwarks washed away. After the gale subsided it continued to blow strong, and being against us we did not make much way for several days when it again favoured us and we soon came in sight of the Heights near Corunna. We kept pushing on at a good rate, passed the Tagus with the Bullen rocks in sight. Weather very fine.

This day we saw a great many porpoises and flying fish, and at night two large fish kept company and played round the vessel several hours. You cannot conceive how beautiful these fish appeared as they darted about, the water had the appearance of silver fire. We tried several times to harpoon them but failed. On the 10th inst. we passed the ever memorable place where Nelson defeated the combined fleets of France and Spain and gloriously fell in the hour of Victory. About 10 at night we dropped anchor in front of the Rock, it being very dark the lights in the town had a very beautiful appearance.

In the morning we had a full view of this formidable place that withstood the united forces of France and Spain during a siege that lasted nearly four years. Above the town stands an old Moorish castle strongly fortified. I have not been on shore. I cannot therefore say much about it. About two miles from the rock, above the village of St. Rook are two rocks called the Queen of Spain's Chair. It is said that during the attack of the junk ships, her 'Most Christian Majesty' sat between those rocks to witness the attack and being confident of success made a foolish vow she would never quit the place until she saw the Spanish flag flying on the rock. After the destruction of the junks, Her Majesty would have to have remained there until doom's day had not the gallant Old Elliott gratified her vanity by hoisting the national flag of Spain.

Opposite the rock, at about eight miles distance stands the town of Algeziras, the place where the junk ships were built. On the African side, the mountains rise to a great height and it has a very barren and wild appearance. There are at present a great number of ships in the bay from all parts of the world. This day we disembarked the men belonging to regiments stationed on the rock. We have some stores to get out, this done we shall sail for Malta.

No. 93. Malta, Fort Ricasoli. 3rd December, 1822.

We sailed from Gibraltar on the 15th. November, wind light and fair. As we passed Europa Point we had a good view of the rock with the garrison called Shooters (Ceuta) on the African coast and the Moorish city beneath, a great many boats with Moors were coming to the Rock, these people keep up a constant trade with Gibraltar and supply the market with all kinds of vegetables, fruit etc. The day after we left Gibraltar we passed Hercules's Pillars, called by the sailors the Asses' Ears. This day the wind became foul and blew strong. On our way up after passing Cape de Gatte we came in sight of Algiers. The city has a very imposing appearance from the water, the houses being built up the face of a high hill and all appeared as white as snow. Several small vessels were sailing in front of the harbour while others were creeping up under the land. After this we met with nothing worthy of notice until we arrived at Malta.

At Gibraltar we took in an old Jew, a native of Jerusalem,

he could not spake a word of any European language. I gave the old Israelite a six man's berth to himself, having stowed all the old chap's luggage away in his berth. He sat, the first two days, watching us with no small degree of suspicion but by degrees we became familiar, but not understanding his language we could learn nothing from him. The 28th entered the Arbour of Valette (Valetta).

The old Jew went on shore and soon returned with some of his countrymen who could spake English, he brought us some fruit and treated us well. His friends told us the old man could not rest until he had returned to thank us for our kindness to him, he had never before been placed alone with Englishmen but he had with people of other nations, who generally behaved rude to him on account of his faith. He could not, he said, have experienced more civility and goodwill from his own people, he should often look back on the voyage with a mixture of pleasure and delight and if ever he saw an Englishman in distress at Constantinople he should feel a pleasure in relieving him.

The men whose regiments were at Malta joined their corps, while the troops belonging to the Ionian army landed and marched into Fort Ricasoli. Here we shall wait until an opportunity offers to take us to Corfu. In getting out the baggage it was observed that several of the officer's chests had been opened and money, plate and jewellery had been stolen to a considerable amount.

A Lieutenant Brown, 80th Regiment and his lady had lost an immense quantity of valuable jewels. The baggage was under lock and key, the key was kept by the first mate, no one could go down unless the mate was with him. On examining the ship forward it was discovered that the sailors had removed a board that partitioned the part they occupied from the hold. On a strict search being made a great deal of the property were secreted in different parts of the ship. The whole of the sailors were removed to the prison at Valette. The ship will be detained some time and will be a serious loss to the owners.

It was lucky for the old Jew that we put him and his baggage together, he had one small box exceedingly heavy, the sailors were very anxious to put this box down with the officer's baggage but the old man would not consent. This box must have contained something very valuable, for the old boy was more particular in stowing it away in his berth than any of the rest. If it had went below, the old boy would have had a very different opinion of the English at parting than he had.

I had forgot to mention in its place that on approaching Malta the first land we made was the Island of Gozae (Gozo) and separated from Malta by a very narrow channel. Into this channel the ship that St. Paul was on board ran into, where he was wrecked as related in the Acts of the Apostles. The little island of Gozae is a very fertile spot, there did not appear a single inch but was under a high state of cultivation and was a pleasing contrast to the barren rock, the island of Malta, that only presented to the eye a huge solid rock of freestone. The climate is delightful and now you are muffled up in your great coats we can smoke a pleasant pipe in our shirt sleeves.

No. 94. Fort Ricasoli, 17th December, 1822.

Valette, the capital of the island is a place of great strength, its harbour is one of the most secure to be met with. An enemy would be blown out of the water in attempting to enter it. Fort Elmo has four tier of guns, the lowest tier ranges with the water, it stretches across commanding the narrow entrance formed by Valette and the fort we are in. Besides the danger of facing fort Elmo, the batteries from Valette and Ricasoli are tremendous. It is also as secure from wind as from an enemy. There is also a good dock yard and arsenal, the batteries on the land side are of prodigious strength. The whole island is one solid rock of freestone, and barren except some small spots round the towns, where the people have made soil by the sweepings of the streets and houses, mixed with decayed vegetables etc.

You might form some notion of the value of manure when I inform you that the 85th Light Infantry Regiment stationed at Cottinaro has two Maltese to each company. These men does all the dirty work, carries the men's breakfasts and dinners to the different guards and run in errands, the only pay they receive is their victuals and the sweepings of the barracks. We have a man who attends regularly at Fort Ricasoli for the same purpose, he told me he makes two dollars per month off the sweepings. He is the most obliging creature I ever met with, he has a boat, if any one wants anything from Valette ever so trifling he will fetch it if it is twenty times a day, he has a small family but what with the sweepings and a few halfpence he picks up with his boat, he contrives to live.

The greatest part of the Maltese are very poor but if you were to judge from the interior of their churches you would imagine them to be the richest people in the world. Not only the poor but what might be termed the respectable tradespeople and mechanics, go without shoes and stockings. The women pay the same disregard to their feet as the men, it is no uncommon thing to meet females without shoes or stockings dressed in a silk skirt and hood that completely covers them except their faces.

This dress has a very simple and modest appearance, but if nature should have been bountiful in her gifts in bestowing on any of the young rogues, a good shape, she has an artful way of favouring you with a glimpse as you pass by letting a part of the hood slip, this the wind carries back, when your eyes are all of a sudden gratified with as charming a young brunette as the heart can desire. But their feet spoil all, from constantly going without shoes they are very large, the toes spread very wide apart and the bottom of the foot is covered with a hard dead skin. If it was not for this, taking them altogether I think the young women to be as pretty a set of dark angels as is to be met with.

The place swarms with beggars of the most miserable description, some of these will follow you the whole length of a street.

Fort Ricasoli lays on the left hand side as we enter the harbour, directly opposite to Valette, it is used as a depot for the Ionian Islands. All troops going to or coming from Corfu are stationed here until there is an opportunity of removing them, it is rather a dreary abode. When the atmosphere is clear we can see Mount Etna. On a small out work, close to the water are four English sailors hanging in gibbets for piracy. My room is about one hundred yards from them, if it should be a windy night I am amused with the creaking of the irons every time I wake. I think I hear you say, what pleasant neighbours.

We cannot leave the fort without a pass, so the only place of recreation is the canteen. Nothing is to be had here but bad wine, no liquors being allowed to be sold in the fort, but we manage to smuggle as much as we want notwithstanding the vigilance of the old fox, the commandant. Our men can get passes twice a week to go to Valette or Cottinaro, besides I take over a party every morning two hours before daylight this is the time we smuggle the liquor. I have the charge of the detachments consequently I can go anywhere without a pass. The seamen have all been released and the ship has sailed. A good deal of the property could not be found, this is a serious loss to the owners. It was impossible to fix the guilt on any particular one as nothing could be found on their persons or in their chests.

No. 95. Fort Ricasoli. 5th January, 1823.

In this letter I am going to take you over to Valette. The distance from our fort to where we land is about a mile, the water is very deep and clear, the bottom being freestone we could see everything beneath us nearly the whole of the way. Being landed, we had to ascend a very long flight of steps, at the top of which is one of those privileged houses that are allowed to sell to the army and navy. This place seems to be the principal resort of the blue jackets and it would not be doing the owner justice if I was not to say that his wines, liquors and cigars are good, and so are the accommodations.

After leaving this we came to the gates, whatever part of the town you want to go to from this is up steep hills, some of the cross streets are so steep that it is necessary to ascend by steps. In one of those cross streets is a famous coffee shop, excellent punch two pence per half pint glass Maltese, a fraction more than three halfpence English. *Segars* seems to be of very little consideration for we smoked during the time we stayed about an hour and the charge was about two grains and a half each or one farthing.

From this we went to St. Paul's Church, this like all other Catholic churches is very grand and as a matter of course they have a part of the wreck of the ship St. Paul was wrecked in. I was told that this church has the distinguished honour of being possessed of the pillar and cats that St. Paul was tied to and flogged during his imprisonment at Rome in the reign of the detestable Nero. These and many other valuable relics the priest will shew to a stranger, but, I being an unbeliever in these things I did not trouble myself about seeing the trumpery.

Our next visit was to the English Hotel, here the High Priest had something to please his visitors, much superior to all the nonsense in the last place we had left, it was a good dinner cooked in English fashion fit for any one with wine for eighteen pence.

After refreshing ourselves we went to St. John's church. It is well worth visiting. One of the hangers on at this church demanded two pence each to shew us round. He took a great deal of pains to explain everything to us in a mixture of Maltese, Italian and broken English. The floor is a beautiful piece of workmanship in different coloured marble representing different figures. There are many small chapels each bearing the name of the country the knight belongs to and many beautiful monuments to the memory of the deceased knights. We were shewn a marble head and dish, it was well executed and resembled the head of St. John.

Whether this was the real head turned into marble to preserve it from the hands of the infidels I could not learn, not being sufficiently versed in Maltese and Italian, and unfortunately our guide confounded the little English he was master of with the other two languages that I had as much knowledge of what he was saying as if he had been a native of Japan. However there seemed to be something extraordinary attached to the history

195

of this piece of marble, for he took a very great deal of trouble to make us understand it, but to no purpose. The gates in front of the grand altar are of solid silver, it is said they were painted to deceive the French when they had possession of Malta. I suspect the truth of the story, the French were not to be so easily deceived by a few cunning monks.

Taking the church altogether it is one of the richest and most beautiful I ever saw. The bells at this church are very large, so are most of the bells at the other churches. At different hours of the day St. John's big bell strikes out, this is a signal for every bell in the island to join in the chorus, this makes such a noise that a stranger would be frightened out of his senses.

On the highest ground stands the Palace, this is occupied by the Governor Sir T. Maitland, when he resides here and by Sir Manly Power the Lieutenant Governor. Here is an English chapel for the English residents, close by is the market place, well stocked with everything, not the growth of the island, for scarce anything grows here, it is brought from Italy, and so cheap is everything that you can with a single halfpenny purchase things at five different stalls.

I have often been taught that England was the finest country in the world, what would you think if you could be transported here with a halfpenny in your pocket and go to a stall for a grains worth of onions, a large bunch half as big as your wrist and receive four grains in exchange. Then a large lettuce costs another grain, a bunch of radishes another grain and so on. Every other article of provisions are alike cheap in proportion.

No. 96. Fort Ricasoli, 19th February, 1823.

I have again had another day at Valette, this time we went to see the Capuchine Friary. The Capuchines are an order of monks who turn their back against everything in this world that gives comfort, ease or pleasure, hence these men wear a horse hair shirt next their skin, their heads are shaved and they wear no hats, shoes and stockings are also dispensed with. They live entirely on charity, but will receive no money. Several of these

'Holy Men' (if I might be allowed the term) are constantly begging from house to house, they carry a bag to stow away the scran. All they can collect is taken to their convent where it is cooked, after which they take their dinner. What is not consumed is then collected and distributed amongst a swarm of beggars who are waiting outside.

They have a curious way of disposing of their dead. When one of their order dies, they have some method of preserving the body, it is then placed upright against the wall one above another like the shelves in a grocer's shop, where you will see the tea cannisters standing in ranks one above the other. But as time destroys everything some of these monks are much altered since they were placed in the niches round the apartment, some are leaning on one side as if tired of standing, others are looking down grinning at the persons who come to visit them, others are looking at you as if supplicating to be released from their standing position.

You would think some of them were or had been in the navy or army, for here is one minus a leg, then his next comrade wants an arm, while a great many seem to have studied Lord Chesterfield for they appeared as if they were bowing to you in the politest manner. Many have their arms held out as if wishing to shake hands, one on the lower tier seemed so pressing that one of my comrades could not pass without giving him a hearty shake, when off came the arm at the elbow joint. Fortunately it was not observed by the person who conducted us he having his attention drawn in another direction.

We next went to the barracks at Florian, the barracks are good. Being now out of the town, nothing presents itself to the eye but a barren white rock except at intervals, a house might be raised when you might see a small tree or two. The 80th Regiment are stationed at this place.

We next took boat and crossed over to Cottinaro, here the 85th is stationed. Having plenty acquaintances in this corps we put up for the afternoon. After visiting the dock yard and other public places. This place is about a mile and a half from Fort

Ricasoli. It is to Cottinaro we go every Sunday to church. This place of worship is near the market place and during the time of morning service the market is in its greatest bustle. This might appear strange to you but it is the case in all the Catholic countries I have been in.

The weather is very warm, every kind of vegetable is in abundance, a person can live much better here for five shillings per week than in England for a pound. Bread about a penny per pound, meat two pence halfpenny, the best gunpowder tea two shillings, coffee (raw) five pence, sugar from three pence to four pence. All kinds of vegetables that are to be met with in England, and many other sorts that you know nothing of, are so cheap that for a shilling you might load a donkey. The climate is healthy but the people are much subject to sore eyes from the whiteness of the rock, particularly in summer.

The city of Valette and Cottinaro is remarkably clean owing to the great demand for soil. The Maltese are generally clean in their persons but from the great quantity of oil and garlic they use their houses do not smell pleasant to an Englishman. It has always been a rule with me when I am in a foreign country to accommodate myself to the customs of the people so far as eating is concerned, I always was of opinion it was the best means to preserve health, thus when I was in the Peninsular I soon accustomed myself to oil and garlic.

This in general is so offensive to our men that, for a long time after arriving in the country they cannot pass the streets, particularly where there are cook shops or those places where oil *chereces* and many other things are sold that more or less partake of oil etc., without expressing their dislike to the fumes that effects their nasal organs. But to me those smells were familiar. Indeed, the first day I went to Valette, I could not refrain dropping in to a cook shop and indulging myself with a platter of fizhongs dressed in oil and well seasoned with garlic.

I let in our canteen man to the tune of a good breakfast one morning. Happening to go in when he was at breakfast he asked me to have some. I knew he did this to have the laugh of me, expecting as soon as I had tasted it I should give over. But in this he was deceived, some soldiers coming in, mine host had to leave the table to serve, by the time he returned there was nothing but an empty plate. Smatch never asked me after, although I have frequently been present when he have been at his meals.

No. 97. Corfu, 11th March, 1823.

The *Rochfort* (80), bearing the flag of Vice Admiral Sir Graham Moore, brother to the gallant Sir John Moore, who fell at Corunna, arrived at Malta, the latter end of February. On the 2nd inst. we embarked on board and sailed for Corfu, where we arrived on the 6th. Before we left Malta the whole of the commuted men were removed from Corfu. On their way they stopped a few days at Fort Ricasoli. I understand they are to join a new regiment now forming for service in Sirra Leon (Sierra Leone), The regiment is to be called the Royal African Colonial Battalion, this is a good job to be rid of these men. Corfu, according to the accounts of the men, begins to alter for the best.

Before we left Malta the carnival commenced on Sunday 17th February. It continued three days. To any one fond of fun this was the time to enjoy it. I had never witnessed anything of the sort before. I took good care to be over to Valette each day before it began. By a general order the British residents and troops are not allowed to mask. About 12 o'clock each day a corps of drums beat through the streets to summon the people, the streets soon became crowded by people of both sex, dressed in every possible way one can imagine. Angels, devils, wild beast, old men and women, young lads and buxom lasses. In short here was as the song has it 'Old and young, grave and sad, deaf and dumb, dull and mad etc.'

Every street was so thronged that we were obliged to elbow our way through the crowd, every now and then saluted by a volley of sugar plumbs, everything that ran on wheels were in requisition, the middle of the streets were crowded with carriages, gigs, cars etc., all were masked except the British. This fun continues until sunset, when the drums again beat and the people disappear for the night.

In the midst of all this merriment there did not happen one single misunderstanding, for foreigners are not like the English who generally get drunk and fight before their feast or revels are half over. Foreigners drink sparingly and always keep in their senses, thus the three days passed over without rows of any kind. Every face seemed to smile, with content, until about half an hour after the carnival had closed, when the whole city, I might say island, was thrown into the deepest sorrow and anguish of mind imaginable.

I will endeavour to describe the cause as clear as I am able. In Valette there are a number of families who consider it improper that the children should be spectators of so much extravagance and folly. Each day they send them to the convent of Jesus Maria and Joseph, where they are amused and entertained by the monks until dusk, when they are let out to go home to their friends.

The children have to pass down a long passage in the centre of which stands an image of the Virgin, here a few priests are stationed to distribute sugar plumbs, sweetmeats etc. to them as they pass. To the poorer sort bread etc. is given. The number of children thus assembled are generally upwards of a thousand.

At the bottom of the passage, there is a turn to the right and a flight of about twenty steps, four or five paces from the steps are a pair of large folding doors that lead into the street. By some oversight the doors were not opened, the children in front, when they came to the bottom of the steps were buried alive by those who pressed from behind, in a short time the space from the doors to the top of the steps was one solid mass of human bodies.

What made it still worse was that a parcel of beggars, follow up the rear, to get share of what is left, so that the poor little creatures in front had no chance to retreat from the danger, but were hurried into it, one on top of the other, until this large space from the top of the steps to the doors were completely crammed with upwards of 500 children. The confusion was beyond description, and before proper assistance would be rendered, upward of one hundred had breathed their last breath.

When the place was cleared and the doors were opened the dead and dying were brought out into the streets, the scene that now took place baffles all description. The street for thirty yards each side of the door were strewed with children, some dead, others dying, and others shewing symptoms of recovering. Women running up and down mad with despair seeking their little ones, and to add to the misery of the scene it was dark. Hundreds of people were carrying lights. When a woman would examine her supposed child she would find it was not her own, it was then laid on the ground and the poor disconsolate mother would rush again amongst the little unfortunates to seek for her own.

I shall never forget this night, cries of despair were uttered by thousands and was heard distinctly at Fort Ricasoli and Cottinaro. It will be sufficient to say that upwards of one hundred were dead, that nearly two hundred were carried to the military hospitals, some died on the road, many others expired during the night, the number of children owned by their parents and carried to their own homes were great so that the number killed and maimed could not be less than 500.

At first the blame was thrown on the monks who are against the carnival, it was said it was done on purpose to try to do away with the carnival, but that cannot be possible, the fault must rest with the person whose duty it was to set the doors open. Sir Parker Carrol, Colonel of the 18th who is in command during the absence of Sir Manley Power, has caused an enquiry to be made, the result I have not heard.

No. 98. Corfu, 5th April, 1823.

I had not room in my last to say that the headquarters and two companies under Colonel Rice are stationed at Corfu, the remainder (eight companies) under Major Campbell, are at Santa Martha. This is not so good a station as Malta, everything is much dearer. Meat is not so good and the markets are not so well supplied. However, I have got to my regiment and am satisfied.

The Ionian Islands is a Greek republic under the protection of Great Britain and consists of seven islands, *viz.* Corfu, Paxo, Santa Martha, Ithaca, Cephalonia, Zante, and Cirego (Cythera). The small island of Fano and Calamas are dependant, the former on Corfu, the latter on Santa Martha. Corfu is the seat of Government. Sir Thomas Maitland is the Lord High Commissioner. The senate or upper house is composed of princes, counts, barons and knights of the order of St. Michael and St. George.

The Legislature or lower house consists of representatives from the several islands. Sir Frederick Adams is at the head of the military and in the absence of Sir Thomas Maitland (or 'King Tom' as the soldiers call him) is the Lord High Commissioner pro tempo. The garrison consists of two companies of the Royal Artillery, one of sappers, a detachment of the staff corps, the 28th, 32nd, 36th, and 51st Regiments, the 28th and 51st giving detachments to Santa Martha.

Corfu is a place of great strength by nature, much improved by art. It has been under several masters, first the Venetians, who defended it against the Turks. Then the Russians, afterwards the French, who held it until the Peace of 1814 when it was handed over to the British. I have been told that the French garrison were reduced to the greatest distress through the vigilance of our cruisers.

The men had worn out their clothing and could get no more, many of the sentries were obliged to wear the hospital dresses. The place were often put to shifts for provisions, the only chance they had of keeping up a supply was by making hazardous trips to the Albanian coast or to Italy, these trips were generally unfortunate being mostly picked up by our cruisers.

The French were obliged to cut a canal a considerable way inland to protect their gunboats and small craft from our boats. This canal was protected by the guns from the citadel, yet our boats would often pay them a visit at night, cut out the trading vessels and tow them out under the muzzles of the guns of the garrison.

The city is called after the island and is small and compact, the main street is wide and kept clean but most of the others are narrow and dirty. It stands in the centre of three strong points *viz.* the citadel, the island of Vido and the bell barracks. These three places are to be strongly fortified.

When complete all the other works will be destroyed as useless. Between the citadel and town stands the Esplanade where the Corfuots take their morning and evening's walks. It is on this place the new palace of St. Michael and St. George stands, it is nearly finished, being built of freestone from Malta, it has a noble and beautiful appearance.

I am quartered in the citadel, from my room I can see the ruins of a town on the Albanian coast, from the flag staff there is a fine prospect over the island, the coast opposite and a large extent of water. The islands of Paxo and Santa Martha, with the range of mountains inhabited by the Suliotts (mixed race of Greek and Albanian origin named after Suli Mountains).

The old palace stands in the citadel, this was formerly the residence of the Governor, but at present it is occupied only by a few of the staff. A large Greek church within the citadel is appropriated to the use of the English where divine service is performed to the troops every Sunday morning.

At an early hour the troops march to church in review order, pile their arms in front of the church. After service the whole garrison march to the esplanade where the major general amuses himself two or three hours in putting them through a field day. Sometimes the men's dinners are ready cooked and taken to church. On these occasions the garrison march into the country and have a sham fight.

The troops return home in the afternoon, swear all the time they are cleaning their things, in the evening get drunk and go to bed. You will say this is a fine way to keep the Sabbath. It cannot be helped, the half of the men are employed through the week in making new roads, so that this is the only day the general can catch us altogether.

No. 99. Corfu. 2nd May, 1823.

The 23rd April being St. George's day, His Majesty's birthday was celebrated, and the new palace of St. Michael and St. George was opened. The day commenced by a royal salute, and hoisting the Independent Ionian Standard. This is a handsome flag; in the centre is the Royal Standard of England, round which are the seven colours of the Ionian Islands; this was to be a grand holiday. The Esplanade was the grand rendezvous where all kind of sport was to take place.

In front of the palace a high pole was set up to the height of fourteen feet from the ground, made smooth by plaining it, and well oiled and greased. Near the top a spar ran across like the yard of a ship, to which was suspended a pigskin of wine, a goat, a lamb and many other tempting things; on the top of the pole was a *doubloon*. All those prizes were to be the property of the man who could climb to the top; to prevent accidents a great quantity of straw was placed at the bottom of the pole. Hundreds tried their luck, to no purpose. Some would get on men's shoulders and vainly hug the post, for as soon as they were left to themselves, down they would come with the run amidst the laughter and shouts of thousands of spectators.

After we had laughed our sides sore, a young Maltese, a fine athletic fellow, came forward amidst the shouts of his countrymen. He had several silk scarves, one of these he fastened round the pole. Leaving a noose to put his foot in, he then fastened another round his body and round the post; by the assistance of other scarves, he contrived to get above the grease. He then had to slip of a jacket and trousers, he was then free of the grease, and having nothing on but shirt and drawers, he climbs to the cross yard in gallant stile, amidst the most deafening shouts I ever heard. After resting awhile, he finished his journey to the top.

The day passed off well, various were the games, *viz.* wrestling, boxing, running, jumping and many other games. The people assembled presented one of the most curious sights I ever saw, Greeks in the dress of the different islands they belong to, Albanians, soldiers and sailors etc. all mingled together, each taking part and striving to be conquerors in the different games. Many surprising feats were performed by the Greeks, who are a fine active robust race. Their riding at full gallop on horseback with a long lance and taking a ring on the point from a line over their heads, is an ancient game in which they excel. Our country men had but little chance with them.

This amusement never takes place without much ceremony, it is announced by a proclamation from the general inviting the knights to enrol their names. The prizes are of great value, an adjutant general of the game is appointed. Captain Wingate, 32nd, whose father lives on Portland place, held this office. A splendid stage is erected for the Lord High Commissioner and his staff, on each side of which are others richly decorated. From the principal stage the line runs across the ride.

The knights having assembled at the starting post, each dressed in ancient costume, some representing the Templars, others in the costume of different ages, everything being ready a bugle sounds, off dashes one of the knights at full speed with his lance erect, as he approaches the ring the lance is brought down, at the same time he rises in his stirrups. If he succeeds in carrying of the ring, the adjutant general escorts him back to the grand stand where the name of the knight and the number of the prize is entered in a book.

I should have told you that the ring is made of stout wire, about three inches in diameter, each ring has three compartments thus:

The whole of the knights have three chances, those who gets No. 1 oftenest are entitled to the best prizes. The best prize was a very beautiful rich sword highly ornamented, this was won by a young Greek who carried number one each time. The other prizes consisted of targets, spears, swords, golden spurs etc. It will be sufficient to observe that the Greeks carried off the most and best prizes.

The game over, the prizes distributed, the knights then escort the general and his lady home, who are drawn by six horses followed by all the Greek nobility and gentry, and officers of the army. All kinds of games continued until dark. Wine and all kinds of refreshments were in abundance. The day passed without a single accident or row.

An illumination took place at night, the palace was all in a blaze, a grand ball was given at the palace by the Lord High Commissioner *pro tempo*. I was on the guard of honour so I was in the thick of the fun all night. Manley of the 32nd was one of the waiters, consequently I came in for some of the good things of the feast. The dancing continued until 5 o'clock when we escorted the Baron Theotokey home, attended by the military bands and all the colours of the different regiments in the garrison, roused all the good people from their morning slumbers, then marched to our barracks.

No. 100. Corfu, 9th June, 1823.

I believe I have told you that the Greek church is the religion established by law here and that the Roman Catholic and Protestant religions are tolerated. The Greek and Roman churches keep the old style. At Easter we had a busy time of it, on good Friday (old style) the Greeks paraded about the town several hours.

I will describe to you one of the Greek processions. First, military band, followed by a large cross on which was painted a representation of a crucified Saviour. Two archbishops and two bishops, mitered and robed. Another cross accompanied by two of the frail daughters of Eve doing penance for their secret sins, their heads were bare, their long black hair flowed in disorder over their backs, their eyes cast on the ground, with their hands crossed on their lovely bosoms, their feet and legs minus stockings and shoes.

Thus they crept along to the tune of the 'Dead March in Saul,' followed by about fifty *papa's* (eastern priests) in their robes with their long snuffy beards, chanting a funeral dirge in ancient Greek, the discord of their several voices and then broken in upon by the sweet and solemn tone of the band, together with the ugly faces they pulled, to get out the notes of their song was enough to inspire one with disgust in place of piety.

The next who followed was the major general and staff accompanied with commanding officers of corps, the Greek nobles consisting of princes, counts, barons, and the knights of the Most Illustrious Order of St. Michael and St. George all dressed in richly embroidered coats, collars, stars and badges of the different orders of knighthood, then followed the undecorated gentry and last of all came the rag-tag and night. I do not know its proper name, the soldiers call it the wood slave. This little creature that I believe to be perfectly harmless is looked upon with abhorrence, it is said, if one of them should run over your leg or arm you instantly loose the use of the member, nay, it is farther affirmed they are fond of p———g on people, and so poisonous is their water that the part becomes an incurable ulcer.

I have often taken them in my hand and found them harmless. They are persecuted the same as the poor inoffensive toad is in England, such is the prejudice of man that although I have brought home a toad in my hand my comrades cannot believe but that it is as poisonous as a viper. I have always found the wood slave very shy, always wishing to shun the company of man.

Scorpions and centipedes are very numerous and we often find them on the walls in the rooms. We have a remedy against the bite or sting of these reptiles, it is simple and every company is provided with it. A bottle of rum is kept, into this every venomous reptile that can be caught alive is put. If anyone should get stung you have only to wash the part with the liquor, the relief is instantaneous and cure certain.

There is a particular sort of fruit grows amongst the rocks called prickly pears, when they are in season we are subject to a troublesome disorder called the prickly heat. It is in appearance like a surfeit in the blood, you become covered all over with blotches. Some have it so bad they are obliged to go to hospital, everyone has it more or less, particularly the first season after your arrival in the country. To have it bad is a good omen for it is said to prevent sickness. Be this as it may I have it very slightly. When a person has the prickly heat, if he takes a drink of anything cold, or receives a sudden fright, or anything should happen to impede or increase the circulation of the blood, he feels as if ten thousand pins were run into his person, followed by a burning heat and then an intolerable itching, that if you had a thousand pair of hands you could find employment for the whole.

The prickly pear is the best remedy for this troublesome disorder, they are much esteemed by our men, who are very industrious in procuring them even at the risk of their lives. A party the other day took a sheet with them and soon returned with a good load. The man who owned the sheet, not suspecting anything, turned into bed in his buff, that is without his shirt. He soon found himself in a terrible plight. The pears are covered with a very fine beard, that adhered to the sheet. The poor fellow was not in bed many minutes before he began turning and rolling, cursing and groaning in such a manner we all thought the fellow mad, every bit of his body, arms, legs etc. were stuck full of the beards that had adhered to the sheet. The consequence was that we were obliged to take him to the hospital.

There is a wind called the *scirroco*, or south, this is the disagreeable evil I have to contend with. It is rather early for it yet, next month we shall have plenty of it, the remittant fever then sets in.

I shall finish this letter by relating a laughable story of a ghost, it was related to me by one of the men who saw it. It was at the close of the sickly season last year, one of the Royal Artillery, supposed to be dead, was one evening removed to the dead house. The hospital sentry's duty was to go every few minutes to rattle the door to prevent the rats gnawing the corpse. About midnight, when spirits are fond of walking, as the sentry was about to rattle at the door, it opened of itself and out walked the man with the sheet wrapped round him.

Away goes the sentry in double quick time to the guard room, but the serjeant on guard being an unbeliever was ordering another man to be put on sentry and the frightened sentry to the main guard for leaving his post. Just at the moment in walked the ghost himself. The serjeant was instantly cured of his unbelief and away he went, accompanied by the corporal and all the men who were awake and left the ghost in quiet possession of the guard room. In a little time the serjeant recovered from his panic, returned with his guard, found the poor fellow sitting on the stool, they wrapped him in a couple of great coats and took him back to the hospital. The man shortly after this recovered and went to his duty.

No. 101. Corfu, 12th August, 1823.

Since my last we have had a grand procession in honour of St. Speridon (or Spero). The body of this saint is kept in a silver tomb in the church of St. Speridon. On the left of the Grand Altar stands the small chapel dedicated to the saint, on the top of the tomb are several small holes resembling key holes. The people kiss the ground in the little chapel, crawl on their hands and knees up the steps leading to the tomb, taking care to strike the forehead and kiss every step, touch the tomb with their forehead and kiss it several times in different places, then apply their noses to the holes and take good hearty sniffs. So very great are the crowd of worshippers on particular days that it is with difficulty the feeble can approach the place.

But the most extraordinary part of the worship of this saint is when he is carried in grand procession. This happens twice in the year, on those occasions his Saintship is taken out of his resting place with great ceremony and pomp, a guard of honour and band attends, the saint is placed standing up right by the grand altar, the guard presents arms, band playing 'God save the King,' the people throw themselves down as well as the crowded state of the church will admit amidst the clang of arms, prayers and incense and a Royal Salute from the battery over the saint's head.

On the glass case is a crown of glory formed of diamonds, a very large one in the centre is said to be a present from the Emperor of Russia. The lower part of the case being open his feet, or at least his boots are visible, these boots are of scarlet cloth richly ornamented with gold embroidery. A large silver dish is placed by the case, to receive the presents of the faithful. Sentries being placed to keep order, the aristocracy in their embroidered coats covered with badges and stars etc. first advance, kiss the boots and throw down their offerings, next the holy sacrament is administered, then the remainder of the day is passed by the devout kissing the mummy's boots, not forgetting the most important part of the ceremony the dollars and *doubloons*, which continues to shower into the large dish to the no small delight of these holy thieves.

All this is going on amidst the greatest confusion, Greeks in their pious zeals struggling and swearing with each other to get up to the saint first, while the soldier enraged at the difficulty he has to keep order curses their eyes and limbs, and is no way backward in giving the most furious a clout under the ear or a poke with the butt of his firelock. The soldier too receives many *dais* in the fist to allow persons to pass out of their turn.

To give you a notion of the misery attending this religious ceremony the church is thronged to suffocation, the glass stands at 92 or more in the shade, the place is full of candles and lamps all in full blaze, a most intolerable smell of incense mixed with stinking breath highly seasoned with garlic. To this add the fumes arising from about fifteen hundred bodies then you will be able to form some notion of what is passing within the walls of the church of St. Spero.

The second day is taken up by a grand procession, this is exactly the same as others I have described, only the saint is carried by colonels and a much greater multitude follows. A salute of twenty-one guns and the clanking of all the bells in the place announces that the procession has left the church. As it passes along the sick are brought out and laid in the middle of the roads under a burning sun waiting for the saint to be carried over them. If this fails to cure the sick it is no fault of the saint but a want of faith on their parts or for some secret sins.

When the saint arrives at the entrance of the citadel he is

rested on the ground, every Greek then prostrates themselves on the earth, the priests, or as they are called *papas*, chants a hymn, the guns at the citadel fire a royal salute, so do the men of war in the harbour who are decorated with all the flags on board, and all the bells are set a ringing.

This takes up about ten minutes. The procession then starts under another royal salute, when they arrive at that part of the ramparts where there is a view of the opposite coast, his Saint-ship is made to face that way amidst great chanting. This was done to bless the Greeks who are fighting the Turks for their independence. After the whole of the town had been peram-bulated, and half the sick had received their death stroke from the powerful rays of the sun, the saint is once more stood up by the side of the altar, when the old trade of kissing his boots and dropping money in the dish again begins and is continued until late the next day when the holy personage is again entombed.

On the day of the procession, one of the frail daughters of Eve done penance, she was a very interesting young woman, the penance laid on this young girl did not differ in any respect from the others I have already mentioned in former letters.

No. 102. Corfu, 3rd October, 1823.

Knowing the jealousy of the Greeks I thought it prudent not to call on Mrs. Pirie without taking Priscilla with me. Mr. Pirie gave us a good welcome, he is a fine looking man and boatswain of the harbour. From what we could learn from Mrs. Pirie, like the rest of his countrymen he is sadly troubled with the green eyed monster. He seemed pleased that his wife had found an old acquaintance and wished us to renew our visits as often as we could. I could not prevail on him to come and spend the evening with us, respecting allowing Mrs. Pirie to visit us alone was out of the question, she is a complete prisoner, never goes out but to his mother's and then she is always escorted there and back by himself. Mrs. Pirie speaks both Greek and Italian to perfection, but she has in a great measure forgot her mother tongue, for I frequently observed she was at a loss to express herself without slipping in a word of Greek or Italian.

She is a doubly good Christian believing in all the articles of the English and Greek churches. I observed a large painting of St. Spero in a gilt frame with a large lamp burning in front suspended by three chains from the ceiling. I remarked to her that the saint was their household God. She very seriously told us that a short time since she had been dangerously ill, all hopes of her recovery was given up, that she lay on her bed, her eyes fixed on the saint praying St. Spero to have compassion on her, when the lamp and picture began swinging she was convinced he had attended to her prayers for from that moment she began to recover. I endeavoured to account for this by natural causes, the same thing happens from the shock of an earthquake so frequent in these islands or perhaps it was only fancy from the weak state of her body and mind borne down by sickness. Mrs. Pirie would not have it so, she was convinced and there was no persuading her.

As I had endeavoured to persuade her she must be wrong, she in her turn endeavoured to shake my unbelief by relating to me the following anecdote. Some centuries ago when the Vinicians (Venetians) were mistress of the Mediterranean and by the power of her arms secured the independence of the Ionian Isles, a plague broke out in a large village a few miles from Corfu. To prevent the disorder spreading, a chain of soldiers were stationed round the fatal place.

The plague had made sad ravages amongst the poor inhabitants, the dead were unburied, almost every one left were more or less infected, their cries and lamentations were heart rending when one night a stranger was observed advancing towards the place. A soldier stopped him but the stranger would proceed telling the soldier he was St. Spero and that he was going to restore the dead to life and heal the sick.

The soldier swore if he advanced another step he would shoot him. The saint, nothing daunted, moved on and the sentry, like a good soldier let fly, but wonderful to relate, the contents of the piece recoiled back and killed the soldier. The saint then went into the town and in a short time the plague was stayed, the dead raised and the sick healed. This done the saint returned to the soldier, restored him to life, then went and laid himself very comfortably in his silver tomb. Everyone was astonished to hear the voice of woe so soon changed to songs of mirth, accompanied by the merry pipe and dance. The soldier's tale soon unravelled the mystery and the hole where the ball entered proved the fact beyond a doubt. I swore it was a lie, got up by the *papas*. Priscilla looked doubtful and Mrs. Pirie crossed herself, said it was as true as the gospel, muttered something in the shape of a prayer in Greek, added some oil to the lamp. I suppose to make an atonement to old Spero, should he be offended at our unbelief.

We have received the news of the death of Sir Thomas Maitland. The Greeks were determined to have a holiday, so they got up a mock funeral, a coffin was laid in state in St. Mark Church in front of the grand altar, many thousand candles were placed round the coffin so as to represent an amphitheatre. When they were all lit up the effect was certainly grand. All the *papas* were employed chanting a solemn dirge, the flags half mast high and the batteries fired minute guns, the Greeks sauntered about in their best clothes. The soldiers drank a glass to the memory of 'King Tom,' got as drunk as lords and went to bed as happy as princes.

No. 103. Corfu, 10th November, 1823.

Sir Frederick Adam is appointed Lord High Commissioner, nothing could have pleased the Greeks better. Sir Frederick is a great favourite, his lady is a Corfuot, her husband and brother are both living in Corfu. The story is that Sir Frederick was caught in such a situation with the lady that left no doubt on the mind of her Greek lord that Sir Frederick had just been measuring him for an enormous pair of horns which everyone knows is a disagreeable appendage to one's brows, particularly in a warm climate.

Whether there was any foundation for the husband's fears

I cannot say. Be that as it may he soon applied and obtained a divorce.

This lady is now Queen of the Ionian Isles, and the ladies, British as well as Greek, consider it an honour to receive a smile from 'Her Majesty.' Like most of the Greek women there is something interesting about her yet she must be content to be placed in the second class, her complexion is dark, features regular, eyes black as sloes so is her hair, but the beard on her upper lip would ornament an hussar.

Sir Frederick, as a general officer is not disliked by our men, he is much altered for the better since the commuted men left this station. At times he is very passionate, when he will vie with any soldier under his command in swearing. A short time since while putting the garrison through a field day on the esplanade one of our serjeants made a mistake. It was noticed by the general, he discharged a volley of oaths at the serjeant, then threw his gold snuff box at him. He is a fine looking man and received a severe wound at Waterloo by which his left arm is disabled.

When the news of his appointment to Lord High Commissioner arrived a high holiday took place, much powder was wasted, all kinds of sports were carried on, on the esplanade, a grand illumination at night with a ball and supper at the palace. The Greeks sang and danced their *papooches* (Oriental slippers) to pieces and the soldiers drank wine until they could put their fingers into their throats and dabble in it. Thus began the accession of 'King Fred,' the second English sovereign of the independent Ionian Islands.

We have experienced a slight shock of an earthquake since my last, those awful visitations are not so frequent here as they are in the southern islands. This one though slight, shook the barracks, made the tiles chatter and the belts and everything suspended against the wall swing backward and forward like the pendulum of a clock.

We have had rather a sickly season this fall, many have died and many more will have to be sent home before they will perfectly recover. So far, I have escaped, although I was sometime

214

in the very focus of the fever. Our hospital serjeant has been sick some time, I had to take his duty. This man has drunk hard in his time, this and the *scirroco* wind has so shook his nerves he will have to be sent home.

I shall close this letter by relating an anecdote of this man as told me by himself. Before I arrived on the station one of the commuted men was shot by sentence of a general court martial, the sentence was carried into execution near the hospital. Ever since poor Sergeant McNeil has been afraid to go out after night. It happened last August that our doctors had been opening a dead man by candle light, they had returned to the surgery, and in putting up their instruments they missed a knife, poor Mack was ordered to fetch it. Doctor Webster saw him change colour, said he had better not go, but rather than it should be thought he was afraid, away he goes. The dissecting room was over the surgery, the only way to go to it was through the long room or sick ward, then up a flight of steps, back over the wards through the cock loft.

This loft was used for a store to keep the spare things in, there was at the time several pewter close-stool pans and chamber pots piled up near the centre of the loft.

Our hero entered the dismal room seized the knife and was returning in triumph when out goes the lamp. He was so terribly alarmed that in hurrying to get back he came in contact with the pewter pots over which he tumbled. He said he never could recollect how he got back to the surgery, but the sick men who were roused by the noise overhead were astonished to see him rush into the ward his hair erect, pale as death, the lamp in one hand and the knife in the other.

The ward is above thirty yards in length and it was the unanimous opinion of every one that he did not make above three strides through it to the surgery. What a dreadful thing it must be to be disordered in the nerves. I have known poor McNeil for many years, what a change. I have seen him in trying moments under showers of shot and shells, when he was as firm as a rock.

No. 104. Corfu, 6th January, 1824.

I was about to describe to you the celebration of a marriage that took place at Corfu between an Albian (Albanian) and one of the females refugees from the Moors. The man is one of the Ionian Cavalry, a small party consisting of a serjeant and twelve men, kept up more for ornament than use, having no duty to perform but giving a man daily for general's orderly. I must omit that part of the ceremony performed by the *papa* in church, not being present. The bridegroom is about thirty, the bride fifteen.

The happy pair accompanied by their friends proceeded from the church to an empty apartment, a short distance from the citadel where preparations on a grand scale had been provided. Chairs and tables there were none, it would have been superfluous to be troubled with them for a Greek can sit is well and as comfortably on his heels with his knees projecting in front, as we can in the easiest chair. Dinner was served up in a large brass kettle round which the party, consisting of the bridegroom and bride, the whole of the men of the corps and a few select friends, formed a circle each armed with a formidable spoon. The contents of the kettle consisted of a goat stewed to rags, well thickened with rice and highly seasoned with pepper and garlic.

After demolishing this a sheep, roasted on a wooden spit was brought in. Having no dish one end of the spit was rested on the ground, the other end held by one of the party. Each person had now changed his spoon for a knife. The work commenced by cutting and hacking until the whole that was done was devoured, the remainder was then placed before the fire to finish roasting. Next came the coffee, *rosolio* and *rojetta* (Mediterranean cordials or liqueurs), with sweetmeats for the ladies who sat squat on their heels, while the men regaled themselves with wine and water (the Greeks never drink wine without infusing plenty of water with it). The song and dance with an abundance of tobacco was kept up until the evening when the remainder of the sheep was devoured.

About 10 o'clock the happy bridegroom and bride were escorted by the *papa*, the fathers and mothers of the new married pair and their friends to their bed chamber, where as a matter of course they were left to themselves. Early the next morning their fathers and mothers (or in the case of death or absence of any of these relations, they are represented by someone else) accompanied by the *papa* who performed the ceremony enters the bed room, rouses the drowsy pair and in the presence of the husband examines the sheets. It is then decided whether the bride was in possession of her virginity, if so the marriage is declared good, but if on the contrary the husband demands a divorce. I blush for some of my fair country women if such a practice prevailed in England!

There has been the ruins of an ancient palace discovered near Castarada. The general opinion is that it has at some remote period been swallowed by an earthquake. There is no account in the records of the islands of such a place, it must therefore be very ancient. Several small pieces of copper coin have been found but they are so much corroded no light can be discovered by them.

There is a missionary from England stationed here. Few, if any of the soldiers ever attend his preaching, twice a week he preaches in Greek, when the Archbishop of Corfu, and most of the *papas*, with a good sprinkling of the Greek nobs generally attend. It is an astonishing fact that not one *papa* on this island can preach a sermon. Their churches are always open, the people go in, cross themselves, go round, kiss several pictures, then cross themselves again and go out. On Sundays, there is service twice, when the *papa* goes through a deal of ceremony at the altar, while repeating the prayers and litany, which they have by heart like a parrot.

They differ from the Church of Rome in several things, first they do not believe in Trans-substantiation, they allow no images to be set up in their churches or houses, but the walls are covered with pictures of saints. They do not acknowledge the Pope's supremacy. Like all other good Christians, they believe all except their own church are wrong and cannot be saved. Mind,

I am speaking of the lower order of the people.

No. 105. Corfu, 12th February, 1824.

When I wrote last, the Greek Christmas had just began, this is kept up in feasting and the poor devils stand much in need of a feast, for Christmas is preceded by a long fast, it lasts all the Advent. The ceremony of visiting and giving presents are much the same as in England, the same might be said of the new year's gifts. On the 6th of January (old style) they have an odd custom of baptising the cross. A large cross is brought to the seaside and thrown in, when instantly in jumps a number of men to get it out. This is not a very pleasant job for the winters here are cold. Besides the two lents before Christmas and Easter, they have two others, one called the Lent of the Virgin, this lasts a fortnight, the other is the Lent of the twelve apostles and continues twelve days. Besides these, if all the other fasts are taken into account, the whole year is one continued round of feasts and fasts.

The other day on going to see Manley, I passed a baker's shop. Hearing an old fiddle going I had the curiosity to peep in, how I was astonished to see five strapping fellows as naked as they came into the world, their nasty greasy pelts as yellow as saffron, the sweat running down their bodies, as if they had been basted with oil or melted butter. These dirty devils were dancing in a long kneading trough, they held on with their hands to something over their heads while the master was scraping a jig out of a miserable old fiddle. I had often been told this is the way they knead their dough, but never saw them at it before. It is seldom I ever put any bread to my mouth since, but I have the picture before me.

We are under orders for Cephalonia and shall move as soon as the transports arrive with the 18th Royal Irish from Malta. After landing the 18th at Corfu, the transports will proceed with us to Cephalonia, calling at Paxo for Captain Bayly's company and at Santa Martha for the remainder of the regiment stationed there, under Major Campbell.

I have been favoured with the perusal of some papers giving the history of our regiment from its first raising to the close of the war in Germany, some seventy years ago. They were the memorandum of Colonel Nowles and presented by him in 1819 to the regiment some short time before his death. I was struck by an anecdote of a young woman who served in the corps and was on two expeditions with it.

The following as near as I can recollect is the colonel's account of the story. (But it must be borne in mind that at the time this young woman entered the regiment recruits were not so strictly inspected as now). The regiment was raised in Leeds and the neighbourhood and was composed of respectable young men principally of tradesmen's sons and aspiring young men in the vicinity. Regiments were thus raised under false pretences, then sold to the Government, the person who incurred the expense was presented with a colonel's commission by way of compliment or to indemnify him for his expenses.

As soon as the government was in possession of the regiment, it was sent on a secret expedition to the coast of France (Rochefort). It was remarked that the young soldier the subject of this anecdote was the first who leaped on shore, but as this expedition was only a diversion it soon returned and was again employed on a similar service. After this it appears the regiment was stationed at Chichester. At this place the young soldier's sex was discovered by the following accident. (It must be remembered at the period this happened the soldier's pay was only sixpence *per diem*, scarcely sufficient to sustain life).

The soldiers were continually committing depredations in the gardens and fields. She in company with her comrade were walking through a turnip field. The soldier drew two turnips one of which he gave to her. They were observed by the farmer who came upon them, the soldier ran but she was seized. In vain she entreated forgiveness from the old churl but he was deaf, she pleaded her innocence by saying it was the other soldier who gave the turnip to her. It was no use, he was determined she should go before her commanding officer. She knew what would follow, she could not strip at the triangle without exposing her sex. The only means she had left was to reveal herself to the old man under a promise of secrecy. After some parleying the old fellow promised when she imparted to him the secret that no one knew but herself.

The farmer was dumb founded, went home, told his dame who was just then setting off for Chichester Market with her butter. Before she had sold half her butter the story was blown all over the market and in a short time, to use 'Corporal Trim's' words to my Uncle Toby, 'There was not one in the regiment from the colonel to the lowest drum boy' that had not heard and told the story over and over an hundred times. The sequel was as follows. She was discharged and married to the man whose fortunes she had so faithfully followed.

The colonel's papers are preserved in the orderly room giving a clear historical account of the regiment from its being first raised down to the time he left it, a document of great value. The records of the regiment during that period are missing. Colonel Nowles served a long time in the corps, he was severely wounded at the battle of Minden, served and was in action several times afterwards under Prince Ferdinand of Brunswick. He was employed afterwards in the Mediterranean, was at the capture of the Island of Minorca, storming of the Star Fort on that Island, who, in company with Captain Moore (the late General Sir John Moore, killed at Corunna), carried the fort at the head of the Grenadiers 51st Regiment. Finally, he was with the regiment in Portugal, from whence it embarked for the East Indies.

No. 106. Argostoli, 10th June, 1824.

At length the expected transport arrived with the 18th. Regiment, we embarked the 20th *ultimo* on board the *Vittoria,* and proceeded to Cephalonia. The other two called at Paxo and Santa Martha for the remainder of the regiment who have joined us at this place.

Sailing out of the harbour of Corfu we passed the beautiful gun brig, the property of the late Lord Byron, his Lordship's remains are on board on its way to England. Lord Byron died a short time since at Missilonghi, he seems to have devoted both his purse and talents to the Greek cause. His poems have inspired the patriotic Greeks with such a love of liberty and thirst for revenge they will never again submit to bondage, the struggle might yet last sometime but in the end the Greek must be successful. I said to a Greek one day 'Byron is dead.'

He replied, 'No, never,' then striking his left breast at the same moment his soul rushed into his eyes, 'he will always live here and in the hearts of my countrymen.' When a Greek speaks of Lord Byron it is as if he was speaking of some superior deity who had visited them from heaven on an errand of mercy. This generation adores him and future generations will ever respect the name of Byron and class him in the highest rank of their immortal heroes.

Sailing down the coast with Paxo on our starboard side we had a good view of the mountainous country inhabited by the Saliots, here the soldier can contemplate with delight the obstinate resistance the brave Saliots made against the power of Ali Pasha. After passing this we came to poor devoted Pargo. The history of its misfortunes and of its noble devotion rather than submit to that most detestable tyrant, the Nero of the present day, Ali Pasha, is of so resent date and must be well known to you. It needs no remark from me. It is impossible for a soldier to pass those places where the tyrant prevailed, and patriotic blood dyed the land, without feeling sensations it would be utterly impossible for me to describe.

After passing Pargo we soon came to the island of Santa Martha. We now left the mainland, sailed between Paxo and Santa Martha, keeping the latter place on our larboard. This island is the Botany Bay of the Ionian Isles for the young refractory officers of the Ionian army. When an officer commits an offence he is placed under the command of Major Temple, Sub Inspector of Ionian Militia and Commandant of the island. From the many reports of the doings and sayings of this man amongst the men of every regiment that has been under his command he must be a complete tyrant.

I know of no man so universally hated and feared, so great is the feeling of dislike against him that his name is never mentioned with respect, he always goes by the name of 'Old Blue Skin.'

Next to Santa Martha is the little island of Ithaca, famous in ancient history for having the sly Ulysses for it's king, and being the solitary place of abode of the chaste Penelope during the long absence of her husband, who figured so conspicuously against Troy. It is also the birth place of Telemachus.

We now make the northern part of Cephalonia, about ten miles down the coast we turn into a bold opening to our left proceed about two miles, we are abreast of the pretty little village of Luxoria. Here we turn short to the right, pass the Devil's point, when ten minutes sail brought us to the town of Argostoli, dropped anchor and in a short time landed.

The 8th or King's Regiment has been stationed here, a part of the 8th took our places in the transport and sailed for Corfu. Captain Elliott's company was sent to the island of Cirego to relieve a company of the 8th. This regiment is under orders for England having served their time on this station (ten years). We had also to send a party of two officers and forty men to Ithaca, this detachment marched across the island to Salmos where they crossed by a ferry to Ithaca and relieved a similar party of the 8th. The other two transports soon arrived after us. By the 27th *ultimo* the 8th. had left the island.

Since Christmas I have had charge of the regimental school. I was put in orders for schoolmaster just before I left Corfu. This is a good comfortable situation particularly as I have a family. I have nothing to do with parades or drill, when the school is over my time is my own. We have a very comfortable room, the winter half year we have an allowance of sixty pounds of wood *per diem*, my wife and children are on the ration list, that is a woman has half and a child quarter ration *per diem,* besides Colonel Rice allows me to take as many Greek scholars as I can get. I go in plain clothes except to church on Sunday mornings and to muster on the 26th of each month.

Argostoli is the capital of the island, it consists of one long street extending itself about a mile from north to south along the lake or arm of the sea fronting the east. In front of the town by the water side is a beautiful walk, when the sun is declining. This place a short time since was a nasty stinking beach. A wall built out in the waters where it is six feet deep, the back part filled up, forms this walk. This will prevent much sickness, much of which arose from the impurity arising from sea weed and filth from the town. This wall will be continued a considerable distance beyond the town northward where there is a wide open space much frequented mornings and evenings, at this place there is a statue of Sir Thomas Maitland, it stands on a pyramid about forty feet in height. It is in contemplation to build a prison on the same principal as the new prisons in England.

Returning to town you pass the Devil's barracks. The next building occupied by the English is the school room, this is occupied by your humble servant, joining this is the orderly room. This was once an immense building covering several acres, it has been destroyed by an earthquake. I believe it was a Greek monastery. Opposite is the hospital, a fine building and an ornament to the town. Farther on is a large house occupied by the officers, it is called the rookery. Next to it at a short distance stands the Commandant's house, near it is another barracks, at the south end of the town is a bridge half a mile in length that crosses the lake. This leads to the soldier's burying ground and into the interior of the island. There is nothing handsome about this bridge, but it is a strong and useful piece of work. About the middle stands a small column erected as the inscription says 'To the glory of the English nation,' with the date of the building the bridge.

Farther to the south, about four miles, at the head of the lake stands the castle, an old Venetian fortification. Here is a strong detachment, it being the only fortified place I have seen, except a battery mounting one heavy gun at the Devil's Point. About three hours distance beyond the castle, stands the bold and majestic mountain, named Jupiter Enos, but from its sombre appearance it is likewise called the Black Mountain.

At the foot of this mountain stands the village of Jerosemo, in the church the Greeks have got the precious body of the renowned Saint Jerosemo, who is carried about the village in grand procession once a year, But more about Jupiter Enos and the saint when we are better acquainted.

On the opposite side of the town across the lake runs a long ridge of lime stone that shuts out the view of the interior, yet a short pleasant walk after you cross the bridge, throws a great part of the island open to view, little is to be seen but ridges of lime stone, but the pleasantest walk is up the hill behind the town, the road runs through olive grove, vineyards and currant gardens. On the top of the hill the eye is delighted with a variety of beautiful scenery. Under the cooling shade of the olive we can sit and enjoy a rich repast. To the west as far as the eye will carry is a bold view of the Ionian sea.

Vessels are always passing to and from the Archipeligo and Italy. Ships of war of different nations convoying or cruising to protect the traders from the bold pirates that swarm in the arches, not forgetting the Turkish men of war and Greek armed vessels watching and playing at hide and go seek with each other.

Another pleasant walk is to the Devil's point, from this for a few *obili* you can cross to Luxoria a distance of three miles by water, here the country is more fertile, wine good and cheap, a large plant resembling the American Mallas is very common.

An artillery man stationed at the Devil's point has surrounded his garden with some young plants, they have taken root and thrive well, it forms a complete barrier to all intruders. It is called by the soldiers Adam's Thread, it takes fifty years to come to perfection, it then throws out a long straight pole from thirty feet and upwards in height.

Out of the top of this pole comes the blossoms that lasts a considerable time, it then seeds and dies. Some of every age might be met with in a short walk from the size of a cabbage plant to a full grown one whose leaves are from eight to nine feet long.

I do not know if I am justified by calling them leaves, for when at their full growth they are full a foot thick in the middle, the point and both edges are armed with sharp pointed thorns, this is the needle, the inside is composed of very fine threads, the inside of the pole makes excellent razor strops.

This is the largest of the seven Ionian Isles, there does not appear to be any trade carried on, it produces oil and wine, but few currants are grown, pomegranates plentiful.

No. 108. Argostoli, 7th August, 1824.

My next door neighbour is an old Switzer, he has been a serjeant in one of the Sicilian Regiments, but is now out of the army, he holds the civil situation of clerk of the works, aged about sixty. His wife, a young Greek about twenty eight. His family consists of himself, wife, seven children, a dog, two cats, and a monkey, a fine hawk, several pigeons, canaries, turkeys and fowls, a little army of guinea pigs and rabbits. Last Sunday his youngest child was christened. I and my family were invited. After dinner the *papa* arrived with the font, it was put in the parlour where was abundance of wine, *rosolio, rojetta*, sweetmeats and sugarplums.

The ceremony began about three o'clock when another *papa* arrived. There was a good deal of prayers and nonsense, when one of the *papas* took the child, blew his stinking breath on the little innocent and walked several times round the fount making the sign of the cross over the child. He then stripped it naked, put it into a large white cloth, the edges of which were decorated with broad white lace.

The two *papas* then caught hold of the four corners and carried the child round the fount several times, mumbling something in Greek. It was then marked with the sign of the cross on the head, forehead, cheeks, back, belly and sides, arms, hands, thighs, legs, and feet with holy oil, then a pinch of salt was put into the child's mouth. It was then carried round again, after which the child was plunged overhead and ears three times in the water. One of the *papas* then put an amulet or charm round the child's neck. It was then dressed without wiping any of the mess off it.

The godfathers and godmothers then each presented the child with money, according to their circumstances, the rest of the company followed the example. This I understood was to be laid by for a marriage portion, for no female can marry unless she is in possession of sixty dollars and seven changes of garments. Not wishing to debar the poor girl of a husband when she came of age I willingly threw in my mite with the rest, then one of the godfathers put a gold chain and cross about her neck and the other a large pair of gold earrings. This was the joint offerings of the godfathers and godmothers. Coffee and cake was then handed round, of which the two *papas* did our host infinite honour. We then left the ladies to the coffee etc., while we regaled ourselves in a back apartment over plenty of excellent old wine that had been kept for the purpose.

Bullinger was no starter, I believe he would drink an hogshead without being drunk, so we kept it up until the cock crew more than thrice, there was abundance left, so we had another turn at it the night after. Bullinger is one of the most singular characters I ever met with, when in company he always engrosses all the conversation to himself, he knows everybody in the island, can spake well of no one unless they are present, no one takes any notice of what he says. In bottom he is a good hearted old fellow.

One day I saw him give a beggar something as he passed him. When he came up to me I asked him who the beggar was.

'Oh' says he, 'dat is de woster b——r in the island, I never give dese b——s anyting, only I curse dem.'

He is a Catholic or rather he professes that religion, one day we were passing the Catholic church, there was a very strong smell of incense burning, I pretended ignorance and asked him what it was.

'Oh,' said he 'dis is de very ting dat keeps me from the church, if it vas not for dat tarn pini I should be one of the petter Christians in all the island, but I never can say my prayers in de church for dat tam smell, it makes me sick.'

This is the sort of character I generally spend an hour with every evening. You may depend I do not fail to enjoy a good bit of fun at his expense.

We have had a smart shake of an earthquake, it drove all the people out of their houses into the street, it passed without doing any mischief, only frightening the people, and amongst them your humble servant. I would prefer the chance of a general action at any time than being buried alive under the ruins of an old house.

The feast of St. Jerosemo has taken place, an officer's guard with most of the officers, started to the village. I obtained leave and went with them. I was well entertained and lodged for the night, the next day the saint was carried about the village.

I accompanied several of our officers to the top of the Black Mountain from which we had one of the finest prospects in the world, the Moria, the Poleponesses of the Greeks, with the plain where the Olympic games were celebrated and a vast extent of country was at once open to the eye.

It was on this mountain where the priests used to sacrifice to Jupiter, a better place could not be selected for such a purpose, for the whole of the inhabitants of the Moria could see the fire. There are some remnants of the ruins left and a spot where a queen has been buried, she was a person of some consequence, Major Ross who is well informed in antiquarian lore, pointed out many things that were interesting to the party, but what pleased me the best was the prospect, I had never before seen anything to compare with it. We returned much delighted to our old friends the *papas* and spent another night under their hospitable roof, the next day joined our regiment at Argostoli.

No. 109. Argostoli, 14th September, 1824.

The *scirroco* wind has prevailed very much this season. It produces a very disagreeable sensation, it paralyses the whole frame, the breath is so much affected one can scarcely breathe, the feet swells so much during the night that in the morning it is difficult to get on one's shoes, it generally sets in about 4 o'clock in the afternoon and continues until 10 or 11 the next morning when a breeze sets in from the west or north-west, this season we have had it blow constantly for forty eight hours, the consequence was that a great number have been sick and upwards of forty have died, these winds are not over yet but their continuance are not of long duration.

Last month our commandant died. I am sitting at my door when the intelligence was brought, minute guns was firing, the *scirroco* had continued three days, the sky was over cast and seemed all of a quiver, the heat was extremely oppressive, not a breath of air, but was as hot as the gleam of an oven's mouth.

In the short space of an hour I had seen five men taken to the hospital and I was about thinking I must strike myself when old Bullinger came up to me gasping for breath, saying

'Dis tam scroco will kills us all, never before did I know a worster time as dis, look at de sky, whoever did see any ting like dis. Crykes tunder veter we shall all die come wid me, it is besser to have a drop of someting goot. Calla Mari! Oh, dis tam *scirroco*, when vil it fenish? I wish the Devil would keep it at home, we have droble enough wid out it, Santa Maria, Joseph.'

Then crossing himself like a good Catholic, he said, 'Come along wid me, bring your pipe, I have someting goot.'

I went with Bullinger to his house. Mrs. Bullinger laid stretched out on an oak settle, with nothing on but her chemise, all the little ones were laying about naked, the hawk was perched on the top of the canary bird's cage all seemed over powered except the monkey, he was perched on the table eating chestnuts. Bullinger had been on board the Pelican gun brig and had got a bottle of rum, or as he called it 'a bottle of the right sort' after taking some of Bullinger's rum, I went and laid down. I soon began to perspire, this relieved me from the oppression I was labouring under.

We buried the commandant the next day, when Colonel Rice had finished the burial service, the Greek *papas* went through

228

some mummery over the grave. Sir Charles Sutton, Inspecting Field Officer of Ionian Militia soon arrived from Corfu to take the command. He is a very good man, he delights to mix with the soldiers and take part in any sport that might be going on. I hope we have got over the worst part of the season, we have now many sick in hospital, but there are but few new cases, another month will put all to rights.

Last week our chaplain paid us a visit, there is but one English parson for the seven islands, once in the year he makes a tour to baptise what children might have been born since his last visit and to marry all the widows who have made up their minds to try their fortunes once more, at the altar of Hyman.

Amongst the deaths this season was Serjeant Lambert an old soldier who had seen much service. To shew the respect our good and gallant old colonel delights to shew to the soldiers who compose the remnant of the late Peninsular Army. I will describe his funeral.

Colonel Rice ordered the whole regiment to attend, and although it is contrary to the usages of the Ionian Army to fire over the grave of the deceased yet the colonel ordered a strong firing party. The cause of not firing over the grave of a soldier in this country is that when the sickly season sets in the number of deaths are generally very great and that so much firing would dispirit the men. Be this as it may I do not think the soldier who falls a victim to climate in the service of his country should be short of the last honour we could pay him.

I must finish this by stating that on the 1st of August, the anniversary of the glorious battle of Minden, the serjeants kept up the day by giving a ball and supper, our funds were rich, nothing of the kind having taken place since we left England. Perhaps you would like to know how the fund for such a purpose is created. Every serjeant on his promotion pays his footing, ten shillings and sixpence and when again promoted to colour serjeant, five shillings, to this is added ten shillings from everyone present. We had a long barrack room decorated with evergreens, devices and mottoes.

229

The supper was served at 8 o'clock, several Greek ladies and gentlemen who visited the room previous to the supper were astonished at the richness and grandeur of the table. The officers had (as they always do on those occasions) lent us their service of plate, and every requisite from their mess, everything that was good, and could be procured for money was provided and cooked by the mess–master.

After the cloth was removed and the customary toasts were drunk our colonel, the justly named father of our corps, accompanied by several of the officers, paid us a visit. I wish you had seen the welcome he received, it is impossible to describe it, here were no forced cheers, it was one simultaneous burst of joy proceeding from the hart, welcoming the best of colonels, the soldier's friend.

I asked Bullinger what he thought of it. 'Dunder wetter, never before did I hear and see such a ting as dis.'

In the course of the colonel's address, Old Bullinger jogged my arm saying 'Vat is dat about de vine?'

I told him the colonel had sent us a hamper of good old port.

'Vat' said he, 'a hamper of vine, Santa Maria Joseph, this is the besser ting I ever know.'

Let it suffice that after the colonel left, several officers remained with us all night. The dance was kept up with great spirit. Music and songs mingled with wine and punch that flowed plentifully, we kept it up until six next morning then broke up. Amongst the company were several Greek gentlemen, one a young man who was in holy orders, they were all delighted, declaring they never before attended a party of this kind where they received such kindness and attention.

There was abundance of everything left, the next evening we finished it up under the shade of the olive tree accompanied by our Greek friends who severally invited us to the next grand feast which took place the beginning of this month, a few miles from Argostoli. In my next I shall say something about it if I do not meet with something better.

No. 110. Argostoli, 5th October, 1824.

The feast I mentioned in my last, to which the Greeks had invited us after our ball, began the 8th September. Argostoli was all bustle, people from the country passing through on mules, well stocked with refreshments. The people of the town too were loading and mounting their mules to join in the throng. I and my family were waiting the arrival of Signor Lusi and family, who shortly arrived with a mule loaded with a pigskin of wine, bread, cooked turkeys, capons and a variety of pots, kettles and pans to prepare coffee, fry meat etc. Jugs, decanters and glasses, pipes and tobacco, *rojetta* and a variety of other cordials with sweetmeats and sugar plumbs for the ladies and children and not forgetting grapes and all kinds of fruit.

A pleasant walk to the Devil's Point brought us to the water where we crossed to Luxoria, where the multitude had assembled. A short distance from the town, at a church where the feast was held we took up our position under the shade of a beautiful olive tree, proceeded to unload the mule. In the vicinity of the church several acres were similarly occupied, a great number of our men were sprinkled up and down amongst the Greeks, of whom many belonged to different islands, in their different costumes, gave it the appearance of a masquerade.

As soon as we were properly settled the table cloth was spread with all kinds of eatables, drink, etc., a variety of melons, grapes, sweetmeats etc. The host then invited his guests to partake of his bounty, after this you are not asked during the day, nothing is removed and everyone takes of what there is, as often as his appetite requires. As often as a dish is emptied it is filled again, decanters are constantly replenished with wine, *rosolio* etc., tobacco and pipes in abundance, a thousand tabors and pipes in every direction while as many different parties are dancing to the simple music, at numerous large fires whole sheep were roasting and a great number of booths, to accommodate those who have it not in their power to bring refreshments with them.

About midday the procession started from the church, when it was followed by the most devout, while those who preferred staying in camp, merely crossed themselves and remained kneeling until it had passed. Signora Lusi and family with my *Signora* and family joined in the procession by following in the wake, while the *Signor* and myself remained, with a few friends who are not so strictly religious as their countrymen are in general, to sacrifice to Bacchus. As the sun began to draw near to the horizon many wended their way homeward, those who lived at a distance had brought their beds, for the feast lasted two days. Our party arrived home before dark, when, after spending an hour at my friend's house, we parted for the night, to renew our visit early the next morning.

The second day was spent the same as the first. Old Bullinger joined us for a short time but as he knew everybody he could not remain long, having to pay his respects to all his friends. Bullinger ran the gauntlet of the feast, drank and smoked with everyone and went home sober as a judge. This old chap would drink a whole regiment of soldiers drunk twice over.

There is in Argostoli a small theatre, we got up a play, it was the 'Recruiting Serjeants,' it was a crowded house. Sir Chas. Sutton and Colonel Rice were present and was much pleased, many of the respectable inhabitants wished to see another performance. I was to have taken a character but Priscilla voted against it, so like a good husband I submitted to her wishes.

Some of our officers have discovered an ancient burying place at Salmos. Many graves have been opened and several curious wrought jugs, lamps and various things have been found in stone coffins. The remains of bodies were found in some of the coffins but being exposed to the air instantly crumbled into dust. An order has been issued to stop the opening of any more graves.

I scarcely know how to spin out a long letter, we are in a manner isolated from the world, but as often as I can scrape up anything I think will be interesting I shall give it you, if it is only to fill up the fag end of a letter. A steam vessel has arrived on this station, it will be employed in conveying the mails to the different islands, and upon any business that requires despatch.

When she first entered our harbour I thought the Greeks would go mad with surprise and joy.

No. 111. *Argostoli, 19th January, 1825.*

We have passed another Christmas, or rather two this time, I have conformed to the old adage 'When you are at Rome do as Rome does.' So far as feasting goes, I never had such a time of it. To give you some idea I must first state I have eighteen Greek children attend the school, whose parents are in a state of independence. From these I am continually receiving presents, but as Christmas drew near, *complimentas*, as the Greeks call it, came in so thick and fast I am puzzled where to stow them. Each of my scholars brought a large loaf made of the best flour, covered with almonds and walnuts in shape resembling a child in swathing bands and weighing from six to fourteen pounds each and wine in abundance.

By twelve o'clock on Christmas Eve I was in possession of seven fat turkeys, five capons, eleven fowls and seven lambs, about a bushel of currants, loads of grapes, sugar and water melons, honey, locust and pomegranates, with a long variety of etceteras. (The lambs and poultry was alive). We had asked all the boys but as Christmas fell on a Sunday we has our dinner on the Monday. I must here remark that although the Greeks are such strict observers of their fasts, they did not object to their children attending.

We had not provided anything for the Sunday yet we dropped in for an out and out good dinner. Next to our orderly room is a cook house with two furnaces and an oven, the two orderly room clerks with a few others had knocked up a dinner, sufficient for thirty people to sit down to. You might form some opinion of what sort of a dinner this was when I inform you that there was cooked twenty pounds of beef, three turkeys and a pig about four months old, besides puddings and every other thing requisite to make up a feast. Two barrack tables were placed in the cook house and dinner laid, but not one of the party came, excepting the two clerks, the corporal of the pioneers and the cook. The few that assembled sent for me and I fetched old Bullinger. We had nothing to do the remainder of the day but enjoy ourselves.

On Monday I had twenty eight sit down to dinner, not including my own family. I found our Christmas pudding to be a novelty to the Greeks, so we were determined to present each of the Greek boys with one on old Christmas day. Their parents were so well pleased they were determined not to be behind hand in returning the compliment, so that by the evening of Old Christmas we were stocked with bread, lambs, turkeys etc., not forgetting currants, of these we had enough to set up a grocer's shop.

The other Sunday, as we were at divine service, a funeral, on a very grand scale passed us, it was the funeral of a lady who had been married several years, but having no children her husband will have to refund to her friends the whole of her marriage portion. I understand it is thirty thousand dollars, besides an immense quantity of wearing apparel. The law, amongst the Greeks, is that a woman on her marriage must have a marriage portion, from sixty dollars and upwards and a suitable number of changes of garments. If there should be children, then on the death of the mother the husband retains the money etc., but on the contrary if as in the case of this lady there has been none, then the whole must be returned.

The Greeks bury their dead in the churches, the body is dressed in all its best clothes, ornamented with gold chains, jewellery etc., as if going to a ball. The body is then put into a coffin, put on a bier and carried to the church attended (if rich) by a great number of priests, chanting as they go along, followed by a great crowd of the inhabitants. After the ceremony in the church the body is stripped of all its finery and put into a grave without a coffin, the earth is well rammed down and the stone is replaced on the top. The corpse has always a new pair of shoes. The poorer sort have a good way of burying their children. When a child dies it is dressed as if going to a christening, put into a tray carried by a boy to a church where it remains with a silver plate along side of it for the charitable to bestow their alms. A sufficient sum is soon collected, then the *papas* commit the body to the earth.

No. 112. Argostoli, 7th May, 1825.

You have, no doubt, heard of the earthquake that has destroyed a great part of the town of Santa Martha. Fortunately, for the people, it gave a longer warning than usual, so that they had time to escape out of their houses before they were buried alive in the ruins, with the exception of the barracks and a few buildings the whole of the town is nearly shook down. The hospital is levelled to the ground, there happened to be only two or three sick, and these being in a convalescent state, were outside the building watching the soldiers going through a field day. Between forty and fifty of the inhabitants are killed and seriously hurt.

We felt it very severely in our island, it happened about eleven o'clock. I had some suspicion that we were about to have a shake, for a few minutes before it happened I observed my fowls moping about and going to roost. I have often laughed since when I call to mind the confusion it caused. Priscilla was doing something at the fire, I was leaning or rather bent forward over the table looking at a book when it began. Priscilla nearly tumbled head foremost into the fire, I was pitched over the table and before I could recover my legs all the boys was running and tumbling over me, making for the door.

In our fright we scampered out amidst the noise of broken earthenware, chimneys tumbling, tiles rattling and falling into the street, the earth shaking, Greeks crossing themselves and calling on the Virgin, soldiers swearing, dogs howling and cats running, in short, everything was on the move, except old Bullinger who was sat down on the green in front of his house cursing the rheumatism.

Fortunately it did not last long or the whole of the buildings must have been shook to the ground. As it was, many houses are cracked from top to bottom, the water was agitated for a considerable time.

As things was again settled Bullinger hailed me. 'Go' said he 'into mine house and bring out de vine, perhaps the Divel vil give us anoder push and shake down dat old house of mine, it is better to have the vine safe.'

I soon brought out a large basket bottle containing about twenty quarts. 'Dat is de ting, now we will drink a little vile ve have time, fetch some tobacco and pipes. Oh dam dis rheumatism.'

As we were blowing a cloud I asked Bullinger what could be the cause of the shakes so frequent in the island.

'Very few people know dis ting' said he, 'I will tell you. It is all through dese tan vicket Greeks, day be no Christians like you and me, dey tink of noting but swearing, cheating, lying and back-biting one anoder all day long, den are always stuffing, it is eat, eat, eat all day long and drink, drink, drink, Got for tarn, vy don't you drink, put me over a glass.'

At this moment a Greek gentleman came up and saluted Bullinger and asked him how he was etc.

'Oh Signor Mataxa, you be a very good Christian to ask after poor old Bullinger. I am very well only for dis rheumatism. Will you take a glass of vine *Signor*? but it is not so good as your vine, your vine is the better vine of any in de island.'

'It is very good, I think it is from Signor Lusi.'

'You be right, you be right, Signor Lusi's, next to yours is de better vine in de island.'

'I will send you some this afternoon Bullinger.'

'Oh you be too kind *Signor*, you be de better Christian in the island, and your fader I remember your fader. Oh vas he not a good Christian, he vas better den de Bishop.'

The gentleman winked at me and wished us good morning, when Bullinger said 'do not trouble *Signor* to send me the vine I vil send Constantine for it '

'No, no, Bullinger I am going home and will send it by my servant.'

'Tankee *Signor*, tankee *Signor*, but I give you much drouble.'

When the gentleman was gone, Bullinger said to me, 'You know dis Signor Mataxa, he is the worster b—— in the island, he only vants me to do someting for him.'

Now I know this gentleman to be one of the most liberal men I ever met with. I never pass his house but I am welcome to go in and partake of the best that can be laid before me. But this is old Bullinger all over, he ever speaks fare to ones face and runs them down behind their backs. Suffice it to say in an hour two men came with a large basket bottle full of good old wine each, one for old Bullinger, the other for myself.

Colonel Chas. Napier who distinguished himself at the head of the 50th Regiment at Corunna, and was dangerously wounded and left on the field for dead, has arrived. He is one of the inspecting field officers of Ionian Militia. He appears to be a regular off-handed soldier, a rigid observer of military discipline. At the same time he has the method of gaining the affections of the soldiers under his command, he is the commandant of the island.

No. 113. Argostoli, 21st October, 1825.

I believe I have never said anything in my former letters respecting the Greek's way of performing the sacrament. I had an opportunity the other day of being present when this ceremony was performed. Next to the schoolroom stands a small church. On the morning in question I observed a great quantity of large loaves being brought, and taken into the church. I expected that something extraordinary was going on from the confounded clatter of the bells from twelve o'clock the preceding night. I was told by one of my Greek boys that a very rich gentleman had about fifty years ago died, and that he had left a large sum of money to be distributed in bread, on the anniversary of his death for ever.

I thought this would be a good opportunity for me to be present. When I entered the *papa* was standing at the altar going through the church service. In one part of the service he unlocked a small door and took out a book, apparently a testament with silver covers. After kissing the outside, he turned round and held it up for the congregation to have a sight of it. This done, he very carefully returned it to its place and locked the door again, the people all the time remaining on their knees, while some lay stretched out on their faces.

At length the wine was produced, when the whole assembly gathered round the altar, some ten or twelve deep. The *papa* stood with the silver cup in one hand and a small silver spoon resembling a mustard spoon in the other. With this he served the wine to the mob about him.

The person who had received the wine then went to the other end of the chapel where a *papa* was stationed with about a wagon load of bread. This was distributed to the people according as they needed it, the wealthy only received a very small loaf, while the poor man with a family got one from six to ten or twelve pounds in weight.

After the *papa* at the altar had served the whole he beckoned to me, but I did not wish to have the spoon put into my mouth after it had ran the gauntlet of the whole congregation. I declined the offer. The old chap then looked round his flock with a very careful eye, then put the cup to his own mouth and swallowed its contents. Then corked it down with a good wedge of bread. I had a small loaf and found it to be the very best quality, like the loaves given away at Christmas.

The *papa* that serves this church lives a few miles in the country. The way he passes his time on a Sunday between morning and afternoon service, weather permitting, is as follows. He gets a Greek to play at cards with him, both sitting at the church door with their backs to the door posts, one leg in and the other out of the church, here they sit gambling for halfpence, sometimes it will happen that a dispute will arise, when the shepherd and his sheep will swear as hearty at each other as a barrack room full of soldiers.

This fall has not been attended with so much sickness as last. We have had a good share of the *scirroco* and have been troubled with many slight shakes, the last happened three days ago, was very heavy, but passed off without doing any damage.

No. 114. *Argostoli, 11th March, 1826.*

I thought I should not during our stay on this island, be able to fill up another letter with anything new, and but for a fracas between Colonel Charles Napier and our commanding officer Colonel Rice, you must have contented yourself with short epistles until we should change our station. The late row is likely to cause us to be removed, as it seemed impossible that a reconciliation can be brought about between the parties.

A short time since I was returning from Colonel Rice's quarters, it was at a quarter before nine in the morning. I heard our buglers sounding the assembly. When I arrived on the parade ground I saw our men assembling in a hurried manner and the detachment of Royal Artillery getting the two field pieces out. Colonel Napier with our adjutant was on the parade mounted. The commandant seemed very much excited.

I ran back and acquainted Colonel Rice with what was going on, he was just going to breakfast. The colonel desired me to order his horse, I hastened back again and found the regiment with the two guns had just moved in the direction of the Devil's Point. By this time the boys had just assembled in school. I left them in charge of Priscilla and off I went after the regiment. When we came to the sandy beach, near to the Devil's Point the mystery was at once explained. Two Greek vessels of war, mounting the one eighteen and the other fourteen guns were anchored inside the Devil's Point. (No vessels belonging to either Greeks or Turks are allowed to enter any of our harbours unless through stress of weather.) It was reported they had ran in to get out of the way of a couple of Turkish frigates who had been chasing them.

Be this as it may the weather was fair and the commandant was not justified in allowing them to remain. They were ordered to go to sea, but refused to go, this irritated Colonel Napier (who by the bye is as hot as pepper). This was the cause of making the hostile movement. The field pieces were placed on the beach, a boat sent to insist on their immediate departure, but it returned with an answer that set the commandant in a blaze.

The pieces were loaded and everything looked as if we should have a fiz at the vessels, when the serjeant told Colonel Napier the pieces would not reach above half way. This was too much for Colonel Napier, he got into a violent passion and just at this moment Colonel Rice happened to arrive. Colonel Rice very mildly asked Mr. Mawdsley our adjutant why he did not inform him the regiment was ordered under arms, when the commandant turned on Colonel Rice and said 'Hold your tongue, hold your tongue, sir.' Colonel Rice then addressed the adjutant, when Colonel Napier, whose passion seemed to increase, said many times 'Hold your tongue, sir, damn'e hold your tongue sir, I will not be trifled with when I am in command, go to the rear of No. 1 gun.'

Colonel Rice made no reply and instantly obeyed the order.

I never was more hurt in my life. Colonel Napier is that sort of a soldier who is sure of gaining the confidence of all under his command, it is a pity he should so far forget himself by allowing his passion to get the better of his understanding. Colonel Rice is the oldest soldier in the regiment and is beloved and respected by every man in the corps. Mr. Mawdsley has not been with us long, but that short time he has been in the regiment has convinced every one he is a soldier's friend, indeed, he is in the full sense of the words, both a soldier and a gentleman, ever ready to check irregularities in a mild way and advising the men for their good. Since this unfortunate affair Colonel Rice has not appeared in public.

The Lord High Commissioner has paid us a visit to settle the business. I believe he did not succeed. It is reported that Colonel Napier offered to apologize to Colonel Rice at the *levée* but that Colonel Rice refused to receive such apology unless it was at the head of his regiment where he had received the insult.

We are under orders to remove to Zante, this move will take place as soon as arrangements can be made.

But I must return to the beach. While the row was going on between the two colonels, the two Greek brigs got under weigh and we returned to Argostoli.

No. 115. Zante, 19th May, 1826.

This is the most fertile and pleasant of the Ionian Islands, its chief produce is currants, the same you make your Christmas puddings of, a great deal of wine is also made, but little if any is exported. There is a brisk trade in oil and a great quantity of the cups of acorns is brought from the Morea, it is called *vallani* and is put in between the casks of currants to fill up.

The town is built under the castle and runs a long way from north to south, the houses are generally well built, the town is crowded with Greeks from the Moria and from different islands in the Arches. Zante is the residence of an Archbishop of the Greek Church and a Roman Catholic Bishop. The castle is built on an exceedingly high hill above the town, from this place the eye is delighted with one of the most delightful views it is possible to conceive.

The whole island appears one large beautiful garden with here and there a house and a few trees scattered up and down.

The prospect across the water is grand. To the north rises the lofty mountains of Jupiter Eros on the island of Cephalonia, to the right stretches the bay of Patrass, then the eye meets the bold projecting point running out from the Morea on which stands the castle of Tornese, at present in possession of the Greeks.

There in front of Zante is the large plain where the Olympic games were celebrated, bounded to the south east by a lofty ridge running out into the sea that shuts out any farther view of the land under the citadel. To the south once stood the ancient city of Zante, there is now no trace left; looking down from the point where the morning and evening gun is fired, this place looks frightful, nothing but an irregular deep yawning gulf presents itself where the ancient city once stood.

The man who keeps the canteen in the castle is blind, what is most extraordinary he does all the business of the canteen without assistance. This man can distinguish colours by the sense of feeling. Ask for any coloured thread or silk he never picks out a wrong colour. The same with the money. There are three sorts of coin current here, the Spanish, Imperial and Venician, all differing in value. Some of the pieces are much worn and would often puzzle a person with a good pair of eyes to distinguish them, but the moment Jerosemo takes a piece of money into his hand he can tell the value of it.

Zante has its saint, the same as the rest of the islands, he is called St. Dioneces and has but one arm. Whether he had been a soldier saint and lost his arm in the wars I cannot learn. A few years ago while the people were perambulating the town with the saint the island was visited by a violent earthquake, attended by a violent hail storm, the hail stones were so large that some measured two inches round and it was observed that those which broke by the fall emitted electric fire.

The 36th Regiment lay here at the time, much damage was done to the town. The officers' mess-room was shook down. I was told by the quartermaster of the 36th while I was in Malta that he was lying on his sofa and by the shock was rolled on to the floor, at the same time his lady was pitched from the balcony into the street. Earthquakes are more prevalent and heavy here than in the other islands, there has been one slight shake since our arrival.

My quarters is at the English chapel, where the school is held. It is close by the water, in front of the harbour. From the chapel windows we have a good view of the shipping in harbour and of those who pass between us and the main land. The Moria might be about twelve miles from us.

I have often been astonished in the morning before sunrise to see the Moria appear so close to us, it frequently happens that the distance does not seem to be more than four miles when this phenomenon happens. Objects can be seen with the naked eye that at other times it would require a good glass to discern them. There is a good harbour and many vessels are constantly arriving for currants.

I should have said when I was about the castle that several gibbets are hanging about the town, four are suspended from one gallows on high ground, near the place where the ancient city stood, others are distributed about, some are pirates, one near the town is a fellow for a burglary and murder.

In some of my former letters I believe I .told you the Greeks are very jealous of their women. Most of the windows in this town are guarded by blinds, in such a manner it is impossible to catch a glimpse of a woman, wile she is able to see everything that passes in the street. The blinds are made of thin strips of deal laid across each other so as to leave just sufficient room to put the end of one's finger through. They project out from the bottom leaving sufficient room to place a cushion to lean on, no respectable female ever goes out without being accompanied by a male relative. The women are about as badly off as if they were in prison. During the carnival (that lasts here six weeks) they have a chance of getting out because they are masked and guarded.

The castle of Tornese has been carried by storm. The Turkish crescent is now flying on the flagstaff. The Turks are besieging Patrass, the Greeks often attempt to get in with supplies by water, but are closely watched by the Turkish men of war. At present there are two Turkish 74's and a large corvette watching the harbour.

Several officers, mostly Germans, are at Zante waiting for a passage for Napoli de Romania to join the Greeks. One of these officers is said to be a near relation of Napoleon, if he is possessed of but half the skill and daring of his illustrious relative he will be of service to the cause of the oppressed Greeks. I wish we could lend them a hand, we would soon turn the scales in their favour.

I have nothing more to add unless I tell you the old tale of religious ceremonies. Processions both Greek and Roman are constantly taking place. Saint Dioneces has been round the town robbing the people, his procession differs in no respect from those I have already mentioned. I should mention I was a gainer of two dollars by his Saintship. I managed to get three large candles, one for myself and one each for the two young ones, we followed in the wake until we came near to Old Paddy Conlon's (an old Irishman who keeps a shop). Paddy soon bargained to give two dollars, a bottle of rum and a craft of wine for the candles. He is a good Catholic and intends to display them at the next procession of his church.

No. 117. Zante, 27th November, 1826.

We have had several violent shocks since my last. Last Sunday morning at about half past seven I was taking a very comfortable nap when I was roused by the most confounded rattle I ever heard. I ran into the passage in my shirt, here I found myself in company with my wife and three Greek ladies, all huddled together trying to open a door to escape. It passed off without doing any mischief and I soon retreated back to my room and dressed myself, but the weather evidently told as plain as possible that we might expect another.

About nine I was spreading the communion cloth when another shake came on, down came about a dozen bricks on the table, and the large board having the commandments etc., sunk one corner about a foot, covering the cloth with about a wheelbarrow of rubbish.

My faith was not strong enough to remain in the 'Sanctum Sanctorum,' so off I bolted, leaping over the rails of the communion. The old Greek proprietor of the chapel was outside with his wife, daughter and a young lady, the same three ladies I found myself in the corner with about an hour and a half before. About half an hour after it began to rain and blow fresh from the south west, when my patron said we might go in. Besides the altar being damaged there were seventy three panes of glass broke in the chapel.

An English missionary and his wife belonging to the Methodist persuasion has taken up abode here and opened a chapel, it is very well attended by the soldiers. How long it will last I don't know, it is something new. He seems to be a very nice sort of a man, his wife is about opening a school for the Greek girls. They are from nearly the same place as Priscilla whose religious sentiments are inclined that way, we are consequently on a very intimate footing.

We have bought a hymn book and go to chapel regularly, several Greeks who understand English attend, one young man told me that he never knew anything of the Christian religion until this man came to the island, that he learned more from him in five minutes, than he could learn from one of their *papas* in a century. The missionary is on good terms with all parties. The prince Comuto (a venerable old man) frequently visits him, and is much interested in getting up a school for the girls of the poor.

No. 118. Zante, 13th January, 1827.

Mr. Croggan, the missionary I mentioned in one of my former letters, has received permission to read the church prayers to the troops on Sunday mornings, but he is not to preach. Mrs. Croggan has got a good school. The Greek *papas* with Prince Comuto, seem to work in good earnest in rendering the missionary and his wife every assistance in their power. I occupy apartments in the house joining the chapel, belonging to, and part of the house, occupied by the Greek gentleman, the owner. Consequently Priscilla spends much time with the old lady and her daughter.

The young lady's name is Andriana, and is a good hearted open girl, about twenty, a regular good looking brunette, rather above the middle size. She has been brought up in all the ignorance and superstition of the country, but her intercourse with the school master's wives, has, in a great measure, withdrawn the veil from her understanding, and she sees things in a different light from her countrywomen. She can neither read or write, as is the case with all the females. She does not disguise any of her grief and trouble from Priscilla. That which most preys on her mind is of course, as is the case with most females of her age a love affair.

The poor girl is betrothed to an old ugly squint eyed Greek gentleman, upwards of thirty years older than herself, there is a young gentleman visits her who has stole the poor girl's heart, but he is ignorant of the conquest he has made.

The law of marriage is very hard, particularly so far as the female is concerned. A Greek gentleman seldom or ever thinks of marriage until he has passed the prime of life, he then takes a young wife. The girl says the man she is to be married to (like all other Greek bachelors) keeps a woman, this woman will continue to live with him until his marriage.

He will then, according to the laws, have to allow her a separate maintenance, or in other words, he will have two wives and two establishments to keep up. All the children he has by the woman before his marriage, are taken to the asylum, a place supported by the public. These children, as soon as born, are taken to this place, the parents never see them to know them afterwards.

Most young people look forward with pleasure to the day of their nuptials, but poor Andriana looks forward with disgust. Her intended husband has been living with his woman upwards of twenty years, nearly two years before Andriana was born.

The last fall passed over comparatively speaking with but few cases of fever. This island, in the whole, is much healthier than Cephalonia. The market is much better supplied with all kinds of vegetables, in short Zante in every respect is much superior to our last station.

No. 119. Zante, 7th April, 1827.

The Greek squadron, consisting of twenty nine armed vessels, sailed past our town the other day, their object is to throw in supplies to the Garrison of Patrass, but the place is too strongly blockaded by a superior fleet of the Turks, consisting of several large double banked frigates.

I have watched their movements several times, the Greeks are very daring, but they have not a vessel of sufficient force to lay alongside one of the regular Turkish men of war. They shew most skill in manoeuvring their vessels, and have several times caused the Turks much uneasiness with their fire ships.

Their method of attack is to advance on the enemy's fleet, until within gun shot, then to bare away close to the wind, the

Turks follow them firing their bow guns. As soon as opportunity serves, the Greeks send a fire ship amongst the enemy, it is laughable to see what a pucker this throws the Turks into, who, as soon as their panic is over, skulk back to their old anchorage.

The Greeks dodged them about several days in this manner, without any apparent injury to either party, when the Greeks grew more bold and hung longer about the van of the Turk. This drew them into a most inequal contest. A couple of fire ships were started amongst the Turkish squadron, but done no mischief, however it gave the Greeks time to benefit by their enemy's confusion and get out of the reach of their heavy guns.

One Greek vessel (a brig) was roughly handled by a large frigate, but from the superior manner which the Greek shewed in manoeuvring and answering the fire of her antagonist it is to be hoped the frigate has good cause to remember the day of the month. Fortunately the brig succeeded in getting away and anchoring for the night in front of our harbour.

A guard of our regiment lay alongside of her all night in a boat to prevent any communication with the island. Our men stated that many of her crew were badly wounded and some dead bodies were committed to the deep during the night. Since, both fleets have left this part. The Turks leaving two 74's and a large corvette in the bay formed by the point of land on which stands the castle of Tornese.

No. 120. Zante, 17th May, 1827.

Since my last, the gallant Lord Cochrane, in his beautiful frigate called the *Hellenus,* with a large gun brig and a steamer, has visited our waters, His Lordship is the Admiral and Commander in chief of the Greek navy. You know his Lordship does not belong to the family of Dolittles, and so has the Musselmen found out to their cost.

The beginning of this month a large strange steamer was seen steaming up under the land, it passed Tornese point, then bore off between the islands of Zante and Cephalonia. Shortly after she was followed by a very large ship and brig, scudding away in gallant style. Just as the Frigate made the point of Tornese, a large corvette bearing the Tripoli flag came round the point, nothing could be better, she just dropped into the Lion's mouth. The frigate proved to be the *Hellenus,* bearing the flag of Lord Cochrane. As the frigate passed her she gave her a broadside, then pushed on and engaged a 74, who had just made her appearance. By this time the gun brig whose name I am told is *Lord Nelson* closed with the corvette, a couple of broadsides done the business.

The corvette was then handed over to the steamer, who had by this time returned. The *Hellenus* had given the 74 a most unmerciful hauling, so that the brig was in good time to polish off the rough work Cochrane had made on her, whilst the *Hellenus* went after another 74, who was under all the sail he could set. Unfortunately she had too much start but the gallant Cochrane did not let her off without leaving his mark on board her. The frigate was obliged to return to secure the two vessels she had left with the brig and steamer. The 74 having hauled down her colours, the whole came to anchor on the spot.

The next day was devoted to repairing what damage was done, when His Lordship sailed off with his prizes. I have not been able to learn what loss the Greeks met with. I am inclined to think that some officer must have fallen for minute guns were fired the day after the fight. Some were afraid it was the gallant admiral, while others were of opinion that it was done to induce the other Turkish 74, who had ran away to return, with the hope that the victors had lost their admiral.

A few days ago a beautiful schooner arrived called the *Unichorn,* she mounts two small brass swivel guns on her quarterdeck, while she appears to carry sixteen. It is said she is a tender to Lord Cochrane. Be that as it may, she passes for a private yacht, belonging to an English gentleman by the name of Lewis, she is one of the smartest craft I ever saw and she has a fine smart dashing crew, all English. This place is completely crowded with unfortunate Greeks who have left the Morea and other parts during the great struggle between the Turks and Greeks. Some are in a very distressed state and are obliged to exist upon charity.

No. 121. Zante, 29th July, 1827.

The Archbishop of Zante died this month. His funeral being of a novel description, I shall trouble you with an account of it. As soon as his death was announced the whole of the churches were put into deep mourning, the body was dressed in full uniform with the mitre on his head and placed in a chair in the Church of St. Sepulchre. The dead Right Reverend Father became the lion of the day, every Greek that could get out visited the church. Curiosity not devotion led me to the church, the place was crowded, a guard was stationed to keep order.

It was the most disgusting sight I had ever seen. By the dint of much squeezing I elbowed up to the place where the body was placed, he was in full canonical robes, one hand held up as if blessing the people, an open book placed in his front, and his pastoral staff leaning across his shoulder, a large silver dish to receive the offerings of the people, near him stood a table on which was placed the head and two hands of St. John the Baptist (I don't know how many heads St. John had, this is the third I have seen, one in Spain, the second in France). Near the grand altar were bricklayers, building a vault. I was glad to escape out of this stinking place, the smell from the body was dreadful.

The second day after his death the prelate was carried round the town in grand procession, sitting in the chair, the stench from the body was insufferable, the weather very hot, the procession was frequently obliged to stop to allow the pious Greeks to wipe the old gentleman's mouth, out of which continued to run a nasty ———.

After they had paraded all over the town they returned to the church when he was lowered into his vault, a book placed in his hand, a candle lit and placed before him. I got a glimpse at the old fellow before he was completely walled up. There he sat in the same posture as I saw him in the church, they had however changed his figured robes and mitre in place of which he wore a black gown and a cap, the same as worn by the *papas*, and he had a book open in his hand as if reading. I could not get the smell of the old chap out of my nose for several days after.

The church continued to be crowded the remainder of the day by the people kissing the head and hands of St. John.

A Russian frigate called the *San Nicholas* has visited the harbour, this was a grand treat for the Greeks, who during the time of her stay continued to visit her in crowds. The Russians belong to the Greek church. On board was a picture of the saint with a lamp burning in front, with a plate to receive the offerings of visitors, this was a nice way to make them pay for their curiosity.

No. 122. Zante, 9th September, 1827.

The missionary Mr. Croggan has met with a hindrance in his work of labour. He was in the habit of going to the castle and preaching to the soldiers. One evening Captain St. Maur sent the serjeant of the guard and a file of men to fetch him from the midst of his hearers, to his quarters. When he arrived, I have the missionary's own words of what passed, Captain St. Maur was sitting with his bottle and glass before him in company with a woman whom he keeps. He told the missionary he would not allow any more preaching in the castle while he commanded, asked Mr. Croggan to take a glass of brandy.

It is not proper for me to relate the conversation that took place, suffice it to say that Mr. Croggan was ordered prisoner to the guard room but was soon released. The next day he was summoned before the commandant, Sir Frederick Stovin, when he was informed that the only religion tolerated in the Ionian Islands is the Greek, Roman Catholic and Church of England.

The commandant signified that when the 90th, the Regiment he is the lieutenant colonel commanding, came to Zante, he would take care none of them should attend his place of worship. If they did, he find some other amusement for them. After a long chat he told the missionary there was in his corps a few drunken rascals that he could do nothing with and if Mr.

Croggan wished he would send them to him to see if he could reform them. Mr. Croggan thanked Sir. Frederick and said he was very thankful. The consequence is the meetings are discontinued and Mr. Croggan is not allowed to read the church service to the troops.

Our chaplain shortly after arrived, I suppose to put things to rights. The chaplain is a very good sort of a man and expressed himself to the missionary that he was very sorry for what had happened. After marrying a few widows, baptising several children and preaching a sermon he returned to Corfu. It is curious that a man like Mr. Croggan should meet with opposition when, if he was doing no good, it was evident he could do no harm.

Colonel Rice is gone to England on leave. Colonel Rice was very partial to the missionary, considering he was doing much good. But different men have different opinions. Had Colonel Rice remained with the regiment I do not think Captain St. Maur would have interfered.

The missionary takes it very quietly, he held a meeting in his room and is attended by several of the soldier's wives. Mrs. Croggan's girl's school flourishes and Mr. Croggan takes comfort in that. He will have more time to complete himself in the Greek language, to enable him to begin his labours on the Morea, where it was intended by the society in England he should proceed as soon as he had sufficient knowledge in the modern Greek tongue.

A Greek has been hanged for murder. The morning before the execution the fellow was brought from his prison put in a church, where he remained until the time of his execution. Jack Ketch sat before him on his heels all the time, wearing a dress of blue and yellow with a large black veil over his head and shoulders, with two large glass eyes to see through. A gallows was set up on the mole, the culprit was mounted on four steps, the rope made fast, the steps dragged from under his feet. When hanging, his feet were not more than three feet from the ground. The hangman then went back from the gallows about ten paces, ran and sprang on the poor fellow's back, caught hold of the rope, pulled himself up until he got his legs on the man's shoulders, here he sat until the poor fellow was dead.

Several convicts has been carried about the town on donkeys with a paper setting forth their crimes, and gallows drawn on the paper. A woman too, who had, it is said, poisoned her husband, stood several hours on a platform in the square. This mode of punishment seemed to have a very bad effect on the prisoners, they had armed themselves against all shame, and came out of prison to go through this part of their sentence with minds made up to show the people by their behaviour they did not care a straw about it.

No. 123. Zante, 7th November, 1827.

The news of the battle of Navarino must have arrived before you will receive this. It will be my business to relate a few of the leading particulars connected between the hostile fleets previous to that battle.

A short time before the battle the Turkish fleet, consisting of sixteen ships of the line, thirty seven frigates, most of which were double banked, between thirty and forty corvettes, sloops, brigs and schooners with a number of transports, all armed, made their appearance between Zante and the Morea. From the castle, the sight was beautiful. Lord Cochrane had got the weather gauge and was hanging about to tempt some of their foremost ships to leave the cluster, but to no purpose.

In front of Patrass lay the *Asia* 80, the flagship of Sir Edward Codrington, with the *Pelican* gun brig. Matters remained thus two days, when on the third morning the Turkish fleet was observed to be steering towards the south accompanied with the *Asia* and *Pelican,* and we soon lost sight of them.

The beginning of October the Russian fleet anchored in front of our harbour to take in water, after completing their water and purchasing vegetables they sailed, and in a few days the French fleet came here for the same purpose. When the French were completed then came the English. Before they had taken in their water an English frigate came from the southard making signals to the admiral, who with the fleet weighed anchor and sailed for Navarino. At this time there was a violent thunder storm.

The frigate appeared in the midst of it, the lightening was flying about in all directions, the thunder rolled in long loud and heavy peals, the frigate firing signal guns and the *Asia* answering her. Such weather always foretells good luck to the British before a battle. I could not but call to mind that the battles of Fuentes d'Onor, Salamanca, Vittoria and Waterloo were preceded by violent storms of lightening and thunder, and of course had calculated on a victory, should the hostile fleets come to an engagement.

On the morning of the 21st October the wind blowing south, two Turkish men of war's boats, manned with Greeks brought the intelligence that the combined fleets under Sir Edward Codrington had burnt the whole of the Turkish fleet. These boats belonged to one of the Turkish line of battle ships, and was, when the action commenced, on a watering party. The Greek seamen watched their opportunity and bolted.

When we consider the allied fleet of England, France and Russia, consisted of only twenty-six sail, mostly of corvettes and brigs, there being only three British, two French and two Russian ships of the line, one 50 gun frigate (French) and six other smaller frigates—the other twelve being composed of sloops, brigs and schooners, and the little tender belonging to the admiral mounting only four small guns—we are apt to think it impossible they should destroy such an enormous fleet consisting of between 130 and 140 sail, as described in a former part of this letter. The Greeks are running mad with joy. One of our brigs has called at Zante from whom we are informed that only one corvette and fourteen gun brigs have been saved from the fire. During the time the British were getting in their water one of the watering party strayed away and broke his quarantine. He is now in prison awaiting his trial, the punishment is death, but it is to be hoped the Government will pardon the man on account of the signal victory.

No. 124. Zante, 3rd February, 1828.

The regiment has removed to Corfu. A medical board has sat to invalid men to be sent home, I am one of the number, we expect to embark in a few days. I have nothing now to write and am busy in selling what things I cannot take with me, and packing up. The packet is about to sail for England, you must not expect to hear from me again until we arrive once more in old England, which I trust will not be long. Mr. and Mrs. Pirie are both well etc.

No. 125. Fort Pit, 29th May, 1828.

On the 1st of June, I shall leave this for London where I shall remain a week with Priscilla's sister, you might expect us to Bath about the 9th or 10th of June. We are all well. My pension is one shilling and ten pence *per diem*. The particulars of our voyage I shall be able to relate to you over a jug of beer. It will be sufficient to say owing to having to call at Santa Martha and Ithaca to deliver and take in stores we did not arrive at Malta until the 2nd of March, here we stayed until the 17th and should have remained longer but for the captain of a man of war laying in the harbour, he ordered us to see and I and my family was near being left behind, being on shore at the time.

Our passage to Gibraltar was a long and tiresome one being seventeen days, here we stayed five days, then sailed for England, this was the worst and longest being from the 8th of April to the 16th of May, coming from Gibraltar to Chatham.

If I do not leave London so as to be home by the 10th June I will write. We are all well and happy that we have got on shore after being cooped up on board a closely crowded transport from the 16th February to the 14th May, long enough to have come from the East Indies.

Appendices

Eight bullets pierced this young man's body. In the full light of glory and in the warm lap of love he died esteemed, honoured, wept, in the blossom of his youth, and in the pride of manly beauty.

Young Gore was a captain in the 51st Regiment and I have heard, a son of the Earl of Arran. He fought at the battle of Vittoria and it was in the town, a few days after the fight that I first saw him, as well as the fair and soft black eyed girl who was the innocent cause of his death.

When the sanguinary and memorable fight was at an end a few officers of necessity remained in the town. In consequence of this battle, the Constitution was published on the Sunday succeeding it, in the main square or market place, with great pomp and rejoicing. In addition to bull fights and public dancing upon the platform erected in the square for proclaiming the constitution, a ball was given in the evening expressly to the British officers then in the town, at which all the inhabitants of consequence attended.

At this ball I first saw Captain Gore, he was then apparently about twenty-two or twenty-three years of age, and as handsome a young man as ever I beheld, his hair was light brown and hung in a profusion of graceful ringlets, he was of a florid complexion, about the middle size, compact yet light, and in the beautiful uniform of the 51st a Light Infantry Regiment, faced with green and gold, he was decidedly the most striking figure in the ball room and in addition to this was the best dancer amongst the English officers—nay as good as any of the Spanish and French who exhibited on that evening their salutatory powers. Whether it was that our English style of dancing at that time wanted something to be added to its grace, by a communication with the continent or not, I will not pretend to say, but certain it is that my countrymen were not so happy in plucking the laurels from the French that night in the dance as they had been a few days before in the fight.

With qualifications such as I have described, it is not to be wondered at if the eyes and hearts of many fair ladies followed the young captain, it would rather have excited wonder if it had not. The warm hearts of the Spanish *Señoritas* are but too susceptible to the charms of love, when his godship dresses in British regimentals.

My friend D——, of the 13th Light Dragoons and I were admiring the waltzes of the evening when he observed to me that the young officer of the 51st was not only the best dancer, but had the prettiest and best partners, 'and' said he, 'I think the lady seems quite smitten with him, they have been partners the whole of the evening.' From this observation I was led to remark the young lady more closely than I had done before, and the result in my mind was, that Captain Gore was blessed with a partner the most bewitching in all Spain, and that he was of the same opinion. She was about seventeen, rather *en bone point* and middle sized, large dark and languishing eyes, black, glossy ringlets, with a beautiful fair skin, she was dressed in the graceful black costume of her country appeared a personification of the beauty of a Castilian romance, her manners were gentle, and with Captain Gore as her partner, she attached the admiration of every one present.

Where is the moralist who has looked into the book of nature, and can say they were culpable in loving each other, although circumstances wholly forbid their union. Let us draw a veil over the weakness of human nature when opposed to such powerful influences as those which surrounded these young persons. Let us not, with the austerity of mature and experienced wisdom, censure, but pity them, circled as they were with a glowing halo of youth and love. They loved, marriage was impossible, she left her father's house and fled to him, while he vowed to protect her with his life even unto the end of it. This happened in about three weeks after the ball.

The father at first knew not of the rash step his daughter had taken, but soon learned the distressing truth, he became almost frantic, and applied to the authorities for their interference, respecting young Gore as a seducer and a heretic. The authorities (a very inferior sort of men, at that time) immediately ordered a serjeant's guard (Spanish) to accompany the father to the quarters of the captain, they arrived—his apartment were on the first floor—and the soldiers were already in the courtyard below. Gore was informed of the intended purpose through a Spanish domestic of the house he lived in. His own servant, a brave and determined soldier, hurried to the apartment in which his master was, with his bayonet drawn, and observed that there would be no great difficulty in driving away the 'Spanish fellows below,' if necessary.

The young lady clung to Captain Gore for protection, and besought him not to give her up, declaring that she would never survive if he suffered her to be taken away. The soldiers were mounting the stairs, Captain Gore was decided. There was very little ceremony in the affair, he and his servant in a few minutes drove them out of the house and secured the door with bolts and locks. Few blows were struck by either the captain or his servant, the success which frequently attends sudden and resolute assaults against superior force, was in this instant manifested, and, considering the opinion which the Spanish soldiery entertained of the British powers, it is not surprising that the guard was ousted.

The defeated soldiers returned to the authorities and related the failure of their enterprise, they were answered by abuse, and their officer having been sent for was peremptory ordered to take his men to Captain Gore's quarters, and force the lady away.

At the same time, he was tauntingly asked whether two Englishmen were equal to a dozen Spaniards.

The guard under command of the officer immediately repaired to the place for the purpose of executing their orders, and demanded admission in the most ferocious manner, but not waiting for reply, the men began to batter the door with their muskets, and apply their shoulders to the panels. The door was too strong for them, they grew more outrageous, and the officer still more abusive to those within, again they demanded admittance, but this was peremptorily refused by Captain Gore. With the Old English maxim in his mind 'my house is my castle,' no doubt he believed he was acting in a justifiable manner, and perhaps he was right in the line of conduct he pursued, because there was a British commandant in the town—and a British officer situated as he was in the theatre of war, would act with perfect correctness in questioning any authority but that of his own nation—however, nobody ever suspected the modern Spaniards of good military discipline, or prudence in their actions. As allies, and under a commander in chief who always listened to the complaints of the Spaniards against his officers or men. The British in the case of Captain Gore were treated in a most unwarrantable manner.

The insolent and impudent officer of the guard was now determined to do all the injury he could, and hearing the voice of Captain Gore inside the door, drew up his men in front of and close to it, then motioning his orders, which were but too well understood, the whole of the Guard fired, the door was not thick enough to resist the bullets, and the unfortunate young man within fell lifeless in a moment. Would that he had fallen a few weeks before, in that battle which defended the rights of Spain, and not thus by the murderous hands of those he defended in that action. He was not a seducer, this his mistress declared over his dead body, and he did not mean to abandon her, as the melancholy catastrophe but too clearly proved.

The young lady was borne almost broken hearted away and placed within the cheerless walls of a convent many leagues from the scene that was the source of all her love and of all her sorrows.

There was never a Captain Gore in the 51st Regiment, if there was a young sub of that name at the time I have quite forgotten, it is certain he could not have been long in the corps. If such an extraordinary circumstance had happened it is natural to suppose that it would have been talked over so much that no man of the regiment could ever forget it. I am lead to suppose that the author of the anecdote penned it many years after the occurrence took place and that Captain Gore must have belonged to some other regiment.

ANECDOTE OF COLONEL MAINWARING

I have not the least doubt of the truth of the following, it has been related to me by many different persons who served under the colonel at the time.

In my letter No. 26, dated from Campa Major 1811, it will be seen Colonel Mainwaring left us on leave for England. He was appointed on the staff and to the command at Hilsea Barracks. At the close of the war he was removed to the Isle of Wight, where he remained in command of the depot until his promotion to major general.

The Riding School in Albany Barracks was used for a chapel on Sundays. It happened one winter that for several Sundays the colonel was very much annoyed by the men coughing, a great deal of which was done for the purpose. The colonel was determined not to be annoyed in such a manner, took the following novel plan to stop it in future. One Sunday after the morning service, the colonel took the opportunity before the sermon to address a few words to the men on the subject.

He began by coughing two or three times, then observing 'Many of us have very bad coughs, and I understand that the reverend gentleman is going to deliver a sermon on a particular subject, such being the case (coughs again) I shall endeavour to suppress mine, if I do not succeed I shall go out and wait until the service is over. Now I would advise everyone who cannot stifle their cough, to go out and walk about until we come out etc.'

Instantly, a great number walked out and the parson got through his sermon with but little noise. The soldiers who went out were chuckling with delight to think they had come the old soldier over the colonel, but they were struck with surprise to find some serjeants outside ready to form them into drill squads. When the service was over and the men formed in the parade Colonel Mainwaring said he would not turn his back on any medical man in England for curing coughs, he knew a remedy that never failed, then turning to the adjutant, said, 'Put all these men to the iron roller and keep them at it 'til retreat beating and every mother's son of them shall dine with Duke Humphry, this day.' The consequence was that afterwards it was very rare to hear a cough during divine service.

The following anecdote happened at Chatham in 1819. The regiment was stationed at Chatham and Sheerness. In the garrison at Chatham was stationed the 1st. Royal Veteran Battalion, 51st and 86th Regiments. One fine sunshiny day as the colonel of the 86th who was field officer of the day was going his rounds, he came to a post where a sentry of the Old Veterans was on duty. Seeing nothing but the box he went up to it. There sat the sentry industriously mending a pair of stockings with his spectacles on. On the field officer enquiring what he called himself, the man with much *sang froid* said he was a sort of a sentry.

The colonel then said 'And I am a sort of a colonel?'

'Well' replied the Old Veteran 'if that is the case, I suppose I must give you a sort of a present.'

The colonel reported the man to Colonel Cristie, the commandant of the garrison and colonel commandant of the 1st Royal 5th. Battalion. Colonel Cristie was for taking no notice of the report. When the field officer wished the commandant to punish the man for the sake of example, stating his own regiment being composed of raw recruits, having just been filled up on their return from India, it would be so bad an example if the man was not punished, he might expect to find the same thing in his own regiment.

Colonel Cristie replied 'Your men, colonel, are all active young fellows, and want no rest like my poor old worn out regiment, I dare say the poor old fellow found the sun to oppressive, however, I'll talk to him about it.'

The following should have been entered at the conclusion of the 112th letter, from Argostoli, but was left out by mistake. A short time before we relieved the 8th or King's Regiment, the following order appeared. It seems that some officer had brought out from England some bulldogs, and was in the habit of amusing themselves at night by hunting down all the dogs and cats they could meet with in the streets. Colonel Napier soon found out what was going on and took this method to put a stop to it.

Garrison Orders Argostoli, 5th August, 1825

Last night the peaceable inhabitants of Argostoli were alarmed by the continual worry of dogs and cats. Should the like again occur, the adjutant of the 8th or King's Regiment will mount a picquet consisting of one private and two subalterns. This picquet will patrol the streets from sunset to sunrise and all noisy dogs they pick up to be delivered over to the commandant's guard.

After this order appeared the sport was discontinued. On another occasion when the soldiers complained of bad wine the following extract of a garrison order appeared.

If the good soldier will keep his senses and not swallow down any poison that a scoundrel will offer him Colonel Napier will see that he shall be provided with good wine, but it cannot be expected that the commandant is going to play the butler to drunkards.

In justice to the brave Napier I must add I never met with an officer who would stand up like him to see a soldier righted. He was a decided enemy to the monopoly of confining the soldiers to the canteen for the purchase of wine etc.

When the warm weather is about setting in a long General Order is received from Corfu confining the soldiers to their barrack rooms during the heat of the day, but this order never was approved of by Colonel Napier (or as we used to call him 'Old Charley') for the General Order was always followed by a Garrison Order, beginning in the following words.

Lieutenant Colonel Napier does not approve of the system of coddling up British soldiers like a pack of old women etc.' Then would follow the commandant's directions how to prevent disease such as never to go out into the sun without a covering on the head, never to stand still in the sun, for the sun hurts no man if he keeps moving etc.

HONOURS OF THE DUKE OF WELLINGTON IN 1845

The Most Noble, Arthur, Duke of Wellington, Marquess of Doura, Marquess of Wellington, Earl of Wellington, Viscount Wellington of Talavara and Baron Doura of Wellesley.

Lord Lieutenant and Cust. Rut. of the County of Southampton, Lord Warden of the Cinque Ports, Constable of the Tower, a Privy Counsellor in England, a Privy Counsellor in Ireland, Chancellor of the University of Oxford and Doctor of Civil Law.

Senior Field Marshal and Commander in Chief of all Her Majesty's Land Forces, Governor of Plymouth, Colonel of the Grenadier Guards etc., Colonel of the Rifle Brigade. A Knight of the Most Noble Order of the Garter, Knight Grand Cross of the Most Honourable Military Order of the Bath, and Knight Grand Cross of the Royal Hanoverian Gulpic Order.

Prince of Waterloo, Duke of Ciudad Rodrigo, Duke of Vittoria, a *Grandee* of the Highest Order in Spain, Marquess Toras Vedres and Count Vimiera.

Captain General of the Kingdom of Spain, Marshal General in Portugal, Field Marshal in Russia, Prussia, Austria, Netherlands and France. Colonel of the 10th. Regiment of the Line in Austria.

Knight Grand Cross of the Most Distinguished Military Order of the Tower and Sword of Portugal.

St. Benevento de Avis, Portugal.

Golden Fleece, Spain.

Charles the Third, Spain.

Maria Theresa, Austria.

St. Andrew, Russia.

St. George, Russia.

Black Eagle, Russia.

William of the Low Countries.

Swedish Order of the Sword.

Read Eagle of Prussia.

White Eagle of Poland.

St. Esprit of France.

St. Ferdinand and Merit, Sardinia.

Elephant of Denmark.

And many others of the Most Distinguished Orders in Europe.

Honours of the Field Officers of the 51st Regiment

Colonel Mitchell. A Companion of the Most Honourable Military Order of the Bath. Gold Medal for Salamanca, Waterloo Medal, Knight of St. Andrew in Russia and Knight of Maria Theresa in Austria (died in 1817).

Colonel Rice. A Companion of the Most Honourable Military Order of the Bath, Gold Medal for Nivelle, Waterloo Medal, Knight of the Royal Hanoverian Gulpic Order.

Major and Bt. Lieutenant Colonel Keyt. A Companion of the Most Honourable Military Order of the Bath. Waterloo Medal.

Major and Bt. Lieutenant Colonel Roberts. A Companion of the Most Honourable Military Order of the Bath, Gold Medal for Vittoria, this officer was so disabled by wounds he was allowed a retired allowance of £500 *per annum*.

Lieutenant Colonel Campbell. Knight of the Royal Hanoverian Gulpic Order, Waterloo Medal.

Lieutenant Colonel Eliot. (In command 1843). Knight of the

Royal Hanoverian Gulpic Order, Waterloo Medal.

Major Mainwaring. Waterloo Medal. This officer's life has been one continued round of hard service. When a boy in jacket and trousers he was on the expedition in Spain under General Sir John Moore and at Flushing. In the Peninsular from January 1811 to the Peace in 1814. Waterloo and storming Cambray the 24 June 1815. In 1817 he went out as *aide de camp* to his Uncle, General Mainwaring to the West Indies, where he remained until after I was discharged, which was in 1828. He obtained his commission as ensign in the regiment in 1810.

The following account of the two unsuccessful attempts to storm Fort St. Cristoval corresponds so closely with Nos. 25, 26 and 89 of my letters, that I cannot forbear copying it as a companion to those letters. The work is entitled *The Adventures of the Connaught Rangers from 1808 to 1814* by William Grattan Esquire late Lieutenant Connaught Rangers in two volumes, London, Henry Colburn, Publisher, Great Marlborough Street, 1847. Every old Peninsular Soldier should read it. The undecorated of the old Peninsular Army is greatly indebted to Mr. Grattan for the spirited manner he has advocated their claims for medals etc. Bath.

11th July, 1847. W. W.

VOLUME 1ST

Page 140. The evening upon which the first assault was made (the 6th. June) the storming party consisted of but 100 men, whilst the garrison of the fort consisted of 150. Dyas at the head of six chosen men (and accompanied by an officer of engineers whose name I forgot and who was mortally wounded while he was in conversation with Dyas), led the advance. The situation of the fort, the bastions that had been disabled by our fire as also the breach were well known to both these officers, but the remainder of the party including the Commanding Officer Major Macintosh, it would appear were ignorant upon points of so vital importance.

The consequence was fatal. The handful of men that formed

the Forlorn Hope, led on by their brave young commander, jumped into the ditch, and proceeded along the curtain of the breach, but unfortunately the remainder of the party allowed themselves to be occupied before a dismantled bastion, which they mistook for the real breach. The ladders were lowered into the ditch and raised against this part of the wall and while the soldiers were endeavouring to place them upright they were cut off almost to a man. Dyas, finding himself unsupported ran back from the breach, and having reached the spot where his companions had been so uselessly, yet fatally employed, found it occupied only by the dead and wounded.

Thus far it was evident that the attack had failed, but it was also proved that it was owing to the misconception which the troops had of the real breach, because that portion of the storming party that had the ladders stopped short at a place where they should not. Dyas, although little acquainted with engineering or not even having had a trial of the ladders, which were but twelve feet long, at once pronounced the breach impracticable. He was immediately ordered to the tent of General Houston who directed the operations on the right bank of the Guadiana, and there he was closely questioned in the presence of the chief engineer (I believe it was Colonel Squires).

In answer to a question put to him respecting the depth of the ditch, he said he conceived it to be twelve feet, and he, one of the most active men in the army, judged of its depth from the great shock he felt when he jumped down. He was not credited and the engineer smiling said that "Certain allowances should be made to young beginners." This was too much for Dyas, but the brave fellow modestly observed that he considered the estimate he had made of the depth of the ditch to be tolerably correct, and from the moment he made up his mind to head the next attack.

When the breach was again deemed practicable, on the 9th, three days after the first attack and failure, Ensign Dyas waited upon General Houston and requested his leave once more to lead the advance. The general said "No you have already done enough, and it would be unfair that you should again bare the brunt of this business."

"Why general" said Dyas, "there seems to be some doubts of the practicability of this business on the last night of our attack, and although I myself don't think the breach is even now practicable, I request you will allow me to lead the party."

The general still refused, then Dyas thus addressed him "General Houston, I hope you will not refuse my request because I am determined if you order the fort to be stormed forty times, to lead the advance so long as I have life." The general fully appreciating the earnestness of this brave and high minded young man, at length acquiesced and Major MacGeechy having volunteered to command the storming party, he and Dyas made the necessary arrangements to reconnoitre the fort that evening.

They made a detour by the edge of the river, and succeeded in reaching unperceived to within a short distance of the fort. Under cover of some reeds, they carefully examined the breach which, to Major MacGeechy appeared a practicable one, but Dyas better informed from experience, combated all the arguments of his companion, and desired him to watch attentively the effects of the next salvo from our batteries, he did so, and appeared satisfied with the result, "Because the wall" he remarked to Dyas "gave way very freely."

"Yes" replied Dyas, "but did you observe how the stones fell without rolling, rely on it if there were any rubbish about the base, or face of it, the stones would roll and not fall." The observation was not lost on Major MacGeechy, but it having been decided that the attack was to be made that night, both the leader of the forlorn hope and the commander of the storming party at once made up their minds for the trial.

At ten o'clock at night two hundred men moved forward to the assault, Dyas leading the advance. He made a circuit until he came exactly opposite to the breach. Instead of entering the ditch as before, a sheep path, which he remembered in the evening while he and Major MacGeechy made their observations, served to guide them to the glacis in front of the breech.

Arrived at the spot the detachment descended the ditch and found themselves at the foot of the breach, but here an unlooked for event stopped their further progress and would in itself have been sufficient to have caused the failure of the attack. The ladders were entrusted to a party composed of a foreign regiment "the Chasseurs Britanniques." These men, the moment they reached the glacis, glad to rid themselves of their load slung the ladders into the ditch. Instead of sliding them between the *palisadoes*, they fell across them, and so stuck fast, and being made of heavy green wood, it was next to impossible to move much less to place them upright against the breach, and almost all the storming party were massacred in the attempt.

Placed in a situation so frightful, it required a man of the most determined character to continue the attack. Every officer of the detachment had fallen, Major MacGeechy one of the first, and at this moment Dyas and about five and twenty men were all that remained of the two hundred. Undismayed by this circumstance the soldiers persevered, and Dyas although wounded and bleeding, succeeded in disentangling one ladder, and placing it against what was considered the breach. It was speedily mounted, but on arriving on the top of the ladder, instead of the breach, it was found to be a stone wall that had been constructed in the night, and which completely cut off all communication between the ditch and the bastion, so that when the men reached the top of this wall, they were, in effect, as far from the breach as if they had been in their own batteries. From this faithful detail it is evident that the soldiers did as much as possible to ensure success, and that the failure was owing to a combination of untoward circumstances over which the troops had no control. Nineteen men were all that escaped.

It may, perhaps be asked by persons unacquainted with these details, what became of Ensign Dyas, and they no doubt will say what a lucky young man he was to gain promotion in so short a time, but such was not the case, although he was duly recommended by Lord Wellington. This was no doubt an oversight, as it afterwards appeared, but the consequence has been of material injury to Ensign, now Captain Dyas. This officer, like most brave men, was too modest to press his claim, and after having served through the entire of the Peninsular war, and afterwards at the memorable battle of Waterloo, he, in the year 1820, ten years after his gallant conduct, was by a mere chance promoted to a company in consequence of the representation of Colonel Gurwood (another but more lucky forlorn hope man) to Sir Henry Torrens.

Colonel Gurwood was a perfect stranger (except by character) to Dyas and was with his Regiment the 10th. Hussars at Hampton Court, when Sir Henry Torrens inspected the 51st Regiment, Colonel Ponsonby and Lord Wiltshire (not one of whom Dyas had ever seen) also interested themselves in his behalf, and immediately on Sir Henry Torrens arriving in London he overhauled the documents connected with the affair of San Cristoval, and finding all that had been reported to him to be perfectly correct, he drew the attention of H.R.H. the Duke of York to the claims of Lieutenant Dyas.

H.R.H. from that consideration for which he was remarkable immediately caused Lieutenant Dyas to be gazetted to a company in the 1st Ceylon Regiment.

Captain Dyas lost no time in waiting on Sir Henry Torrens and H.R.H. the Duke of York. The Duke received him with his accustomed affability, and after regretting that his promotion had been so long overlooked, asked him what leave of absence he would require before he joined his regiment. "Six months if his royal Highness did not think it too long."

"Perhaps," replied the Duke, "you would prefer two years." Captain Dyas was over powered by this considerate condescension on the part of the Duke, and after having thanked him, took a respectful leave, but the number of campaigns he had served in had materially injured his heath and he was obliged to retire on the half pay of his company.

Page 221. The author of the *Adventures of the Connaught Rangers* speaking of a Lieutenant Mackie of the 88th who had volunteered the forlorn hope at Ciudad Rodrigo, and like poor

Dyas, had been over looked, quotes the four following lines from *Johnny Newcombe.*

'I know a man, of whom 'tis truly said,
He bravely twice a storming party led,
And volunteered both times—now here's the rub
The gallant fellow still remains a Sub.'

These four pithy lines have relation to Ensign Dyas 51st. Regiment.

It is not generally known who the author of *Johnny Newcombe* is. I have heard that General Lygon amongst many other officers was the author. But the real person was Lieutenant Colonel Roberts 51st Regt. It was written with his left hand the colonel having lost his right hand at Lugo. When the 51st with its brigade lay in the apple orchard near the village of Eschellar, I was employed by Paymaster Gibbs in doing some writing. The colonel and paymaster were staying in the same house in the village, thus I had frequent opportunities of seeing the manuscript, when left by myself in the room I was employed in. It was at least the original so far as it was then completed, written backwards so that I was obliged to hold it before a glass to make anything of it.

This good old war officer is frequently mentioned in my letters. In the 53rd letter there is an account of his being wounded on the day of the storming of St. Sebastian, in repelling the advance of three *Corps de Armie* who had crossed the Biddasoa to relieve St. Sebastian. Colonel Roberts never joined again, being unfit for service. I understand this fine old soldier received £500 for life for the many wounds he had received but did not long enjoy it. His iron constitution gave way like thousands of others to the fatigues and privations necessary attending the life of a soldier on active service.

W.W.

Page 111. The author in closing his account of the Battle of Fuentes D'Onor says:

On the 12th left the position we had occupied for eight days and returned to our old quarters at Nave d'Aver. As we passed over the ground between that village and Posobello, we traversed a part of the field of battle, which we had not before viewed, except at a distance, too great to distinguish distinctly the objects with which it was covered. This was the ground upon which the 7th Division, and the troops that were forced from Posobello, had fought, it was strewed with horses and men. (See my 23rd letter).

In general the bodies of both were in part devoured by the eagles and vultures, but there was one figure amongst them that remained untouched, as if it was too horrible for them to approach. This man who in his lifetime must have been of enormous size presented the human figure under a frightful aspect, he was swollen to the size of a horse and I cannot account for this extraordinary enlargement of his frame, which was not partial but general. This giant arrested our attention for several minutes and we stopped to survey him distinctly, the flesh was quite green, except the face, which was black, he had been shot through the head perhaps. It would be difficult to convey a description of the frightful spectacle this man offered to our view, and the recollection of him haunted me for weeks afterwards.

Mr. Gratton has written so much about Ensign Dyas 51st and Lieutenant Mackie 88th being passed over without promotion. What is to be thought of the following statement of Sergeant Button 9th Foot? He is one of the remnant of the old Peninsular army and was present in the following actions, sieges, storms, besides affairs and skirmishes.

Roleia, 17th August, 1808.—Private.
Vimiera, 21st August, 1808.—Private.
Corunna, January, 1809.—Private.
Busaco, 27th September, 1810.—Corporal.
Fuentes d'Onor, 15th May, 1811.—Serjeant.
Ciudad Rodrigo, January, 1812.—Serjeant.

Badajos, 17th March and 16th April, 1812.—Private. Volunteered Forlorn Hope and was promoted to serjeant.

Salamanca, 22nd July, 1812.—Serjeant.

Vittoria, 21st June, 1813.—Serjeant.

St. Sebastian, August and September, 1813.—Serjeant. Volunteered Forlorn Hope lost left leg and severely wounded right thigh by grape.

He was ten years eight months in the 9th Foot. His brilliant service was rewarded by a pension of. What, 3/6 per day? No, only a paltry 1/3 per day. This fine old veteran is now employed is a toll collector in the Bath Turnpike Trust, and might be seen any day at some one of the Turnpike gates about Bath.

W. W.

Bath, 14th July, 1847.

LEONAUR

ALSO FROM LEONAUR

AVAILABLE IN SOFTCOVER OR HARDCOVER WITH DUST JACKET

THE JENA CAMPAIGN: 1806 *by F. N. Maude*—The Twin Battles of Jena & Auerstadt Between Napoleon's French and the Prussian Army.

PRIVATE O'NEIL *by Charles O'Neil*—The recollections of an Irish Rogue of H. M. 28th Regt.—The Slashers— during the Peninsula & Waterloo campaigns of the Napoleonic wars.

ROYAL HIGHLANDER *by James Anton*—A soldier of H.M 42nd (Royal) Highlanders during the Peninsular, South of France & Waterloo Campaigns of the Napoleonic Wars.

CAPTAIN BLAZE *by Elzéar Blaze*—Elzéar Blaze recounts his life and experiences in Napoleon's army in a well written, articulate and companionable style.

LEJEUNE VOLUME 1 *by Louis-François Lejeune*—The Napoleonic Wars through the Experiences of an Officer on Berthier's Staff.

LEJEUNE VOLUME 2 *by Louis-François Lejeune*—The Napoleonic Wars through the Experiences of an Officer on Berthier's Staff.

FUSILIER COOPER *by John S. Cooper*—Experiences in the 7th (Royal) Fusiliers During the Peninsular Campaign of the Napoleonic Wars and the American Campaign to New Orleans.

CAPTAIN COIGNET *by Jean-Roch Coignet*—A Soldier of Napoleon's Imperial Guard from the Italian Campaign to Russia and Waterloo.

FIGHTING NAPOLEON'S EMPIRE *by Joseph Anderson*—The Campaigns of a British Infantryman in Italy, Egypt, the Peninsular & the West Indies During the Napoleonic Wars.

CHASSEUR BARRES *by Jean-Baptiste Barres*—The experiences of a French Infantryman of the Imperial Guard at Austerlitz, Jena, Eylau, Friedland, in the Peninsular, Lutzen, Bautzen, Zinnwald and Hanau during the Napoleonic Wars.

MARINES TO 95TH (RIFLES) *by Thomas Fernyhough*—The military experiences of Robert Fernyhough during the Napoleonic Wars.

HUSSAR ROCCA *by Albert Jean Michel de Rocca*—A French cavalry officer's experiences of the Napoleonic Wars and his views on the Peninsular Campaigns against the Spanish, British And Guerilla Armies.

SERGEANT BOURGOGNE *by Adrien Bourgogne*—With Napoleon's Imperial Guard in the Russian Campaign and on the Retreat from Moscow 1812 - 13.

Lightning Source UK Ltd.
Milton Keynes UK
UKOW04f0131291017
311819UK00001B/23/P